WITHDRAWN BY THE
UNIVERSITY OF MICHIGAN

Comparative Democracy

Comparative Democracy

POLICYMAKING AND GOVERNING COALITIONS IN EUROPE AND ISRAEL

Gregory M. Luebbert

New York   Columbia University Press   1986

Columbia University Press
New York Guildford, Surrey
Copyright © 1986 Columbia University Press
All rights reserved
Printed in the United States of America

Library of Congress Cataloging-in-Publication Data

Luebbert, Gregory M.
Comparative democracy.

Bibliography: p.
Includes index.
1. Coalition governments—Europe. 2. Coalition governments—Israel. 3. Comparative government.
I. Title.
JN94.A979L84 1986   320.94   86-4165
ISBN 0-231-06298-2

This book is Smyth-sewn.
Book design by J.S. Roberts

For My Parents

Contents

Tables	xi
Acknowledgments	xiii
Abbreviations	xv
Introduction: Governing Coalitions and Democratic Politics	1

Part One
Policymaking and Governing Coalitions

Chapter One: Varieties of Multiparty Democracies	9
Legitimacy	12
Consensus Building	17
Elite Attitudes Compared	21
The Institutional and Historical Bases of Consensual Politics	29
Chapter Two: Policymaking and the Imperatives of Party Leadership	45
Party Leaders and Policy Politics	45
Policy Profiles	53
Policy Principles and Party Preferences	60
Bargaining and the Limits of Tolerance	62

Contents

Chapter Three: Party Leaders and Governing Coalitions   67
     Consensual Democracies   68
     Conflictual Democracies   70
     Dominated-Competitive Democracies   71
     Undominated-Competitive Democracies   83
     Minority and Majority Governments   87

Part Two
Governing Coalitions in Four Types of Democracies

Chapter Four: Israel   93
     Origins of the Party System   93
     The Governments, 1950–1975   105
     Summary   147

Chapter Five: Denmark   149
     Origins of the Party System   149
     The Governments, 1955–1975   158
     Summary   184

Chapter Six: Finland   187
     Origins of the Party System   187
     The Governments, 1955–1965   197
     Summary   217

Chapter Seven: Finland as an Unconsolidated Democracy, 1966–1982   219
     The Sources of the Transformation   219
     Corporatism, the Party System and Government Formation   225
     Unconsolidated Democracy   229

Chapter Eight: Conclusions   233
     Theory and Evidence   233
     Finland, Italy, Corporatism and the Problem of Regime Stabilization   241

Appendix A: Methodological Notes   249
     Limits of the Theory and Selection of Test Cases   249
     The Dependent Variables   252

Contents

Identifying Parties and Governments	252
The Empirical Procedures	255
Appendix B: Case Summaries for Sweden, Norway, the Netherlands and Italy	257
Notes	295
Bibliography	313
Index	327

Tables

1.1	Distribution of Multiparty Democracies	11
1.2	Modal Positions of Left and Right Party Sympathizers	16
1.3	Attitude to Existing Political Order, Bureaucrats and Parliamentarians	23
1.4	Attitude to Existing Socioeconomic Order, Bureaucrats and Parliamentarians	25
1.5	Administrators' Perceptions of Conflict	26
1.6	Perceived Conflict in Problem Resolution	28
1.7	Indicators of Societal Corporatism	33
1.8	Trade Union Membership in Industrial Democracies	35
3.1	Composition of Israeli Governments, 1950–1981	74
3.2	Composition of Dutch Governments, 1945–1966	77
3.3	Governments in Competitive Democracies	86
3.4	Minority and Majority Governments	88
8.1	Consolidated Results	247
B.1	Policy Profiles of Swedish Parties	259

Tables

B.2	Relationships with the Social Democrats (1956)	260
B.3	Relationships with the Social Democrats (1960)	262
B.4	Relationships with the Social Democrats (1964)	264
B.5	Relationships with the Social Democrats (1970)	265
B.6	Relationships with the Social Democrats (1973)	266
B.7	Policy Profiles of Norwegian Parties	267
B.8	Relationships with Labor (1961)	268
B.9	Relationships with the Conservatives (1963)	269
B.10	Relationships with the Agrarian Party (1969)	271
B.11	Relationships with Labor (1971)	272
B.12	Relationships with Labor (1973)	273
B.13	Policy Profiles of Dutch Parties	274
B.14	Relationships with the KVP (1956)	276
B.15	Relationships with the KVP (1959)	277
B.16	Relationships with the KVP (1963)	278
B.17	Relationships with the KVP (1965)	279
B.18	Policy Profiles of Italian Parties	280
B.19	Relationships with the DC (1955)	281
B.20	Relationships with the DC (1957)	282
B.21	Relationships with the DC (1958)	283
B.22	Relationships with the DC (1962)	285
B.23	Relationships with the DC (1963)	286
B.24	Relationships with the DC (1964)	288
B.25	Relationships with the DC (1968)	289
B.26	Relationships with the DC (March 1970)	290
B.27	Relationships with the DC (August 1970)	291
B.28	Relationships with the DC (1973)	293

Acknowledgments

This book began as a paper that I wrote in 1980. Over the years, the work has gone through so many revisions that it now bears only the faintest resemblance to that first paper. In transforming the paper into a book, Alexander George, Gabriel Almond, and Seymour Martin Lipset provided me, as friends and advisers, with a wealth of intellectual insight and encouragement.

That I owe a great intellectual debt to the works of Giovanni Sartori, Marty Lipset, and the late Stein Rokkan is evident from the chapters that follow. Professor Sartori's influence, however, goes beyond his published works. It was he who, as a then Stanford faculty member, opened my eyes to the opportunities for the theoretical and comparative study of democracies and the use of rational choice models.

At Stanford, Berkeley, and in Europe, I have benefited from the thoughtful comments of Stefano Bartolini, Jean Blondel, Hans Daalder, Guiseppe Di Palma, Lawrence Dodd, Robert Keohane, Joseph LaPalombara, Arend Lijphart, Gary Marks, Gary Myers, Robert North, Mogens Pedersen, Giovanni Sartori, and Kaare Strøm, and Henry Valen. Monique Klück provided invaluable help as a research assistant at the University of Leiden. Daniel Verdier has done the same and more at

Berkeley. I owe a special debt to Vinod K. Aggarwal who, first as a fellow graduate student at Stanford and now as a colleague at Berkeley, has been a source of friendship and intellectual stimulation.

Stanford University and the American-Scandinavian Foundation provided financial support for dissertation research. A National Science Foundation–NATO postdoctoral fellowship and a grant from the Institute for International Studies, University of California, supported further research at the University of Leiden. The Political Science Department at the University of Leiden provided an exciting environment in which to undertake research. I owe special thanks to Hans Daalder for arranging my stay in Leiden. On other occasions the Institute for Social Research in Oslo and the European University Institute in Florence have provided important assistance. The Political Science Department at the University of California, Berkeley, graciously provided me with a year of leave after I had been on the faculty for only one year.

Abbreviations

Frequently cited sources are abbreviated as follows:

BLT	Berlingske Tidende
DHK	Divrei Ha-Knesset
DV	Davar
HA	Ha-Aretz
HB	Ha-Boquer
HSB	Huvudstadbladet
HZ	Ha-Zofeh
JP	Jerusalem Post
MA	Ma´Ariv
Nk	Nordisk kontakt
PTK	Politiken
SDB	Svenska Dagbladet

Comparative Democracy

INTRODUCTION

Governing Coalitions and Democratic Politics

In most Western democracies, elections do not decide who will govern. Who will govern is instead decided by coalition negotiations among political parties. In these negotiations, all of the most fundamental conflicts in a society are brought to life as parties and the factions within them struggle to gain support for their most cherished policy ambitions. For political elites and the news media, the negotiations become almost an obsession. This is not surprising, for it is assumed with some justification that it is in these negotiations that the central issues of politics are decided: Who will govern? Who will benefit? and, Who will pay? We also assume that the negotiations are a critical indicator of the health of the polity. Media observers and political scientists alike assume that protracted negotiations and minority governments are signs of a debile polity. Calls for constitutional change, democratic and otherwise, invariably follow.

With so much importance attached to the making of governing coalitions, it is not surprising that a large body of literature has sought to understand how such coalitions are made.[1] Most of this literature has concentrated on predicting the party composition of coalitions and, by corollary, the amount of legislative support a coalition will enjoy. This literature has remained deficient in several ways. I have discussed some of these deficiencies elsewhere.[2] The most basic criticism that can be made is that the authors of the literature have forgotten the ultimate worth of a theory. That worth is in the explanation it provides, not the predictions it makes. Predictions confirm explanations. Thus, the value of a theory of coalitions is not mainly in predicting which parties will form a government in a given country. It is in what the theory reveals about political leaders, parties, the party system, and the polity itself in a given country. It is by this criterion that a theory should be judged.

Because the making of coalitions is so central to the working of multiparty democracies, a theory of coalitions should make a major contribution to a theory of democratic politics under multiparty conditions: What are the ambitions that a party leader brings into negotiations? How does a leader resolve his ambitions when they are in conflict? Which policies do leaders and their followers make decisive in their calculations? How do parties resolve policy conflicts? Which policies are negotiable? Which are not? How is this influenced by the larger policymaking process that characterizes a polity? What is the relationship between the structure of the party system and the size of the government that emerges? Between the structure of interest groups and the government that emerges? Between the political culture and the government? Why do some democracies regularly have minority governments while others have bare majority governments and still others have oversized governments? Why are some democracies governed effectively by minority governments while others lurch from crisis to crisis with them? When is a majority government a prerequisite of effective government? How can we explain the differences among countries in historical terms? What sort of constitutional engineering can help compensate for the instability of governments in debile democracies? All of these questions are essential to a theory of democratic politics under multiparty conditions. A theory of coalitions should provide answers to them. Thus, as we improve our understanding of coalitions, we should also improve our understanding of democratic politics. The challenge is to do this within the context of a single, coherent theoretical framework.

This book tries to do just that. In part one, I develop several models of democratic politics and a model of party leadership behavior. These models respond to the questions I have just posed. From them, we can derive some predictions of the party composition and size (minority, minimum winning, and oversized) of coalitions in multiparty democracies. Empirical support for these predictions will provide a corresponding amount of support for the models.

If we want to create a potent explanation—one that finds order in chaos by grasping the common experiences of politicians—we must anchor the theory in observed behavior. In this book I have attempted to do that. In the following chapters I will develop a theory that is deductively formulated. But it is the product of countless movements back and forth from the theory to the empirical evidence to the theory. In making the theory, I scrutinized cases of government formation in the Weimar Republic, the Federal Republic of Germany, Iceland, Belgium, the Netherlands, Norway, Sweden, Denmark, Finland, Israel, and Italy. Once the theory had been developed in its final form, I then returned to the evidence at a much more detailed level and tested the theory against the experiences of Norway, Sweden, Denmark, Finland, Italy, Israel, and the Netherlands.

Insofar as the theory is based on observation of the same experiences against which it is tested, it is as much an inductive interpretation of those experiences as it is a deductive theory tested against them. This approach makes possible a theory with greater explanatory power, but only at a price. The movement from theory to observation to theory violates one of the traditional tenets of deductive theory: that the theory should be tested against behavior not observed in the making of the theory. The reply can only be that comparative political scientists, especially those concerned with whole polities, do not live in an ideal world. There are not so many multiparty democracies that the ideal standards can be maintained.

Scrutiny of descriptive accounts of coalition making in many democracies quickly reveals that the meanings politicians attach to making coalitions change from country to country. Because previous coalition theories have been drawn from theories of games and decision making and then tested against aggregate data sets, these different meanings have been obscured. Lacking an understanding of these different meanings, theorists have assumed that politicians everywhere try to simplify their tasks by, for example, always striving to create a minimum-majority coalition or always negotiating in a "margin-dependent" fashion with ideologically adjacent parties.[3] These maxims have undoubtedly been more widely employed by political scientists than by politicians. In fact, politicians must juggle multiple and conflicting ambitions. It is these ambitions that give coalition making its meaning for politicians.

Among them are the ambition to be in government; to be in a majority government; to gain acceptance of their parties' policies; to minimize policy concessions; to maintain party unity; and, above all, to retain their positions of leadership in their parties. Perhaps others could be added to the list, but I have found these sufficient. Party leaders constantly weigh these ambitions as they negotiate with each other and with their followers. Negotiations are the means by which they learn and reconcile their ambitions. How they reconcile them depends on the democracy they are blessed or burdened with. This means that we must classify democracies. In the next chapter I will use a typology to make these classifications. It is this typology that ties coalition making to important features of the polity, including the structure of the party system and interest groups, the policymaking process, and the elite political culture.

With their ambitions reconciled, politicians are able to evaluate the amount of policy dissonance they encounter in negotiations in terms of its effects on their ambitions. In chapter 2, I will provide a simple scale that allows us to distinguish the amount of dissonance that exists in a bargaining relationship. Application of the scale, of course, requires that we know which policies parties value most. This, too, will be discussed in chapter 2. Given the ambitions and the bargaining relationships, we can make inferences about how much dissonance politicians will tolerate in a coalition in a particular kind of democracy. These inferences can be made with a rational-choice model. With these inferences we can predict the party composition and legislative strength of governments. And we can understand why governments of a particular size regularly occur in some democracies but not in others. We can also understand why minority governments can be highly effective in some countries and ineffective in others, and why some countries can only be governed by majority governments.

The predictions have been tested against the experiences of sixty-seven postwar government formations (including 302 bargaining relationships) in Israel, Denmark, Sweden, Norway, Finland, Italy, and the Netherlands. These countries were selected because they provided the most demanding tests of the theory. This is discussed in detail in appendix A. The chapters in part two include all of the cases from Denmark, Israel, and Finland. To include all of the cases from all seven countries would have required a second volume. Instead, the Swedish, Norwegian, Italian, and Dutch cases have been abstracted in appendix B. These cases were selected for abstraction because they are less demanding of the theory than comparable countries (Norway and Sweden vs. Denmark); or cover comparatively brief periods (the Netherlands vs. Israel); or exhibit no system change (Italy vs. Finland). The abstracts allow students of these countries to check our understanding of the critical policy issues that were on the table when these governments were negotiated. The abstracts omit much background information on the context and evolution of issues and party politics. The comprehensive studies on which the abstracts were based are identical to the studies in part two and are available from me.

In chapter 7, the theoretical framework is used to analyze the institutional changes that have made Finland more governable since the middle 1960s. In the concluding chapter, the test results from all seven countries are discussed, and Finland's experience of more effective governance is contrasted with Italy's largely failed efforts so that we might better understand the preconditions of improved governance in such conflictual democracies.

Part One
Policymaking and Governing Coalitions

CHAPTER ONE

Varieties of Multiparty Democracies

Democracies differ in the extent to which they encourage parties to cooperate with each other. They also differ according to whether they encourage cooperation in the government or outside it. The incentives for cooperation a democracy offers decisively influence the way in which party leaders understand their choices and thus indirectly determine the government formation outcome. The different incentives are ultimately the result of different experiences in the transition to mass democracy and of different patterns of interest-group organization. I will turn to these more remote causes later. But first we must understand the more immediate incentive structures that distinguish democracies. The simplest way to do this is with a typology built on two variables: regime legitimacy and the role of the opposition parties. I will distinguish between regimes with widespread legitimacy and those without it; between regimes in which the opposition plays the classical role of opposition and those in which this role is accompanied and tempered by efforts to participate in policymaking. Where the opposition fulfills the second role, I will say that the democracy is characterized by consensus building.

Figure 1.1. The Typology of Multiparty Democracies

Consensus Building

	Yes	No
Legitimacy Yes	Consensual	Competitive
Legitimacy No	Unconsolidated	Conflictual

When the two variables are dichotomized, the result is a typology of democracies such as appears in figure 1.1. The first democracy I will refer to as a consensual democracy; here the regime enjoys widespread legitimacy, and the role of the opposition is such that the policymaking process is characterized by consensus building. The second system I will refer to as competitive: here, too, legitimacy is unchallenged, but the opposition does not play a role that yields a consensus-building policy process. The third system, the conflictual system, suffers serious challenges to its legitimacy and lacks consensus building. The fourth system, the unconsolidated, suffers a lack of widespread legitimacy, but displays consensus building in policymaking. Table 1.1 is a comprehensive but not exhaustive distribution of Western European and other multiparty systems in this scheme in the postwar period and as otherwise noted.

Differences among political systems on the two dimensions are in reality matters of degree. They also fluctuate over time. The consensual systems have undoubtedly become less consensual under the strains of the economic crises of the 1970s and 1980s. Many scholars have argued that most democracies have suffered a decline in legitimacy as they have grappled unsuccessfully with these crises.[1] Still others have implied that democracies that suffered serious challenges to their legitimacy in the 1950s from large Communist parties have gained in legitimacy as these Communist parties have moderated their opposition to the political system.[2]

Whatever the merit of these interpretations in particular cases, the fact that the differences are matters of degree and that changes have occurred can create problems in classify-

Table 1.1: A Distribution of Some Multiparty Democracies

Consensual	Competitive	Conflictual	Unconsolidated
Norway	Ireland	Weimar Republic	Finland (1967–present)
Sweden	Israel	Finland (1945–1966)	
Denmark	Germany	2d Spanish Republic	
	Belgium	4th French Republic	
	Netherlands	Italy	

ing systems. For example, the scholarly consensus is clearly that Norway, Sweden, and Denmark have—with some fluctuations—shown the characteristics that define the consensual system.[3] But it is possible, to a limited degree, to impute these characteristics to other democracies, in particular to the Netherlands during its consociational period.

Direct, quantitative measures that could be applied across time would solve these problems of classification. But sophisticated measures of most of the concepts that will be used in this chapter are depressingly elusive. This is in spite of the fact that many of the concepts—antidemocratic party, established legitimacy, corporatism, consensus building—are among the mainstays of comparative political science. In the absence of reliable quantitative measures, our only recourse is to proceed by defining the concepts qualitatively in a way that accentuates the differences among democracies. These definitions can then be supplemented by a range of available evidence—direct and inferential, quantitative and qualitative, historical and contemporary.

Before returning to the dimensions of the typology, one final point is in order. It is that the hypotheses I will offer in subsequent chapters are deductively related to the typology. Consequently, if the similarities among, say, the Scandinavian systems, and the contrasts between them and all others, are not validly construed, the hypotheses will of necessity be proven wrong. This could happen in two ways. If the consensual systems are not similar, there will be unexpected variations in the performance of the hypotheses within the type. If the consensual systems are not distinct from all others in the theoretically relevant respects, the hypotheses that draw distinctions between outcomes in consensual and other systems will be disconfirmed. The hypotheses could be wrong for reasons unrelated to the typology; but if the typology is invalid, the hypotheses cannot possibly be confirmed. Ultimately, then, the best check on the validity of the placements is to be found in the tests of the hypotheses.

Legitimacy

In the main, we are not likely to disagree about which systems have established legitimacy. But the key word is "established." Just how established must the legitimacy be before the system is judged to have it? The discriminant I will employ is drawn from Giovanni Sartori's study of parties and party systems. I will say that a system lacks established legitimacy when an antidemocratic party possesses what Sartori has called "blackmail potential." A party has blackmail potential "whenever its existence, or appearance, affects the tactics of party competition and particularly when it alters the direction of the competition—by determining a switch from centripetal to centrifugal competition either leftward, rightward or in both directions—of the governing-oriented parties."[4]

Sartori has used the notion of blackmail potential in regard to antisystem rather than antidemocratic parties. Here, the narrower usage is more appropriate. Many parties have been antisystem parties without being antidemocratic. They reject a particular set of democratic arrangements, but not democratic arrangements as such. Rather, they want constitutional changes—to a parliamentary or presidential or federal system—but do not want to end democracy. The French Socialists in the Fifth Republic's first years and the Democrats-

66 in the Netherlands in their early years were such parties. The Belgian communal parties have been antisystem, but not antidemocratic. The challenge such parties make to the legitimacy of the existing institutions, especially in the Belgian case, is a serious one, but different in kind from the challenge presented by an antidemocratic party.

By antidemocratic, I mean that the party would, if it could, change not only the policies and personnel of the government, but would bring to an end competitive politics. Whether this is true of a party is notoriously difficult to determine if the party has been excluded from power or admitted only in very restricted circumstances. The problem is compounded because the party in question is often divided between a reformist wing anxious to participate in normal parliamentary politics and an unreconstructed wing determined to remain in total opposition. Moreover, the reformist wing can be accused of hidden intentions: of playing by the constitutional rules because those rules are "the only game in town." All of these difficulties arise with particular force in any attempt to classify the Finnish and Italian Communist parties since the early 1970s. There is simply no consensus among students of the parties.[5]

Few would dispute, however, that the debate over the democratic status of the Finnish and Italian Communist parties has been a conspicuous feature of party competition in their societies. Whether they are sincere democrats or adroit impostures need not be resolved. The fact that their democratic credentials are widely questioned, that many observers and many of their opponents remain unconvinced of their democratic commitment, is sufficient. Sufficient, that is, to profoundly affect the patterns of government formation—and not simply because the parties are kept out of power or allowed only limited access to it. The impact is more subtle and far-reaching than that. A democracy will therefore be said to suffer a lack of established legitimacy when the party system contains an anti-democratic *or doubtfully democratic* party with blackmail potential.

Thus, a system is conflictual or unconsolidated when it includes an antidemocratic or doubtfully democratic party *and as a consequence* experiences centrifugal competition. The simple existence of such a party does not result in placement in one of these types. A country such as Sweden, which has a doubtfully democratic party in the Communist party, is not one of the types, because party competition has remained centripetal. Likewise, the simple occurrence of centrifugal competition, such as that provoked in Denmark in the 1970s by the antitax Progress party, does not result in placement in the conflictual or unconsolidated types.

In practice, multiparty democracies are always a mixture of centripetal and centrifugal competition. Even so, it is not difficult to distinguish the dominant character of competition in the countries that appear in table 1.1. Several criteria are available to help us make this distinction. Since the centrifugal competition of importance is that induced by antidemocratic parties, the first question is whether the legislature contains such a party with the potential or actual ability to obstruct the passage of legislation on a regular basis. In more precise form, the question amounts to this: does the existence of an antidemocratic party numerically undermine, according to the party's position, the legislative potential of the democratic left or right? An antidemocratic party of the left that can obstruct the success of the democratic left (or center-left) clearly has blackmail potential. *Pari passu,* an antidemocratic party on the right that can have the same effect on the democratic right (or center-right) has blackmail potential.

When the antidemocratic party has such a presence in the legislative arena, at least some of the democratic parties will be compelled to challenge it directly in the electoral arena, and centrifugal competition will by definition ensue as the democratic parties escalate their ideological appeals. By the criterion of legislative influence, Italy and Finland have had antidemocratic parties with blackmail potential. For there can be no question that the two Communist parties and the Italian neo-Fascists have had such legislative influence. On this count, the Weimar Republic (because of the Communist, German National People's, and Nazi parties), the French Fourth Republic (Communist party), the Spanish Republic (monarchists, Communists, some socialists, and CEDA), Spain again from 1977 until the 1982 election defeat of the Communist party, and post-Caetano Portugal (Communist party) qualify as democracies without established legitimacy.

In contrast, in Norway, Sweden, Denmark, Israel, the Federal Republic of Germany, the Netherlands, Belgium, Austria, and Ireland, antidemocratic parties have rarely or never had obstructive potential. In these countries such parties have generally remained small, suffered a secular decline, or even disappeared across the postwar period. In the countries where centrifugal competition has been dominant, these parties have prospered in the electoral arena. Across most of the postwar period, they have either held their own or experienced a gradual increase in electoral support.[6]

Where centripetal competition has been dominant—and this is another indicator of the direction of competition—the distribution of self-placements among voters with party identifications on the left-right scale has been approximately normal. Self-placements have peaked near the center of the scale and declined sharply toward the extremes. Thus, the modal position of major party identifiers on the left-right scale has been closer to the center than to the ends of the scale. On the other hand, in party systems suffering centrifugal competition, there exists a major party—one with obstructive potential in the legislature—whose sympathizers are closer to the ends of the scale than to the center.

This is brought home by the values reported in table 1.2. These values measure the modal position of party sympathizers of the most leftward and rightward relevant parties in each society in the early and middle 1970s on a left-right scale. The most left value is 1, the most right value is 10, and the median is 5.5. Discounting the special case of the United States, two groups are apparent in this data. The first consists of Switzerland, Germany, Austria, Great Britain, and the Netherlands.

Table 1.2 Modal Positions of Left and Right Party Sympathizers

Country	Left Pole	Right Pole	Distance
United States	Democrats (5.7)	Republicans (6.4)	.7
Switzerland	Socialists (4.6)	Catholics (6.9)	2.3
Germany	Social Democrats (4.5)	Christian Democrats (7.0)	2.5
Austria	Socialists (4.9)	People's party (7.5)	2.6
Great Britain	Labor (4.4)	Conservatives (7.2)	2.8
Netherlands	Labor (4.2)	Christian Historical (7.2)	3.0
Italy	Communists (2.5)	Neo-Fascists (8.2)	5.7
Finland	Communists (2.3)	Conservatives (8.1)	5.8

SOURCE: Sani and Sartori, "Frammentazione, polarizzazione e cleavages," table 2.

The second group consists of Italy and Finland. The modal values of the parties in the first group are adjacent to the median. The values of the parties in the second group are adjacent to the ends of the scale. Under the circumstances, it is not surprising that parties in the first group have found centripetal competition the most gratifying, while democratic parties in the second group have consistently felt the centrifugal pull of the votes to be gained closer to the ends of the scale.

The strength of this centrifugal pull is apparent in the extraordinary scores for Finland and Italy reported in column 4 of table 1.2. These scores measure the distance between the left and right mode in each country. Keeping in mind that the scores have been calculated only for parties with obstructive potential, it becomes obvious that the incentive to compete centrifugally is a function of the distance between the left and right mode, and that on this count, too, Finland and Italy are in a class by themselves.

We thus have four criteria by which legitimacy can be gauged: the obstructive potential of undemocratic parties in the legislature; their long-term electoral performance; the distribution of party sympathizers on the left-right scale; and the degree of polarization of the party system. Taken together, they provide ample justification for distinguishing between, on the one hand, Norway, Sweden, Denmark, the Federal Republic of Germany, Israel, the Netherlands, Belgium, Austria, and Ireland; and on the other hand, Finland, Italy, Weimar Germany, Republican Spain, the French Fourth Republic, post-Franco Spain, and post-Caetano Portugal.

Consensus Building

The second dimension of the typology is the role of the opposition. The classical role is for the opposition parties to oppose: to criticize the government's policies; to offer alternative policies; to weaken the unity and resolve of the government, especially if it is a coalition; and ultimately to replace the government. In varying degrees, all opposition parties play this role.

There is a second role, however, that the opposition plays simultaneously in some political systems. In this role the opposition parties are as much concerned to influence and participate in the shaping of public policy as they are to bring down the government. Where such a role is practiced, the objective of bringing down the government is often no more than a long-term one. Indeed, one could say that it is often less than that, because while it exists at the rhetorical level, day-to-day parliamentary tactics are generally not related to such a strategy. Rather, tactics are more reflective of the short-term goal of influencing policy.

It is important to note what does not explain the existence of this role: the structure of the party system. It is not, as might superficially seem to be the case, an artifact of a party system in which one party has a seemingly permanent governing majority. The three Scandinavian democracies—Norway, Sweden, and Denmark—make the point well. It is in these three systems that the role of consensus building has been most fully developed; and it has been a fairly constant feature in spite of party-system changes. It was practiced by the Norwegian opposition parties in the 1950s, when the Labor party appeared to have a permanent majority. It was practiced by them after

1961, when the Labor party lost its majority and governed as a minority. Labor practiced it when it went into opposition after the 1965 election. The same can be said of Sweden, in spite of the gradual erosion of Social Democratic dominance. The Danish party system has always been rather more even—one cannot speak of the gradual decline of a once-dominant party—but the role has been characteristic of Danish politics.[7]

It is in Scandinavia that consensus building has become a norm of postwar politics. The instances of interparty cooperation in Sweden on tax revisions in the 1960s, 1970s, and in 1980–81 are among the more conspicuous demonstrations of the practice of consensus building. So are the numerous interparty agreements on defense expenditures, taxation, housing, and welfare in Denmark in the 1960s and 1970s.[8] Such agreements are important for their frequency—they are common in consensual systems—and for the issues with which they deal. These were at the time among the most contentious issues that parties had to confront—they dominated national elections and political debate. But they were not of such importance that failure to reach a broad cross-party agreement would have threatened the integrity of the regimes. They were simply the pivotal issues of normal, partisan national politics.

In consequence, they did not provide the basis for regime-defensive cooperation. The agreements reflected the comparatively positive evaluation that is attached to interparty cooperation as a norm of behavior and a desirable end in itself in consensual systems. It is this high value attached to positive, nondefensive cooperation across the government-opposition divide that distinguishes these systems. This valuation derives from the combined effects of extreme corporatization of interests and an unpolarized party system. The party system is itself a product of a particular type of transition from oligarchic to mass politics. In the final section of this chapter I will discuss the manner in which corporatism and an unpolarized party system taken together induce consensual values. It is only in such systems that a political scientist could seriously assert, as Ulf Torgersen has of Norway, that "for all practical purposes, the cooperation between the party leaders has been as effective as it could possibly be."[9]

In other systems one frequently observes government and opposition cooperation on secondary matters. Likewise, one observes it occasionally when issues must be dealt with that go to the very foundations of the political and social order: periodic defense and foreign policy cooperation in Israel and Finland and the 1958 School Agreement and the *Pacte Communautaire* of 1977-78 in Belgium are typical of the variety of cooperation that appears in seriously threatened and, especially, consociational political systems.[10]

While Dutch consociationalism might lead one to consider the Netherlands a candidate, or at least a former candidate, for the consensual system type, I have placed it in the competitive cell. I have done so because cooperation among Dutch parties has been mainly *within* oversized governments rather than between the government and opposition, even if the latter has occasionally participated in policymaking. The distinction must be borne in mind, for it is precisely the existence of these oversized governments that we are trying to explain. In this connection, it is important to note that in his analysis of Dutch consociationalism, Lijphart raises to the status of a rule of Dutch politics the autonomy of the government from the parliament: "The cabinet enjoys a large measure of independence, based on the attitude that it is the government's right to govern. This semi-separation of powers is based not on constitutional provisions but on informal, but nonetheless deeply ingrained, political practice."[11]

In the words of a former Catholic party leader discussing government formation and the subsequent legislative session in the Netherlands, "Parliament can influence government policy only before, not during, the 'ride.' "[12] Comparatively speaking, the Dutch parties have had fewer opportunities in parliament than parties in consensual systems to influence policy.

Dutch consociationalism was distinguished not only by the comparative infrequency of government-opposition cooperation, but by another characteristic as well: the more limited range of issues on which such cooperation as did occur took place. In consensual systems consensus building takes place on issues that are neither secondary nor decisive for the survival of the regime. Rather it occurs on issues of an intermediate range: they are issues that dominate national politics, but are not of such weight that they actually threaten the integrity of the system should a broadly acceptable compromise not be found. Lijphart repeatedly emphasizes that in the Netherlands cooperation was activated only by the appearance of issues that "seem insoluble and likely to split the country apart. . . . The Netherlands cannot be called a consensual society, not even by the most generous stretch of the imagination. Consensus exists within each of the subcultures rather than among all four blocs. . . . In The Netherlands, both the degree and the extent of political consensus are very limited, but one vitally important element of consensus is present: the desire to preserve the existing system."[13]

This sort of cooperation is defensive in nature and more limited than that which occurs in systems characterized by consensus building. We do find periodic summit conferences of party leaders in the Netherlands for the purpose of addressing contentious issues—just as we do in Denmark and Sweden. But the nature of the issues is entirely different. In the latter they deal with defense policy, economic policy, taxation, and so forth. In the Netherlands they have dealt with such regime-fundamental issues as the settlement of the school question and the adoption of universal suffrage in 1917, the outbreak of World War II, and the question of Princess Irene's right of succession in the wake of her conversion to Catholicism and marriage to a politically controversial Spaniard in 1964.[14]

I have not said much about the unconsolidated type. On the face of it, it seems implausible that a democracy would be characterized simultaneously by consensus building and uncertain legitimacy. Yet Finland since the mid-1960s fits the description. As we shall see, the institutional basis of consensus building is provided by an extreme corporatization of interest groups. Finland experienced a rapid and far-reaching process of corporatization in the 1960s. In chapter 7, I will examine this process and the way in which it forced Finnish political elites to adopt consensus-building patterns of behavior in spite of the polarization that remained in the party system. This peculiar combination of attributes—consensus building based on corporatism pushing political elites to cooperate, plus extreme polarization in the party system discouraging cooperation—has had important consequences for both government formation and the entire balance of power in the system. The most important consequence has been in transforming the power of the Finnish presidency, the one institution that exists independently of the interest groups and the parties. The peculiar attributes of the system have allowed the President to gain a decisive voice in the formation of governments. Because of the influence of the President's personal predilections, prediction becomes impossible. When it comes to the unconsolidated system, the value of the typology is this: it allows us to understand why it is that an individual politician's personal preferences can be decisive only in an unconsolidated democracy. In doing so, it reinforces our understanding of the irrelevance of personal preferences in all other democracies.

Elite Attitudes Compared

We can safely anticipate that political elites will express high levels of satisfaction with what they do, with their political institutions, and with the prevailing social order. They are, after all, elites. Nonetheless, there should be differences across systems. In particular, we should expect substantially higher levels of satisfaction in Sweden than elsewhere, if the preceding discussion of the consensuality of Swedish politics accurately portrays reality. The assumption is that to the extent that a political system is able to generate widely embraced compromises, dissatisfaction with the social and political order and calls for reform should be low in a comparative perspective. Alternatively, to the extent that a system is not characterized by consensus building, to the extent that broad compromise is not the norm, and especially to the extent that parts of the political elite feel excluded from policymaking, calls for reform should be comparatively high. We are fortunate in having data that allow us to make at least a limited test of these propositions. The data are from the seven-nation study of the "Political Culture of Bureaucrats and Politicians" conducted by Thomas Anton and his colleagues at the University of Michigan. Professor Anton was responsible for the research on Swedish elites, and it is on his data and conclusions that we shall concentrate.[15]

Table 1.3 compares the satisfaction with the existing political order expressed by bureaucrats and parliamentarians in five nations. The response scale runs from 1 to 5. The table provides the percentage of each national elite that falls within each response category along with mean scores. Only Italian respondents expressed substantial dissatisfaction with the existing political order and a desire for institutional change. The Swedish respondents stand in sharp contrast: 79 percent of Swedish administrators and 64 percent of Swedish politicians desired little or no change. What is most striking is that the satisfaction experienced by Swedish politicians is only slightly less than that experienced by Swedish administrators. For the table reveals that politicians elsewhere are usually more dissatisfied and more interested in change than are their bureaucratic compatriots. But nowhere else do politicians come as close as in Sweden to the administrators' level of satisfaction: almost two-thirds of Swedish politicians indicate little or no interest in institutional change.

> This level of disinterest in political reform is perfectly understandable for the Social Democrats among the Swedish respondents, in power for four decades at the time of these interviews (1971). It seems less understandable for members of the then opposition parties, who presumably should have a vital interest in at least a change in government. That such interest was so

Table 1.3 Attitude to Existing Political Order, Bureaucrats (B) and Parliamentarians (P) (in percent)

	Britain		France		Germany		Italy		Sweden	
	B	P	B	P	B	P	B	P	B	P
(1) Passionate, total rejection	—	—	—	2	—	—	—	5	—	—
(2) Rejected, ameliorative reform proposed	—	3	1	13	1	1	14	22	—	2
(3) Accepted, ameliorative reform proposed	27	48	46	62	45	58	54	67	20	33
(4) Accepted, little inclination to change	73	44	53	22	54	38	31	5	67	50
(5) Passionate affirmation	—	5	—	—	1	3	1	—	12	14
Total Percent*	100	100	100	99	101	100	100	99	99	99
Mean Scores	3.7	3.5	3.5	3.0	3.5	3.4	3.2	2.7	3.9	3.8

SOURCE: Anton, *Administered Politics*, p. 138.
*Percents do not always equal 100% because of rounding.

poorly reflected in these conversations suggests, again, how fundamentally content and remarkably unified in outlook all members of the Swedish elite seem to be. It also reflects the fact that, for opposition party members, being out of office does not necessarily imply being out of power. Opposition partisans serve on parliamentary committees, are appointed to Royal Commissions, and otherwise enjoy the perquisites of national policy office. In this context, a change in partisan control of government might well seem one among a number of "minor" changes.[16]

Another indication of the comparatively very high level of satisfaction among the Swedish elite emerges from table 1.4, which compares elite satisfaction with the existing social order in six nations. Again, the Swedes are all by themselves close to the very high end of the acceptance continuum. When the two most positive acceptance codes (4 and 5) are combined, "no other group of administrators comes closer than 25 percentage points of the Swedish level of societal affirmation, and no other group of politicians comes closer than 32 percentage points of the Swedish level of politician satisfaction." The level of support for society and its political institutions is extraordinarily high among Swedish elites. "Indeed, Swedish elite satisfaction is so high compared to other national elites that we can almost think of Sweden as a deviant, Panglossian state."[17] Or, alternatively and more realistically, we can think of it as a consensual political system.

Of even more direct concern for us is the seven-nation data on administrator perceptions of conflict. All respondents were asked the following question: "Some people say that in politics and society generally there is always conflict among various groups, while others say that most groups have a great deal in common and share basically the same interests. How do you feel about this?"[18]

In table 1.5 responses to this are compared. The question was not asked of parliamentarians, but in view of the close correlation between the previous views of bureaucrats and parliamentarians, it seems safe to assume that in rank order and magnitude the views of parliamentarians correspond

Table 1.4 Attitude to Existing Socioeconomic Order, Bureaucrats (B) and Parliamentarians (P) (in percent)

	Britain		France		Germany		Italy		Netherlands		Sweden	
	B	P	B	P	B	P	B	P	B	P	B	P
(1) Passionate, total rejection	—	1	—	2	—	—	—	5	—	7	—	—
(2) Rejected, ameliorative reform proposed	2	21	3	12	—	6	9	21	7	29	1	4
(3) Accepted ameliorative reform proposed	44	42	77	80	46	53	56	55	35	41	20	23
(4) Accepted, little inclination to change	50	21	19	6	51	38	33	16	57	22	66	66
(5) Passionate affirmation	3	15	1	—	3	3	2	2	1	—	13	7
Total Percent*	99	100	100	100	100	100	100	99	100	99	100	100
Mean Scores	3.5	3.3	3.2	2.9	3.6	3.4	3.3	2.9	3.5	2.8	3.9	3.7

SOURCE: Anton, *Administered Politics*, p. 139.
*Percents do not always equal 100% because of rounding.

Table 1.5 Administrators' Perceptions of Conflict (in percent)

	Britain	France	Germany	Italy	Netherlands	Sweden	USA
Consensus is typical	30.1	16.4	14.6	24.8	19.1	41.6	21.7
Neither, both	25.7	57.0	25.4	18.3	20.6	22.3	19.4
Conflict is typical	44.2	26.6	60.0	57.0	60.2	36.1	58.9
N =	(113)	(79)	(130)	(93)	(68)	(305)	(124)

SOURCE: Anton, *Administered Politics*, p. 141.

rather closely to the views of their national colleagues. The interpretation of the responses is complicated somewhat by the differing definitions the respondents assigned to "conflict." For Italian administrators conflict was mainly defined as class conflict (62%). This was also the case with the British respondents (52%). The German bureaucrats interpreted conflict as interest-group conflict (44%) and class conflict (34%). The Swedes see conflict primarily in terms of competition between interest groups (47%) or as an exchange of ideas (41%).

> Bearing in mind these differences, it remains clear that Swedish administrators, far more than their counterparts in other systems, perceive their society to be structured by common rather than competing interests. None of this should be taken to mean that Swedish administrators do not perceive these group-intellectual conflicts to be real or serious. Swedish administrators simply perceive less conflict in their nation's politics than do administrators elsewhere, and they therefore conclude that common interests are more likely to characterize social relations.[19]

This is most clearly brought out by table 1.6. When asked to discuss "the most important problem" facing the country, Swedish administrators were the *least* likely to mention conflicting interests in discussing either the problem or possible solutions to it."[20] Again, interpretation of the responses is slightly complicated. In some countries the interviewees were asked to identify the most important problem in their area of responsibility; for others, the question referred to the most important problem facing the country. It is reasonable to assume that in the former instance the question would tend to elicit more technical, non-political responses that deemphasize the role of conflict. According to Professor Anton, this probably accounts for the relatively low saliency of conflict revealed in table 1.6, except in the Netherlands and the United States, where administrators give conflict a prominent position even within the scope of the narrower question.[21]

From this point of view, however, the Swedish re-

Table 1.6 Perceived Conflict in Problem Resolution (in percent)

Perceived Conflict	Britain	France	Germany	Italy	Netherlands	Sweden	USA
Very prominent	6.8	4.5	3.8	4.0	13.3	1.7	23.4
Important	13.6	3.6	7.5	7.0	21.3	9.0	15.3
Present	23.7	25.5	27.1	14.0	16.0	13.7	19.8
Minimal	37.3	36.4	28.6	36.0	32.0	28.4	20.7
Absent	18.6	30.0	33.1	39.0	17.3	47.2	20.7
N =	(118)	(110)	(133)	(100)	(75)	(299)	(111)

SOURCE: Anton, *Administered Politics*, p. 142.

sponses are especially telling, for in Sweden the question was posed in highly political terms: "What do you think is the most important problem for the Swedish Cabinet and Parliament to try to solve today?"[22] That nearly half the sample could respond without even mentioning conflict at all is a powerful indicator of the consensual environment of the Swedish political elite: "Conflicts exist, and they are real enough, but they amount to debates among members of the same social family over the best means of furthering a common goal that all are presumed to share. In no other country are such views nearly as pronounced or as characteristic of a governing elite."[23]

The Institutional and Historical Bases of Consensual Politics

I have said that consensual systems are distinguished from all others by their normative commitment to consensual behavior and that this normative commitment is itself a product of extreme corporatism and an unpolarized party system. It should be clear that the commitment is not an automatic corollary of consensus-building behavior. Consensus-building behavior can arise, as in an unconsolidated system such as Finland's, when the corporatization of society leaves interest groups in possession of policy vetoes. The system can then become one of mutual policy checkmate, and the choice is between deadlock and mutual damage or consensus building; between immobilization and cooperation across the government-opposition line. In such a system, consensus building may be a fact, but politics is certainly not consensual, because there exists no normative commitment to cooperation.

The normative commitment develops only when extreme corporatism is combined with an unpolarized party system. It is sufficient to say that an unpolarized party system exists when the system has legitimacy—when it does not suffer from the presence of an antidemocratic party with blackmail potential. Certainly the distance between parties can be tremendous even in the absence of an antidemocratic party. But the presence of an antidemocratic party adds not just a difference of degree, but a difference in kind; disputes turn not only on policy, but on the very right of each party to participate in policymaking. As we shall see, such a difference has important consequences for government formation. How certain systems came to be legitimized while others have continued to experience legitimacy problems is rather well understood.[24] In general terms, legitimacy was acquired where societies were able to make the transition to mass democracy without the institutions of mass democracy becoming synonymous with the instruments of class, linguistic, religious, and other conflict. I will return to this.

What must be explained is how hypercorporatism and a historically smooth transition leading to legitimacy and an unpolarized party system could result in the consensual norms that are characteristic of Scandinavian politics. An understanding of the causes of these norms will later be critical to our understanding of the immediate cause of government formation. As well, it will allow us to extend our understanding of government formation beyond an ahistorical deductive model and beyond the analysis of a few distinguishing features of postwar politics, to an explanation that sees government formation as ultimately a product of more causally distant but fundamental social structures and the developmental experiences of the nineteenth and early twentieth centuries.

We have few cross-national measures of corporatism. Most scholars have concentrated on a single country, and those who have not have found the search for functional equivalents to be slow going. More important, perhaps, corporatism has meant different things to different scholars. Some have equated it with incomes policies; others with means to control or suppress the working class; others with structural attributes of governments and trade unions; and still others with interest group participation in government commissions, committees, and so forth.[25]

As I am going to use the term, corporatism is an institutionalized pattern of cooperation between interest groups and the executive of the central government in the formulation, implementation, and administration of public policy. In a corporatist relationship, an interest group does not perform only a consultative or advisory role, and its right to participate is not questioned. Rather, it "participates directly in the authoritative allocation of values" as one among several participants in decision making as a matter of right and routine.[26] This definition is meant to embrace much more than the making of incomes or economic policies, although these are a core aspect of corporatism.

The integration of an interest group into the decision-making process is dependent on its cohesiveness, or its ability to behave predictably, and the size of the group's representational base, or its ability to legitimately claim to speak for a part of society and thereby contribute to consensus when agreement is reached. With these two aspects of groups in mind, we can begin to identify the most corporatist democracies. We can then supplement evidence of the structural attributes of interest groups with some scattered evidence on actual group participation in policymaking.

The most appropriate starting place is with a well-known measure devised by Philippe Schmitter. It gauges the degree of organizational centralization and associational monopoly among trade union confederations. We know that the structural attributes of trade unions mirror accurately the structural attributes of employer organizations.[27] In Schmitter's measure

> two core structural characteristics of the trade union movement—(1) the degree of organizational centralization and (2) the extent to which a single national central enjoys a representational monopoly—are combined into a single rank ordering. The organizational centralization measure . . . is based on information on size of (con)federation bureaucracy, existence of strike funds, and degree of control over member associations. The degree of organizational monopoly was derived from recent data on the number and distribution of union (con)federations,

as well as on information on whether blue- and white-collar workers were grouped in the same peak association ... or in separate ones.[28]

The rank-order scores are reported in Table 1.7. By this measure, Austria, Norway, Sweden, Denmark, and Finland are the most corporatist Western democracies. Austria is first; Norway is second; and Denmark, Sweden, and Finland are tied for the next rank.

In Scandinavia, centralization by the employers forced the trade unions to respond in kind. In Finland, the reverse was the case. In Norway and Sweden, centralized trade union confederations (*Landsorganisasjonen,* or LO) have been created. Even in Denmark, where an earlier urban development led to the creation of craft unions, there has been a similar movement toward centralization, although the structure is complicated by craft divisions.[29]

On both sides of industry, centralization is shown by the control the confederations have over their members. Individual unions cannot strike without prior permission from the LO, and individual firms cannot institute a lockout against the dictates of the employers' association. Although there is generally some small scope for further bargaining at the plant and industrial level, agreements are usually binding for the labor market as a whole. In Sweden, the government, the LO, and the employers' association have often preferred that the government remain aloof from these negotiations. In Denmark and Norway, the government has frequently been an active participant.

The 1973 Norwegian negotiations provide a good example of this practice. An ad hoc committee consisting of representatives of the government, the LO, the employers' association, and organizations of fishermen and farmers was established to discuss price increases and wage restraint. The final agreement included an increase in government subsidies of 250 million kroner a year, to prevent public utility rate rises; a reduction of total government spending of 100 million kroner in 1973; increased government subsidies for basic consumer

Table 1.7 Indicators of Societal Corporatism

Country	Simple Rankings		Combined Rankings
	Organizational centralization*	Associational monopoly†	Societal corporatism‡
Austria	1	3	1
Belgium	3	(9)	7
Canada	(13)	(9)	(11)
Denmark	(8)	(1.5)	(4)
Finland	(5)	(4.5)	(4)
France	10	(14)	13
Germany	9	6	8
Great Britain	(13)	12	14
Ireland	(13)	(9)	(11)
Italy	(13)	(14)	(15)
Netherlands	2	(9)	6
Norway	(5)	(1.5)	2
Sweden	(5)	(4.5)	(4)
Switzerland	(7)	(14)	9
United States	(13)	(9)	(11)

SOURCE: Schmitter, "Interest Intermediation."

Note: Rho = 0.52.

* "A composite score of indicators of (con)federal powers to engage in collective bargaining, to support strikes with own funds, to maintain a large staff, and to collect dues from members." Scores for Switzerland and Canada calculated by Philippe Schmitter.

† "A compound additive score with three components: (1) presence of single national labor (con)federation equals 1; presence of two national (con)federations or one national plus important non-affiliated unions equals 2; presence of three or more national (con)federations equals 3; (2) joint organization of manual and nonmanual workers equals 1; manual and nonmanual organized separately into national (con)federations equals 2; manual and nonmanual organized separately with no nonmanual national (con)federation of importance equals 3; and (3) no stable factions within national (con)federation(s) equals 1; stable faction within national (con)federation(s) equals 1.5."

‡ "A combined rank ordering of organizational centralization and associational monopoly." The organizational centralization measure was created by Bruce Headey, "Trade Unions and National Wage Policies."

goods of 175 million kroner per consumer price index point increase if the index exceeded a specified amount by September 15, 1973. In exchange, the LO agreed to accept only 45 percent compensation for the cost-of-living increase that had occurred since the previous agreement.[30]

The distinctiveness of Austria, Sweden, Denmark, Norway, and Finland is confirmed by another measure: the percentage of the labor force that is represented by a trade union. In each country economic interest groups representing the industrial workers and their employers have virtually complete coverage, and the same is true of producer cooperatives in the agricultural sector. In addition to cooperative organizations, farmers in each nation have strong interest groups to represent their general economic interests.

Whereas Schmitter's rank ordering indicates the organizational cohesiveness of the trade union movement, the size of the labor force covered indicates the representational base of the movement. A combined measure could be created, but it would be superfluous, because by this indicator, too, Austria, Sweden, Denmark, Norway, and Finland occupy the first five positions. Table 1.8 shows that in each of these countries well over half of the labor force is organized. The lowest of the five are Denmark, Finland, and Norway, with about 60 percent of the labor force in a trade union. Ranking next are Belgium, with 48 percent, and Great Britain, with 40 percent. Without attaching too much importance to the precise percentages, a basic distinction does seem to emerge between Austria, Norway, Sweden, Denmark, and Finland and all other Western democracies, especially when the measures of organizational cohesiveness and representational base are juxtaposed. For when they are, we see that it is only in these five countries that trade unions combine exceptional cohesiveness with a broad representational base.

Such cohesiveness and broad base allow for a political role of deeper and more enduring importance than is possible in other democracies. This is seen most clearly in the integration of groups into politics in their representational role on committees that formulate policy and on the boards and agencies that implement and administer it.[31] In Norway, organizations have institutionalized rights to participate in all phases of government policymaking as representatives of spe-

Table 1.8 Trade Union Membership in Industrial Democracies

Country	Percentage of the Labor Force Organized
Sweden	80
Austria	66
Denmark	65
Finland	60
Norway	60
Belgium	48
Great Britain	40
Ireland	36
Japan	35
Netherlands	33
Germany	31
Canada	27
United States	23
Italy	20
Switzerland	20
France	17

SOURCE: U.S. National Foreign Assessment Center, *National Basic Intelligence Factbook* (Washington, D.C., 1977); cited in Charles L. Taylor and David A. Jodice, *World Handbook of Political and Social Indicators*, vol. 1, *Cross-National Attributes and Rates of Change*, 3d ed. (New Haven: Yale University Press, 1983), table 2.9.

NOTE: Date for the data is circa 1975. "The data refer to the percentage of the labor force that belongs to organized trade unions. The labor force consists of both employed and unemployed persons who are employers, persons working on their own account, salaried employees, wage earners, unpaid family workers, and members of producers' cooperatives."

cific interests. In more than 1,000 government committees, organizations are represented in approximately 50 percent by about 2,000 representatives. "In ministries organized around economic interests like the ministries of Industry, Fisheries, Trade and Agriculture, along with ministries of Local Government and Labor, Consumer Affairs and Government Administration, and Church and Education, a large majority of committees at the national level have representation of organized interests."[32] Thirty-three percent of the members of committees even in the ministries of Defense and Foreign Affairs are representatives of organized interests.[33]

Economic producer groups—the trade unions, employer associations, and organizations of agriculture and fisheries interests—dominate the Norwegian committee system. More than 90 percent of the representatives from organized interests are from economic groups. The LO alone was represented on 270 policymaking committees in 1979, and the Confederation of Industry had representatives on 100 committees. Cultural and humanitarian groups were represented on only 67 committees at the national level; youth, sports, and recreation groups on 14; and religious groups on 6.[34] Thus, participation is overwhelmingly weighted toward economic interests, but it is the participation of these groups that is the core of corporatist democracy insofar as it is economic, and related social policy, questions that are the core of politics in industrial democracies. As well, as corporatist institutions contribute to a consensus on economic and social policy questions, they help to defuse noneconomic conflicts that are often connected.

A study of Denmark reveals the same high level of interest group incorporation. Lars Johansen and Ole Kristensen distinguished among four types of committees: those engaged in universal regulation (Ministry of Justice, income taxes, and environmental protection); specific regulation (agriculture, labor, commerce, and so forth); the production and supply of public services (education, social welfare, defense, health); and the direction and coordination of the public sector (Prime Minister's office, Treasury, foreign affairs). In 1975, the percentage of committees in each area with representatives from interest organizations (excluding local and institutional interests) was as follows: universal regulation (N = 119), 42.7 percent; specific regulation (150), 76 percent; public services (353), 52.1 percent; and direction and coordination (45), 40.5 percent.[35]

In Sweden and Norway, the right of groups to be involved in the policymaking process is guaranteed through the *remiss* system, a procedure whereby a ministry contemplating a legislative or administrative action of concern to an interest group must consult the relevant groups.[36] Perhaps more important still in Sweden has been the role of royal commissions.

Multiparty Democracies

> In the first place, royal commissions play a very great part in Swedish legislative and political work. Practically all important questions which are brought before parliament have at one time or another been studied in a royal commission.... Groups and interest organizations are given very full representation on such commissions and are thus able to use this device already at an early stage in order to reach agreement with political parties, with other groups and with administrators. The tendency is to attempt the greatest possible amount of agreement already at this stage.[37]

Gunnar Heckscher, speaking of Swedish economic interest organizations, asserts that "it is regarded as more or less inevitable that groups of this type . . . should exercise a power almost equal to that of parliament and definitely superior to that of parliamentary parties."[38]

It is the political consequences of such extreme corporatism that are of decisive importance. The most important consequence is that the cabinet, the parties, and the legislature are only some of the numerous and important sites of fundamental social and economic decisions. Nothing illustrates this more clearly than the previously discussed 1973 round of wage negotiations in Norway. This means, in the first place, that interest groups have a range of alternatives for the expression of their concerns beyond the above institutions and that parties are consequently under less pressure, and are exposed to fewer inducements, than they otherwise would be, to take maximalist positions. Further, and still more important, because virtually every societal interest is organized and guaranteed access to policymaking, and indeed must frequently be relied on to implement and administer policy, the range of policy choice that political leaders confront is reduced. This reduced range facilitates cooperation and compromise because it constrains greatly the range of potential disagreement at the outset. It discourages the politics of outbidding, because any party that seeks to enhance its appeal to one group by moving toward the periphery of the range simultaneously alienates a host of other well-organized and politically dangerous groups.

In reflecting upon why supporters of the Norwegian opposition parties had not united for a frontal attack on the then Labor government, the late Stein Rokkan, writing in the early 1960s, concluded:

> The explanation is very simple: the opposition may have been losing in the fight for votes, but the interests it represents and the causes it stands for can still be defended through other channels of influence on government decision making. Votes count in the choice of governing personnel, but other resources decide the actual policies pursued by the authorities. . . .
>
> To understand the strategies of government and opposition we have to analyze the bargaining processes between the giant alliances of such associations and corporations. The vote potential constitutes only one among many different power resources brought to bear in these bargaining processes . . . no single group dares to rely exclusively on its electoral machinery. . . .
>
> Even if they lose in competition for votes and seats, they can still bring their organizational resources to bear on the actual policy decisions of the government. . . . The crucial decisions on economic policy are rarely taken in the parties or the parliament: the central arena is the bargaining table where the government authorities meet directly with the trade union leaders, the representatives of the farmers, the smallholders and the fisherman, and the delegates of the Employers' Association. . . .
>
> At least in matters of internal policy, the government can rarely force through decisions solely on the basis of its electoral power, but has to temper its policies in complex consultations and bargains with the major interest organizations.[39]

Where, as in Scandinavia, corporatism compels any government to formulate policies that take into consideration a broad range of competing interests, the range of governmental choice is narrow and the prospects for interparty agreement are correspondingly enhanced.

Given the way in which the Scandinavian systems cluster at the top of the measures of organizational cohesion and representational base and our more general knowledge of the distinct patterns of interest intermediation in these systems, it seems reasonable to consider them a class apart from others on this dimension, to distinguish them as "hyper-corporatist." From the preceding discussion, it should be clear that hyper-corporatism contributes to the existence of a consensual political system by structuring interests in a manner that encourages compromise and by lessening the representational burden on the parties and party system. But it is equally clear that hyper-corporatism alone is not sufficient to explain the existence of a consensual politics, for both Finland and Austria share the hyper-corporatism of Norway, Sweden, and Denmark.

It is, therefore, necesary that we seek other variables on which Norway, Sweden, and Denmark are distinguished. The first of these is the nature of the historical transition from oligarchic to democratic rule. I will simply distinguish between a smooth transition and a rough transition. By smooth, I mean that the transition was made without civil war, without an authoritarian interlude or reversal of *domestic* origins, and without the creation of permanent or semipermanent subcultures based on a sense of exclusion from the political system. Contrarily, a rough transition is one in which one or more of these historical experiences obtained.

Now, it is a fairly straightforward matter to classify political systems according to their historical experience in these terms. In the first place, and I will discuss this further below, Norway, Sweden, and Denmark had, by these criteria, very smooth transitions indeed: none experienced civil war; none experienced a domestically derived authoritarian interlude or democratic reversal; and none generated political subcultures based on a sense of exclusion. Per contra, Finland and Austria, the two other hyper-corporatist societies, had very rough transitions. Both experienced intense, brutal civil wars. In the case of Finland, the war itself laid the basis for the creation of an excluded minority (the Civil War Reds), and this exclusion remains evident to this day in voting patterns. The transitions were rough in other respects, as well. Austria had an authoritarian interlude as well as a civil war. Finland had a semiauthoritarian interlude with the rise of the Lapua Movement in the 1930s and the outlawing of the communists. So it is clear enough that Finland and Austria fall into the class of polities that experienced rough transitions from oligarchy to democracy.[40]

Elsewhere the transition was rough also: Germany had its suppression of socialists and the *Kulturkampf;* the failed revolution of 1918–19; and, of course, the most brutal authoritarian interlude of all time from 1933. France also had democratic reversals and for a long time an excluded minority, practicing Catholics. Italy, of course, had a rough transition: an authoritarian interlude and, until 1891 and Pope Leo XIII's encyclical, *Rerum Novarum,* an excluded minority, practicing Catholics. As well, one must add for both Italy and France, until at least the postwar period, the working class. This leaves three European states besides Norway, Sweden, and Denmark that experienced transitions that were, by the criteria employed, smooth: the Netherlands, Belgium, and Ireland.[41]

The importance of a smooth transition is that it makes more likely, but does not necessarily *cause,* cooperation and resolution of conflict by compromise. Such a process has a cumulative effect: trust and a sense of common purpose are enhanced; permanently aggrieved social groups are not created. In contrast, the consequence of a rough transition is a diminished sense of trust and common purpose and polarization as excluded groups are created. Speaking of Norway, Torgersen has asserted that

> consensus rather than dissensus has been the prevailing condition. Just to give a brief summary: political consensus was the rule almost until 1884. With the exception of the period following 1814 [the year of the transfer of sovereignty from the King of Denmark to the King of Sweden] and the sharp rupture of the political peace resulting from labor unrest in 1848, there was substantial agreement on most questions until 1884 [the year in which parliamentarianism was established], followed by a cooling off period that ended sometime before 1905 [the year of independence]. This was followed by a relatively peaceful period until the end of World War One, when the labor movement was

radicalized, and finally joined the Comintern in 1920.... The situation in the twenties changed very soon, however.... [An] extremely speedy deradicalization brought the party from membership in the Comintern to the Cabinet in the course of four years.... [In 1884] the political system was changed from one dominated by civil servants to a parliamentary system, but without leaving any unresolved deep conflicts, and without essentially threatening the legitimacy of the system. In a sense there is a basic similarity between [1884 and 1920]: in both cases the tension was reduced after a short time. The political system was in both cases able to incorporate new movements and new elites in an extremely rapid fashion.[42]

Ulf Torgersen's general characterization of the Norwegian transition can be extended to Denmark and Sweden. In both instances new groups were rapidly incorporated into the political system with minimal political conflict.[43] At no point did such conflict as did exist threaten the integrity of the political system. There was in neither system a significant element of reaction, much less the prospect of a democratic reversal. Indeed, conservatives voluntarily handed over power to new groups, and usually did so under only comparatively modest pressure.

Torgersen concludes that "Norway is relatively free of internal political tension because it has been that way all of the time."[44] This is indeed one part of the explanation of the existence of consensual politics in Scandinavia. But, by itself, the nature of the transition is not a sufficient explanation of the appearance of consensual politics, for it only explains why there would be a certain propensity toward consensual politics, why such politics is possible, rather than why it actually appears. After all, the Netherlands, Ireland, and Belgium had, by our criteria, smooth transitions, but lack consensual politics.

In order to understand why a historical process that *could* lead to consensual politics *did* lead to consensual politics, it is necessary to combine it with the impact of hyper-corporatism. Hyper-corporatism, too, creates a strong propensity toward consensual politics; but when combined with a rough transition to democracy, as in Austria and Finland, it is not sufficient, because the rough transition itself generates social forces that militate against consensual politics. A smooth transition by itself creates the possibility of consensual politics, because it erects few obstacles, or fewer than there otherwise would be, to such politics. But if it makes consensual politics possible, it does not, by itself, *induce* the behavior of consensual politics. That inducement is provided by the corporatist institutions. Corporatism induces it by narrowing the range of policy choice and pushing political leaders toward the center and thereby toward each other in the policies they advocate. Consensual politics, it would seem, then, requires both hypercorporatism *and* a smooth transition from oligarchic to democratic politics. It is only among the three Scandinavian political systems that these two features are combined.

Our historical understanding can be refined by considering in comparative perspective the extent to which politics during the transition from oligarchy to democracy was dominated by a liberal political and economic ideology. In sharp contrast with much of Western Europe, the Scandinavian countries never experienced an extended period of liberal domination. Late and rapid industrialization in Scandinavia prevented the emergence of a powerful urban bourgeoisie before the mobilization of the peasantry and working class. In other countries that experienced a smooth transition—the Netherlands, Belgium, and Ireland—the bourgeoisie was the principal agent of the liberal political and economic ideology. Throughout Scandinavia, however, liberal parties were notably ineffective in their struggles against the predemocratic oligarchs in the absence of an alliance first with the peasantry and later with the peasantry and the working class. Liberal-peasant alliances were behind the push for parliamentarism in Norway and Denmark. A liberal-peasant-working-class alliance was required to obtain the same end in Sweden. In Norway, Sweden, and Denmark an alliance of all three groups was responsible for the extension of the suffrage. In none of the countries was there an interval of more than fifty years between the establishment of parliamentary government and the coming to power of the first Social Democratic government.[45]

The essential point is that the necessity of such alliances and the brief period between the victory of the parliamentary cause and the coming to office of the Social Democrats left little time for liberalism to assume a position of ideological dominance. In those countries where liberalism was able to assume a dominant position, it deepened the gulf between the middle and working classes and slowed the depolarization of politics once working-class parties gained political power.

To discuss the strength of liberalism in the transition essentially is to make a more refined inquiry into the smoothness of the transition. Weaker liberalism distinguished Norway, Sweden, and Denmark from other systems that had smooth transitions: Belgium, the Netherlands, and Ireland. And it provides an explanation for the comparatively de-polarized politics of Scandinavia. Strictly speaking, however, extreme corporatism and a smooth transition alone seem necessary and sufficient to explain the existence of consensual politics in Scandinavia insofar as it is only in Scandinavia that they are found in combination. If we attempt to sort out democracies according to these variables, a clear pattern emerges: all consensual democracies have extreme or hyper-corporatism and a smooth transition (Norway,Sweden, Denmark). Competitive democracies lack hyper-corporatism, but have a smooth transition (Belgium, the Netherlands, Ireland). All conflictual democracies lack hyper-corporatism and have a rough transition (inter- and early postwar Finland, Italy, Weimar Germany, interwar Austria, the Third and Fourth French republics, and so forth). And the only unconsolidated democracy, Finland since the mid-1960s, has hyper-corporatism and a rough transition. Contemporary Germany appears superficially to be an exception to the generalization that all competitive democracies have smooth transitions. In fact, it simply makes the point that, given a thoroughgoing Nazi revolution, defeat, foreign occupation, a new international balance, and permanent partition, anything is possible. Including a fresh start.

I have said little about another superficially anomalous case, Austria, because it consistently falls outside the scope of our theoretical concerns. Austria belonged to the conflictual type during the years of the First Republic. Then, from 1945 to 1955, it was an occupied country. It makes no sense to classify it during these years because its politics were so heavily conditioned by the occupation and the precarious international balance. The fragile international balance and its legacy were reflected in the Grand Coalition, which lasted until 1966. The political system was not a "normal" one during these years because the competition and conflict that usually occur in a democracy were intentionally suppressed. Elections, although deciding which party would gain the premiership, were not contests, even in principle, about which parties would govern. It was understood in advance that, whatever the electoral outcome, the government would consist of the Socialist and Catholic People's parties.[46]

From the end of the Grand Coalition to the 1983 election, the system was a multiparty one in the electoral arena, but not in the legislature and in government formation. During these years there were only two relevant parties. With the exception of the brief minority government of 1970, one party—either the Catholics or the Socialists—always succeeded in winning an absolute majority of seats. It was, then, effectively a two-party democracy.

It became a multiparty democracy for the first time as a result of the 1983 election, in which the Socialists lost their majority and were replaced in government by a Catholic-Liberal coalition. It is only at this point that it comes within the scope of the theory. Obviously, it does so as a fourth case of consensual democracy. That it became consensual without having experienced a smooth transition hardly undermines my interpretation of the historical origins of the various types of democracy. Austria, like postwar Germany, simply makes the point that revolution, war, defeat, occupation, and a radical change in the balance of power allow for a break with the burdens of the past.

CHAPTER TWO

Policymaking and the Imperatives of Party Leadership

Party Leaders and Policy Politics

Conventional coalition theory has assumed that parties make many policy preferences decisive in government formation and that these preferences are without a definite pattern. The image of a large number of preferences derives from a failure to distinguish between the preferences that are important for the course and length of negotiations and the preferences that are decisive for the final outcome. The latter, I will attempt to demonstrate, are few in number. Even if the number of pertinent preferences is small, the problem of identifying them remains. The important question is: Which policy preferences? As one reads historical accounts, there seems to be no pattern to the decisive preferences. Their realm embraces all manner of political questions: foreign alliances, economic policy, taxation, welfare programs, religious education, divorce, marriage, abortion, land reform, and more. This apparent lack of a pattern is surely one reason coalition theorists have been reluctant to address the role of policy conflicts in coalition negotiations.

I will argue that there is a simple pattern to the relevant preferences. Before that pattern can be appreciated, we must consider why, contrary to the stereotypical image, the number of decisive preferences is actually quite small—seldom more than five per party. This smallness of number derives from the several and conflicting goals that party leaders experience in multiparty systems. These goals include the desire to retain the leadership, to maintain party unity, to participate in a government, to participate in a majority government, to preserve policy preferences, to see the preferences enacted as public policy. The manner in which leaders reconcile these goals is conditioned by the relationship of reciprocal control in which they are bound with party activists and the parliamentary party. In the short-term, leaders largely control the question of participation and therefore access to the benefits of participation. In the somewhat longer-term, however, parliamentarians and activists control the tenure of party leaders. I assume that leaders are motivated above all by a desire to remain party leaders and that this means that they will always strive to minimize party disunity and, in particular, the extent to which the question of participation becomes entangled in intraparty disputes.

They will, therefore, attempt to rest the party's attitudes toward participation on preferences that produce the least disunity. So that, if they decide against participation, activists and parliamentarians will endorse this decision because of the policy concessions that would otherwise have been entailed. Or, in the case of participation, so that they will agree that the policy price paid in joining the government was not excessive. From this perspective, the leaders' task is to insist on preferences that are sufficiently focused that they generate the widest possible support within the party, but sufficiently vague and opaque that they do not engage in government formation the disagreements that are a constant feature of any party.

The policy preferences that parties advance can always be divided into two types: first, preferences that embody contested principles of policy or program direction; second, preferences that concern timing, amounts, rates of change, and contingencies. The first type of preference is normally accompanied by the second; but frequently the second is not accompanied by the first. In either case, the contention is that only preferences of the first type are decisive in government formation. From this point of view, for a party that advocates an increase in agricultural subsidies, it will be the increase rather than the particular terms—which will virtually always be negotiable—that will be decisive. Likewise, for a party opposed to abortion, the decisive preference will be reduced availability of abortions rather than the particular circumstances under which they will and will not be available.

Principles of direction will be decisive because they minimize disunity by deriving from the most widely shared values within a party and because they directly engage the party's most basic sense of purpose. In contrast, preferences that concern timing, amounts, rates of change, and contingencies derive from a range of tactical, legal, economic, technical, and other calculations that virtually always generate dissension. They are consequently a weak platform for leaders to rest their leadership on.

It makes little sense for leaders to make acceptance of such secondary preferences the *conditio sine qua non* of their party's participation in government. For such a demand is likely to weaken the leadership's position within its own party. It is likely to alienate legislators and activists. And to the extent that it reduces the opportunities for patronage by reducing the prospects of government participation, it is likely to reduce the leadership's ability to stay in power and open it to the attacks of counterelites within the party. Such commitment is likely also to make it more difficult for the legislature to function by transforming it into an arena of Hobbesian confrontation. For democratic parties, prosystem parties, who conceive of themselves largely in terms of accomplishing certain substantial ends for their constituents, this is a disincentive of considerable weight. Finally, because they are not related to the deepest predispositions of the party, such leadership commitments are likely to encounter not merely indifference from large segments of the party, but outright opposition. Commitment will thus increase the probability of factionalism within the party and thereby further undermine the leadership's ability to remain in power. Leaders will find it exceedingly difficult to justify nonparticipation in government in terms of policy preferences a large part of the party is indifferent to or actually opposes. Consequently, it will always be in the leadership's interest to take a hard line in government negotiations only on policy preferences that will have widespread support among legislators and activists.

The number of determining issues will be kept small not simply because it is only the major issues which are fungible for the leadership. The number will be kept small, as well, because not participating in government has high costs. Most of the time, payment of these costs can be justified to the parliamentary party and the central committee or leadership bureau, as the case may be, only if the leadership can point to very dear policy preferences that would have to be surrendered. Failure to participate always carries with it the threat of leaving the party politically weaker and still further from its goals. The dilemma of the German Social Democrats in the Weimar Republic is classical. It demonstrates the potency of such considerations even in an extremely divided and polarized political system. Participation with bourgeois parties risked alienation of left-wing activists to the Communists. On the other hand, many argued that failure to participate risked handing the government to the far right and that one could, in any event, accomplish more in the government than out.

> Among them were [Otto] Braun and [Karl] Severing, who as long time members of the Prussian [State] Government could better appreciate the value of active participation in government. Severing kept urging his friends to enter a coalition with the bourgeois parties. To insist on a specific policy as the *sine qua non* of a coalition seemed to him unrealistic and impractical. Moreover, he thought it unlikely that an advance understanding could be reached with the German People's Party, the spokesman of heavy industry, on working hours,

industrial safety, workers' insurance and workers' rights. "Will these problems be settled more favorably for the workers," he pleaded, "if the influence of heavy industry remains unchallenged in the cabinet, or would it not be better from the viewpoint of labor if Social Democrats would participate in the shaping of policies . . . ?"

Otto Braun's advice was in a similar vein. Speaking from practical experience, he pointed out that advance agreements on detailed government programs were pointless. Strong men would always obtain a consideration of their viewpoints without any advance commitments, while weak men would be overruled in spite of all such arrangements.[1]

There is the risk that if a party is not in the government, its opponents will be free to implement their own policy preferences. What may be worse, there is the occasional risk that the opponent will implement the party's policy preferences—or close approximations of them—and thereby make inroads into its constituency by demoralizing its activists. In this connection the profound dilemma that the French Communist party faced in the summer of 1981 vis-à-vis the election of François Mitterrand is instructive. The Communists could remain in opposition and preserve their policies, but risk handing leadership of the left to the Socialists, or they could subordinate their preferences and share leadership with the Socialists. Governments make a steady stream of decisions—frequently on issues that cannot be foreseen at the time of government formation. Only through participation can one be certain of the opportunity to exercise influence on these decisions, even if it is only a defensive or blocking influence.

Party leaders, especially those who represent their parties in negotiations, have unique and powerful personal incentives to limit the number of issues that might preclude participation in government: the opportunity to occupy ministerial positions. Typically, these positions represent the pinnacle of a political career, and their attraction to men who have spent much of their lives striving for them can hardly be overestimated. The career incentive also plays a role for the members of the parliamentary party, who—sometimes in conjunction with the party central committee—usually make the ultimate decision on whether the party will participate on the available terms. Some parliamentarians will have the opportunity to go into the government. Others will have the opportunity to move up in the parliamentary party hierarchy as a result of the vacancies created by government participation. All will benefit politically from the greater access to the governmental machinery and resources afforded by party participation.

Political parties in multiparty systems based on proportional representation almost always have a strong sense of identity based on certain convictions in one or a few spheres of public policy: social policy, economic policy, religious policy, rural affairs, foreign relations, and such. There is likely to be a great deal of agreement on these convictions and the related policy preferences—indeed, the convictions are likely to be what attracted members to the party in the first place. But as one moves away from the policy questions directly related to these convictions, and especially as one moves away from the policy sphere of the convictions, policy consensus, even in well-disciplined parties, breaks down. To take a single example, the Conservative party in Norway has long been concerned mainly with economic and foreign policy questions, and on the central questions of economic and foreign policy, there is a high level of consensus within the party on what constitute proper party positions. In areas removed from these spheres, the consensus dissolves. On the question of abortion, for instance, the party is deeply divided. So much so that the leadership has found it expedient to declare that legislators should follow their consciences. There is nothing in the party's intellectual traditions to give members guidance in reaching common policy conclusions on such a matter. In consequence, the basis for creating a consensus within the party on the matter hardly exists.

The necessity of focusing on only a limited range of issues is prevalent in well-disciplined parties, such as the Norwegian Conservative party, but is especially great when a party is deeply factionalized.

Imperatives of Party Leadership 51

> Whenever in Israel diverse factions . . . have been held together in a single bloc . . . the energy needed to maintain the cohesion of such a unit has been tremendous. The leaders of such a bloc . . . must constantly be on their guard to settle such internal differences as may arise, or else some new or unresolved issue can polarize the factions within the bloc and lead to a split and dissolution of the unit. In order to do this, many differences between component factions must either be resolved in advance, or left unresolved by an understanding that the *status quo* will be maintained and the disagreement de-emphasized. The larger the bloc . . . the greater the likelihood that a number of policy areas may be "depoliticized" for the sake of the bloc's cohesion. . . . Since a large number of potential options for the group's action could lead to a split in that group, only a few options are left which the bloc can safely exercise without the risk of internal disruption.
>
> This was the case with the Religious Front. The only area where it could safely operate without risking dissolution was in the area of demanding greater state concessions to religion.[2]

The Religious Front might well have been particularly fractious, but on this score the difference between it and other parties is in degree rather than kind, and its experience illustrates clearly the general rule that a leadership's injudicious choice of issues always carries with it the danger of a counter-action.

It is normally the case that party leaders choose very carefully indeed those issues on which participation in government will depend. Many other issues will certainly play a role in negotiations: they can be used as inexpensive concessions, bartered, brought to the fore to demonstrate concern for a party faction. But, as a rule, even in fairly polarized systems, coalition bargaining is substantive and pragmatic, despite the presence of much ideological rhetoric. As a general rule, the parties initially present all of their major platform planks as demands. In the early stages the formateur, or especially the informateur, if he is employed, is inundated with dozens of mutually incompatible demands.

In a polarized system, in one recovering from a

"shock election," or in one with factionalized parties, this first stage can last a long time indeed. This is because the leadership must demonstrate its sensitivity to the desires of the party militants. It implies no trivialization of the process to say that this is a kind of ritual engaged in by virtually all party leaderships. Militants are often a very small minority in a party. But precisely because they are so committed they both pose a threat to the leadership and perform valuable services. Leaders who, by dint of their long parliamentary experience and need to cooperate with the leaders of other parties, are often the most accommodating of party members, are thus in the position of needing to reaffirm their virtue in the eyes of the least accommodating of party members. This takes time.

It is only then that the serious interparty bargaining begins. After several rounds of preliminary talks with the formateur, sometimes in the form of multiparty roundtables, each party which intends to bargain seriously has settled on a few major programmatic issues which it will press in the talks. What makes the talks so long, difficult, and complex is generally not the lack of goodwill among elites, but the fact that negotiations must appear the way they do in order to satisfy the members whose orientations are still largely attuned to the vocal, symbolic, and ideological aspects characteristic of each respective political subculture. It is wrong to assume that, because interparty negotiations take a long time, much is being negotiated among the parties. Most negotiation in cases of protracted government formation takes place between leaders and their followers and among rival factions within parties.

These generalizations will be tested indirectly in part two when derivative hypotheses about government-formation outcomes are tested. But the immediate point is that they seem to obtain whether the basis for within-party competition and bargaining is policies or personalities or both. In parties in which factional competition is intense, government formation provides an often ideal occasion for one faction to seek to sabotage another. This seems to be more significant for the course of government formation than for the final outcome.

Certainly these generalizations pertain mainly to democratic parties. Yet it is precisely for these parties that the problem of identifying the determining policy preferences is so pertinent. For parties of the antidemocratic variety, identifying the policy commitments that preclude government participation hardly requires theoretical analysis. The theoretical challenge is posed by the behavior of those parties which do not choose to be parties of permanent opposition and are not compelled to be by their attitude toward the democratic order. They are parties which in the postwar period have entered and left government with some regularity. They value government participation. For them, the questions are mainly: At what cost? For what gains?

Policy Profiles

It follows that if the objective of leaders is to minimize disunity, they will limit the decisive preferences not only to contested principles of direction, but to those principles that are of the greatest concern to their parties. These principles are to be found in the areas that form the core of a party's identification. I have called these areas of identification a party's profiles.

Parties have most commonly acquired profiles by translating societal cleavages into lines of party conflict during the years before and just after the adoption of universal suffrage and, especially, the introduction of proportional representation. As Lipset and Rokkan observed, the introduction of proportional representation had the effect of consolidating—almost freezing—party systems.[3] It tended to guarantee most then-existing parties a place in the system, but it limited the opportunities they had to radically restructure the party system. The limited opportunities derived from the absence of a threshold above which a party could deliver an electoral knockout blow to its rival—as it could in a plurality system.

Because it stabilized party systems composed of existing parties, proportional representation also tended to stabilize the presence in the party system of the cleavages that had initially precipitated the parties. The stabilization of the lines of conflict gave parties an enduring character. Parties came to see themselves and were seen to be mainly concerned with certain types of issues, even though they were regularly required to take positions in other matters. The lines of cleavage remained relevant to parties long after the initial disputes that had given rise to the parties had receded.

This was partly due to the stability of proportional representation. But it was also due to the continuous processes of socialization and competition within parties and the durability of the underlying conflicts within the society at large. As with any organization, the processes of individual socialization and competition meant that men advanced in a party to the extent that they acquired the right concerns and ideals. Those who wished to rise accepted the dominant values and concerns of the party and were rewarded accordingly. Deviants were denied advancement as conformity—learning, if one likes—became more important at every higher level.

Thus, the conserving effects of socialization and competition have tended to reinforce the conserving effects of proportional representation. The result has been fairly stable party systems composed of parties with rather constant policy focuses and varying amounts of value cohesion within the areas of focus. This conservatism, however, has been premised on, and has required, the durability of most societal cleavages. This durability itself has derived from the simple fact that no Western society has ever been able to escape the consequences of the rise of the nation-state, the commercialization of agriculture, and the industrial revolution. All cleavages have had their roots in these three processes and have survived on the legacies of them.

Parties have acquired profiles on socioeconomic, constitutional, producer-consumer, cultural/ethnolinguistic, regional or center-periphery, ethical/religious, and foreign policy cleavages. With the exception of the ethnolinguistic cleavage, each of these is evident in every Western society. Not all, however, have been translated into lines of party opposition in every society. Whether they have been has depended on their relative intensity in the society at large, the historical sequences of mass mobilization, and considerations of organizational and electoral strategies, especially the payoffs of alliances and mergers and the costs of splits and lost support. In general, it appears that parties found a cleavage most profitable in the electoral arena, and were most likely to bring it into the party system when it was coincidental with and reinforced by a second cleavage.[4] The most consistent exception to this has been the socioeconomic cleavage, which has needed no reinforcement.[5]

The socioeconomic cleavage has, of course, involved conflicts over the relative distribution of burdens and benefits across classes and the management of the market economy in its impact on this distribution. All parties in the Western world have had to take a position—and acquire a profile—on socioeconomic issues, because these issues directly engage the well-being of all social groups regardless of their other identifications. The universality of the profile simply reflects the primacy of class conflict over time in Western societies. The varieties of party systems have been a function of the extent to which the socioeconomic cleavage has been supplemented by other cleavages.

In the main, the parties who earlier acquired constitutional profiles on conflicts over personal liberties, the suffrage, and the form of the national polity subsequently lost these profiles through desuetude, for the great constitutional issues were generally resolved at the same time the party systems were coming into existence. The constitutional cleavage has survived, however, where antidemocratic parties have prevented the legitimization of the constitutional order.

The producer-consumer cleavage has involved conflicts of interest between the primary and secondary/tertiary economies, between the farmers of the countryside and the merchants, between workers and industrialists of the cities. In its broadest terms the cleavage reaches back to the Middle Ages and was acknowledged at the time by the existence of separate estates for the nobility (country) and burghers (cities). The commercialization of agriculture and the industrial revolution deepened these conflicts and across Europe produced distinct rural-urban alignments in legislatures. The farmers, for their part, saw themselves as defending not just economic interests but an entire way of life premised on ascription and family and in conflict with the achievement and individualism of the city.[6] The core of the dispute, however, was economic: agrarians wanted to sell the products at the highest possible price and buy what they needed from urban industry at the lowest possible price. In the twentieth century, this conflict has taken the form of disputes, among others, over price supports, rationalization, land reform, and national investment strategies and tariffs on imported agricultural products.

Ethical/religious cleavages have, after the socioeconomic, provided the most common lines of conflict in Western party systems.[7] The substance of the conflict has varied according to national circumstances. In the countries that experienced the Counter-Reformation, the conflict has centered on the role of the Catholic church in public affairs. In nations split by the Reformation—France, Belgium, the Netherlands, Germany, and Switzerland—the cleavage has been between Protestantism and Catholicism. Where the Reformation was thoroughgoing—as in Scandinavia—conflict has arisen from rejection by orthodox evangelicals of the extreme latitudinarianism of the established Lutheran church.

Foreign policy cleavages have been very nearly as common as ethical/religious cleavages in Western party systems. Nineteenth-century struggles between pacifists and militarists, the Russian Revolution, the Second World War, the Cold War, and the growth of supranational institutions have been the primary precipitants of these cleavages. The most basic policy conflicts have been over alliance memberships, neutrality, critical bilateral relationships, participation in regional organizations, and basic military strategy. The foreign policy cleavage has not been the exclusive property of the left, but it has been the most common source of division among left parties. In the same way the relatively late mobilization of the working class resulted in most other cleavages separating bourgeois parties before the emancipation of the working class, the occurrence of the Russian Revolution after the mobilization of the working class led everywhere in Europe to the breaking up of socialist parties.

The center-periphery cleavage has arisen where one or more other cleavages have been regionalized; where socioeconomic, cultural, and other differences have separated territories within a single nation. In its most extreme form the cleavage resulted in secession, as in the division of Ireland and Great Britain and the breakup of the union of Norway and Sweden. The cleavage has tended to enter the party system in nations with a single dominant city, as in Norway (Oslo) and Finland (Helsinki) and in which outlying areas have had only weak cultural ties to the city or have found it difficult to maintain competitive industries. Denmark, with Copenhagen overwhelmingly dominant at the turn of the century, makes the point that a single dominant city was not sufficient to produce the cleavage in the party system when outlying areas were relatively prosperous and communication and transportation fairly easy.

In policy terms, center-periphery conflict has above all taken the form of conflict over strategies of national economic development. Defenders of the center have typically advocated allocations of investment on the basis of calculations of national efficiency. Such calculations necessarily lead to even greater concentrations of interest in the center at the expense of the periphery. Defenders of the periphery, in contrast, propose strategies based on local criteria. The conflict between national and local criteria is mirrored in debates over the distribution of public services and cultural amenities.

The last cleavage in Western societies, and the one least common in the countries that concern us, has been the cultural/ethnolinguistic cleavage—the conflict between minority and majority language communities. In no Western society has the cleavage been significant in the party system when it has not been reinforced by another cleavage, generally the center-periphery or constitutional. In Spain and Belgium both have reinforced it and pushed it into the party system. In Norway, the linguistic conflict between New Norwegian and Classical Norwegian was strengthened by the parallel center-periphery conflict. In Finland, the line of conflict between the upper class of Swedish-speakers and the lower class of Finnish-speakers was reinforced by socioeconomic conflict.

Most party systems were established in the second half of the nineteenth century and the early years of the twentieth century and have survived to the present with only modest changes. And the changes that have occurred have conformed to the same pattern that was apparent in the establishment of the early parties. New parties have either entered the party system directly with a new cleavage or, more frequently, have come about by breaking away from an older party as a result of a new cleavage or an intensified disagreement on an old one. Because the attitudes a party has assumed when it has been engaged by a new cleavage have become virtually synonymous with the party, these attitudes have also become the ones that legislators and activists gain the most psychological and material benefits from advancing in government. In consequence, they are the attitudes with which leaders can most reliably count upon the loyalty of their followers. They are the attitudes that led men and women to join the party in the first place, so that the psychic benefits that accrue from consistency are strong. Because they are so important to the party, the careers of party members—and especially of party leaders—are more likely to suffer from disunity on related questions than on any others.

Two points must be stressed. First, assigning a profile to a party does not imply that the party is indifferent to the issues outside the profile. On the contrary, the party is quite likely to have very real and well-articulated preferences on these extra-profile issues. But the profiles a party acquires reflect its *raison d'être*. The second point is that as the profiles can be known, except in the case of the most recent parties, from the parties' origins and experiences prior to the period for which we wish to predict behavior, relying on them in order to identify the preferences that will be decisive in government formation need not be tautological.

Although in this chapter I have emphasized the formative importance for party systems of the early twentieth century and the enduring quality of cleavage lines, the model I have applied is not a static one. It explicitly recognizes the appearance of new cleavages and accounts for the appearance of new parties during the postwar decades. It does not assume that a cleavage is of constant importance. The evidence of the studies in part two and appendix B is that only the socioeconomic cleavage has been persistently important. The importance of the other cleavages has fluctuated according to the socioeconomic change, environmental events that make them more or less salient, and political calculi about the mass-marketability of specific issues. Within the model, cleavages—and even parties—are free to come and go.

The most efficient explanation for the fluctuating importance of cleavages appears to be socioeconomic change, either development or decay. Development has reduced the intensity of linguistic conflicts in Norway and Finland. But in those countries, and in Sweden, development has also accentuated the center-periphery cleavage. In contrast, decay, or at least perceived stagnation, has accentuated the reinforcing linguistic, religious, and center-periphery (regional) conflicts in postwar Belgium.

In the Netherlands, socioeconomic development weakened the religious cleavage, reduced electoral support for the religious parties, and thereby deprived the Catholic party of its dominant position. The lines of political competition once were trilateral and ran among a religious center led by the Catholics and an anticlerical left and anticlerical right. Competition now is more bilateral and pits a left against a right that is, in practice, also partly Christian Democratic. Whereas their electoral support and the cleavage lines once allowed the Catholics to play off socialists and liberals against each other without clearly aligning with either, the Catholics now—within the Christian Democratic Appeal—must make a clear choice of a coalition with either the left or the right.

In Israel, socioeconomic development reduced the importance of the old, preindependence divisions within the left and right even more than it reduced the divisions between the left and right. The result was the gradual consolidation of the two camps into the Labor Alignment and Likud. If anything, however, development has accentuated the clerical-anticlerical conflict in Israel. Whereas the cleavage was once moderated by the Labor party's ability to balance the claims of clerical and anticlerical foes, the consolidation of the left and right have deprived Labor of the ability to do this.

In none of the case studies of coalition negotiations, which cover the period from approximately 1955 to 1975, is there any indication of a postmaterialist cleavage at work. That there is no indication of such a cleavage in party negotiations does not mean that the cleavage did not exist or was not coming into existence at the mass level. Indeed, we know from other research that in at least some other countries such a cleavage was beginning to appear within mass publics and was having at least a slight resonance in some party systems. But in the democracies studied here, at least through 1975, it had not had enough of an impact on the party system to become a significant line of conflict in coalition negotiations.[8]

Policy Principles and Party Preferences

The essential propositions can now be drawn together. Only preferences within profiles will decisively influence attitudes of leaders toward participation in a hypothetical government; preferences outside the profiles will always be irrelevant to the final outcome of negotiations. Within the profiles,

Imperatives of Party Leadership

only those preferences that leaders find most fungible will be decisive. These will be the preferences that elicit the broadest party unity, or—more accurately—minimize disunity. Because they do so, they will also be the preferences that minimize the vulnerability of leaders. The preferences will virtually always be fundamental programmatic principles that concern the direction in which public policy in a particular area should move.

Preferences based on principles of direction will offer incumbents the lowest level of threat to their tenure because they are preferences that derive from the values that are relatively constant and widely shared in the party. Contrarily, preferences that concern amounts, rates of change, contingencies, and further programmatic elaboration of previously established principles derive not only from shared values, but from the extent of the commitment to the values and from a broad range of exceedingly complex technocratic calculations. They thereby almost always generate dissension.

As a practical matter, this definition of relevant preferences will, for any particular party at a particular time, reduce to a handful the number of preferences that are decisive. And because of their utility to leaders and their importance to parties, leaders will insure that they are highly salient. Henceforth, the references I make to policy preferences will be limited to this small set.

In parties with comparatively coherent belief systems, agreement exists not only about the important concerns and related values, but also about the nature of basic policy preferences. These parties naturally have a stronger sense of identity than do deeply factionalized, nonideological parties. In the case of the latter, a looser interpretation must be attached to the notion of a profile. For such parties, profiles are equivalent only to historically determined foci of policy concern and a minimal set of shared values within the area of concern: party leaders frequently find that the consensus within the party does not extend from agreement on what should concern the party and the basic values to agreement on what specific policies should be pursued in the area of concern.

This, however, is of no consequence for our understanding of government formation. The import of a nonideological character and factionalism is in neither the absence of profiles nor the unidentifiability of preferences when the preferences exist. Instead, it is in the frequent absence of a preference within a profile, because the party is prevented by its deep factionalism and comparative lack of ideology from creating an internal consensus. Such parties simply have fewer decisive preferences when a government is being negotiated, because there is less that they can agree on. In extreme cases, the decisive preferences that such parties do have generate consensus only across the spectrum of the dominant factions. As well, these preferences will fluctuate more frequently in response to the changing balances of power within the party.

Bargaining and the Limits of Tolerance

It is now possible to capture in a simple ordinal scale the bargaining relationships that can exist between the formateurs' party and each other party represented in the legislature.[9] The relevant preferences of the formateurs' party and another party can be tangential, convergent, or divergent. They are tangential if they address different issues and are sufficiently unrelated that party leaders do not consider them to be incompatible. Such a relationship can exist when, for instance, the formateurs' party is concerned with wage indexation or consumer subsidies and the second party is concerned with the status of a minority language.

I will say that policy preferences are convergent when the two parties are concerned with the same issues and advocate principles of direction that tend toward each other. If, for instance, the two parties are concerned with the issue of wage indexation and both endorse the principle of guaranteeing that wages will be tied to prices, even if by somewhat different formulae that yield different rates and amounts of wage catch-up, the preferences are convergent. In contrast, if one of the parties opposed the principle of indexation or advocated the abandonment of it, the preferences would be divergent. Preferences are divergent when two parties focus on different issues but advocate mutually exclusive preferences or focus on the same issue and advocate directionally incompatible preferences.

Two kinds of such relationships can exist, and the distinction depends on the nature of the compromise that the two parties would require before they would be willing to govern together. A compromise can be implicit or explicit. In the case of an implicit compromise, the parties are willing to agree to disagree. They might agree that the government will ignore the disagreement by having no policy on the point of contention. They might—as parties often do—further agree that if the issue arises in the legislature, they reserve the right of a free vote. Another option is for the parties to announce that they have agreed to place a moratorium on the matter for a certain length of time, after which the parties will be free to reconsider their participation in the government in light of the preferences that exist at that time. Yet another option is for the parties to agree to a period of cabinet or committee study. Or the parties might agree to the issuance of a statement of such ambiguity that each is able to interpret it as not violating its preference. If the leaders involved are so inclined, the opportunities for creative procrastination are virtually limitless. Whichever approach is chosen, the decisive point is that the parties do not, by forming the coalition, obligate themselves to support a policy that is at variance with their respective preferences. This is a divergent relationship based on an implicit compromise.

In contrast, in a divergent-explicit relationship, one or both parties demand a preference change—mutual or unilateral—as a quid pro quo of participation in a coalition. What is important is that in such a relationship one or both parties must obligate themselves to support a government policy that is at variance with their prenegotiation preferences.

It is self-evident that the leaders of the formateurs'

party will prefer tangential and convergent preference relationships and that they will prefer implicit compromises to explicit compromises. It is also reasonable to expect that a tangential preference relationship will be preferable to a convergent preference relationship. The reasoning behind this is in the simple need for leaders to preserve the distinctiveness of their parties in a normally crowded multiparty field. It follows from their concern to maintain their distinctiveness that party leaders will, all other things being equal, prefer cooperation with a party whose preferences are tangential to cooperation with a party whose preferences are convergent. The latter will require that a party share with another party advocacy in government of the policies that the party most highly values. This follows necessarily from the nature of the relationship and the definition of relevant policy preferences. Insofar as parties who advocate the same preferences tend to compete for the support of the same pool of voters, cooperation based on convergent preferences will require that the formateurs' party give one of its most menacing competitors access to governmental resources and will enhance the competitor's image as a legitimate alternative recipient of electoral support.

I propose that we can predict the size and party composition of government-formation outcomes by specifying the formateurs' limits of tolerance in consensual, competitive, and conflictual systems in terms of the scale of bargaining relationships. The size and composition will be determined by the availability of parties who have bargaining relationships with the formateur's party which are the same as or more preferable than the hypothesized limit of tolerance. The hypothesized limit applies to the least favorable relationship that exists between the two parties within their entire set of relevant preferences. If the parties have convergent preferences on one issue and divergent-implicit preferences on another, the bargaining relationship is divergent-implicit. When this relationship is equal to or more favorable than the hypothesized limit, it is expected that the formateurs will include the second party in the government. The formateurs will always be willing to proceed to the limit of tolerance, but not beyond it. The government that emerges is, in this view, a by-product of the prevailing constellation of bargaining relationships and the systemically determined consequences that the formateurs find attached to different levels of tolerance.

The building blocks of the theory of government formation are now in place. In chapter 3, by means of a continued analysis of the goals of party leaders, I will derive the hypothesized limit of tolerance for each system type. The theory of relevant preferences and the ordering of the types in the typology of bargaining relationships can, within the context of the entire theory of government formation, be viewed as axioms. They are axioms in two senses: (a) their validity will be tested indirectly rather than directly; and (b) if they are invalid, it will be impossible to confirm the hypotheses presented in chapter 3. In deriving the hypotheses I will assume that: 1) the first goal of party leaders is always to remain party leaders; 2) party leaders always seek to minimize policy compromises. In the course of deriving the hypothesized limits of tolerance and afterward, it will be possible to derive some predictions concerning the distribution of minority, majority, minimum-winning, and oversized governments. We can thereby obtain a preliminary test of the general theory.

CHAPTER THREE

Party Leaders and Governing Coalitions

The conventional wisdom is that among the politically responsible sites in multiparty democracies, the cabinet is by far the most important for the making of basic public policy. We generally assume that the parliament merely ratifies and that parties, because of multipartism, can formulate only preferences rather than policy. In the main, this is correct. But the assumption does not apply in consensual systems. In these systems, the cabinet is just one among several sites capable of formulating coherent policies. For the consensus-building mechanisms that derive from hyper-corporatism and the normative commitment to consensual politics that derives from hyper-corporatism and an unpolarized party system make possible the effective development of policy in legislative committees, national commissions, roundtables of government, party and interest group leaders, and extra-governmental conclaves of party leaders.[1]

In competitive and conflictual systems, too, it is possible to formulate policy outside the cabinet; but it is also a great deal more difficult, because the systems lack the mechanisms fostered by hyper-corporatism and the normative commitment produced by hyper-corporatism and an unpolarized party system. Lacking such mechanisms and commitment, it is possible for parties and the interests they represent to insure influence on policy outcomes only through party participation in the government; because final policies frequently reflect a consensus on the kinds of issues that I have defined as government-formation relevant that is no broader than the bare minimum required to obtain legislative approval. It is also the case that such systems function a great deal more effectively when they have majority governments. Indeed, in the absence of a majority government, such systems are able to implement new policies with only the greatest difficulty, because they lack, or have only weak versions of, the extra-cabinet mechanisms and institutions that are so important to policy formulation in consensual systems.

Consensual Democracies

Because the existence of well-developed consensus-building mechanisms and the normative commitment to their use means that ultimate policy outcomes will be generally satisfactory, whether reached in the cabinet, parliament, or outside of both, the leaders of the party forming a government have little incentive to create majority governments, if they must do so at the cost of policy sacrifices. The point to appreciate is that in consensual systems, the consensus-building mechanisms fostered by hyper-corporatism provide alternative sites for resolving interparty differences. And the decisive feature of these systems is that it is always in a party leader's interest to defer compromises on those major issues I have defined as government-formation relevant to these alternative sites. Because party concessions will not then be party-to-party concessions, and therefore highly risky for party leaders, but will also be concessions among the interest groups directly concerned with the government and parties, and consequently much less threatening to party leaders. The structure of the system itself, therefore, provides party leaders with a strong inducement not to compromise relevant preferences in government formation. This will be especially the case if the compromises entailed are explicit compromises. For the immediate goal of the leaders is to retain and strengthen their control of the leadership. Compromising the party's most deeply held preferences does not contribute to this.

Moreover, the normative commitment to consensual politics that derives from hyper-corporatism and an unpolarized party system means that there is only a low danger that the government will threaten the interests a party represents, if that party remains in opposition. Consequently, parties have little *defensive* inducement to compromise for the sake of being in government. Just as a potential member has little defensive inducement to participate, the formateurs will have little defensive inducement to compromise for the sake of creating a majority government, because the consensual norms and institutions permit a minority government to govern quite effectively. And, as well, although there is always some danger that the opposition parties will compel the minority government's resignation, the danger is comparatively small in consensual systems, precisely because the institutions and norms allow opposition parties to influence policy without recourse to a change of government.[2]

An implicit compromise will not be as threatening to party leaders as an explicit compromise will be, but it still will not provide them with a fundamental gain, because the structure of the system, for all of the reasons outlined above, still means that they do not need to compromise preferences at the government formation stage in order to create a viable government or later have an influence on policy.

To sum up, neither the formateurs nor other party leaders have an incentive to compromise those policy preferences that I have defined as government-formation relevant in government formation. Only governments based on tangential and convergent preferences are justified in terms of the benefits they provide and the costs they impose on party leaders. Neither carries costs in terms of policy compromises. And both will strengthen the leaders' positions by providing additional established support for a party's preferences and thereby enhance the weight of those preferences in final policy development. Having such partners in government rather than merely in the legislature will provide parties with more reliable partners when future negotiations occur on preferences that are not relevant to government formation. The inference to be drawn, therefore, is that the limit of tolerance in consensual systems will be provided by convergent preferences. The formateurs' party will make governments only with those parties whose relevant preferences are tangential or convergent. All parties with such relationships will be included in the government; all others will be excluded.

Conflictual Democracies

The two defining characteristics of a conflictual system are the absence of consensus-building institutions and the presence of an extremely polarized and centrifugal party system. The consequences of the first characteristic are that conflicting principles of policy direction must be resolved largely in government formation or the cabinet and that defensive participation in government is encouraged. But the consequence of the second characteristic, centrifugal competition induced by the presence of an antidemocratic party, is invariably acute party-system polarization. The arguments of politics turn on the rules of the game—the way in which decisions are made and enforced—and on who can legitimately make decisions, as much as on the content of the decisions themselves. As parties challenge one another's legitimacy, a process of reciprocal de-legitimization ensues, which compels parties to move away from each other and to emphasize their radical distinctiveness in policy terms. In the process they expand the space of competition. In consequence, the autonomy of party leaders and the security of their tenure are drastically reduced.[3]

Compromise among parties is, therefore, made more difficult on three counts: 1) polarization makes it objectively more difficult, because compromises must cover a greater distance; 2) even when obtained, it is comparatively more difficult to persuade parliamentary parties, factions, and activists to accede to the sacrifices a compromise entails; and 3) the tenuousness of party leaders' positions makes them more reluctant to strike the kinds of bargains that provide counterelites with ideal justifications for assaults on their leadership positions.[4]

The difficulties notwithstanding, some government must be formed; and it will be a specially felt responsibility of the democratic parties to form it, because of their sense that the system cannot function—indeed, cannot survive—if they do not participate. The acute polarization will require that the relationships on which governments are based entail some type of compromise, if parties are to be brought together in a coalition: tangential and convergent preferences will exist only occasionally and insufficiently. At the same time, explicit compromises are likely to be extraordinarily difficult to obtain. In contrast, an implicit compromise—an agreement to disagree—deflects these difficulties. In principle, it permits of the participation of all democratic parties. Thus, the prospects of a coalition of working size—often of majority size—are greatly improved. At the same time, an implicit compromise avoids the difficulties in persuading followers to follow, in overcoming the objective distances that separate parties, and in preserving leadership positions. It does so in all instances because no policy preferences have actually been altered. The inference must be, therefore, that the limit of tolerance will be the divergent-implicit relationship. Finally, I will assume that, when two or more parties meet the limit of tolerance but refuse to serve together, the formateurs' party will always prefer to govern with the party or parties that provide the larger number of parliamentary votes.

Dominated-Competitive Democracies

In contrast to consensual systems, basic policy agreements in competitive systems must be reached in the cabinet. In contrast to conflictual systems, competitive systems do not suffer the debilitating effects that make the construction of coalitions so difficult in conflictual systems. This distinct combination of attributes has the consequence of allowing the structure of the party system—whether it is dominated or undominated—to profoundly affect the way in which party leaders act on their goals. It is only in competitive systems that the structure of the party system has significance. As it will become apparent, it is not possible for dominance to be of consequence in consensual systems because parties can influence policy without participating in governments; it is of no consequence in conflictual systems because polarization places severe limits on the autonomy of party leaders.

A dominated system is one in which party leaders assume that no majority government is possible in the foreseeable future that excludes a particular party. The party without which a majority government cannot be formed is the dominant party. We have had four such competitive systems in the postwar era: Israel, from about 1950 to 1974; Germany, in the 1950s; the Netherlands, from 1945 to about 1966; and Belgium, since about 1973. In the Israeli case, the dominant party was the Labor party. In the German instance, it was the Christian Democratic Union/Christian Social Union (CDU/CSU). In the Dutch case, the dominant party was the Catholic People's party (KVP); the KVP's dominance derived in large measure from its congruence of views with two smaller Protestant parties. In Belgium, the dominant party has been the Flemish Christian Social party (FCP). As in the Netherlands, domination has been based on a nearly perfect congruence of views with another party, in this instance the Walloon Christian Social party (WCP).

The Dutch and Belgian experiences are important in making the point that the number of legislative seats a party controls is not by itself always decisive in creating the perception that it is dominant. Equally important are its position on the left-right and other relevant dimensions and the perception that the opportunity to break it away from its rocklike collaborators, as in the Dutch and Belgian experiences, does not exist. An additional requirement is that the party system be composed of more than three majority-relevant democratic parties.[5] I will have more to say about this last requirement later.

Domination alters the pattern of government formation in competitive systems in two ways. First, the limit of tolerance will be *lower* in a dominated system than it will be in an undominated-competitive system. The second difference is that dominated-system governments will consistently be *larger* than undominated-system governments. It is paradoxical that a lower limit of tolerance would lead to a larger government. The paradox can be resolved by apprehending the manner in which domination alters the context in which party leaders pursue their goals.

The first and essential point to appreciate is that in a dominated system the only opportunity a party has for influencing public policy is by participation in a coalition with the dominant party. Moreover, and this is equally essential, any one party is typically expendable. That is, the dominant-party formateurs can, because of their party's typically central ideological position, choose from among two or more parties to construct a winning government. Let us consider the Israeli cases in table 3.1 to demonstrate this point. A minimum-winning government required control of sixty-one Knesset seats. Consequently, in each of these governments, at least one party was superfluous. Indeed, in all of the governments except those formed in 1961, 1963, and 1974, two or more parties were expendable. As table 3.2 reveals, a comparable pattern of governments with unnecessary parties is also evident in the Dutch experience. The majority requirement was fifty-one before 1956 and seventy-six thereafter. In all cases except 1946 and 1959, at least one party could have been eliminated.

The German experience is more ambiguous, because the period of CDU/CSU dominance was shorter (about 1953–1961), the number of governments was fewer, and the CDU/CSU absorbed some small parties. We have three governments during this period: 1953, 1957, and 1961. In 1953, the CDU/CSU was a single vote short of a Bundestag majority. It formed a government with three other parties: the Free Democrats, the

Table 3.1 Composition of Israeli Governments, 1950–1981

	Knesset Seats Controlled
1950–1951	
Labor (Mapai)	48*
Religious Front	16
Progressives	5
Sephardim	4
	73
1951–1952	
Labor	50
Mizrachi	2
Hapoel Mizrachi	8
Poalei Agudah Yisrael	2
Agudah Yisrael	3
	65
1952–1953	
Labor	50
Hapoel Mizrachi	8
Mizrachi	2
Progressives	4
General Zionists	20
	84
1953–1955	
Labor	50
Hapoel Mizrachi	8
Mizrachi	2
Progressives	4
General Zionists	20
	84
1955–1958	
Labor	45
Achdut Haavodah	10
Mapam	9
National Religious Party (NRP)	11
Progressives	5
	80
1958	
Labor	45
Achdut Haavodah	10
Mapam	9
NRP	11
Progressives	5
	80

Table 3.1 Continued

	Knesset Seats Controlled
1958–1959	
Labor	45
Achdut Haavodah	10
Mapam	9
Progressives	5
	69
1959–1961	
Labor	52
Achdut Haavodah	7
Mapam	9
NRP	12
Progressives	6
	86
1961–1965	
Labor	46
Achdut Haavadoh	8
NRP	12
Poalei Agudah	2
	68
1965–1967	
Labor (Mapai/ Achdut Haavodah)	49
Mapam	8
NRP	11
Poalei Agudah	2
Liberals	5
	75
1967–1973	
Emergency War Governments	Omitted
March 1974	
Labor	54
NRP	10
Independent Liberals	4
	68
June 1974	
Labor	54
Independent Liberals	4
Citizen's Rights Movement	3
	61

Table 3.1 Continued

	Knesset Seats Controlled
October 1974	
Labor	54
NRP	10
Independent Liberals	4
	68
1977–1981	
Likud	45
NRP	12
Agudah Yisrael	4
	61
1981–Present	
Likud	48
NRP	6
Agudah Yisrael	4
Tami	3
	61

SOURCES: *Keesing's Contemporary Archives* and chapter 4 in this book.
*Labor figures include affiliated Arab lists.

German party, and the Refugee's party. Together, these three parties had a total of 90 Bundestag seats. The government thus had a majority of 333 out of 487. Any two of the coalition partners could have been removed. In 1957, the CDU/CSU received an absolute majority and formed a government by itself. By 1961, the system had been reduced to three parties, the CDU/CSU had lost its majority, and the Free Democrats were now a necessary component of a majority.[6]

What is especially striking about these dominated systems is what happens when domination ends. The German system was transformed from dominated to undominated by the reduction to three parties: oversized governments ceased to appear. More tellingly, in the Netherlands and Israel, which did not experience comparable reductions in the number of parties, oversized governments also ceased to be formed. Excluding the 1972 caretaker, we have six Dutch cases. Five of these have been minimum-winning. The 1967 cabinet (with a majority

Table 3.2 Composition of Dutch Governments, 1945–1966

Governing Coalition	Seats (Lower Chamber)
1946–1948	
Catholic People's party	32
Socialist party	29
	61
1948–1951	
Catholic People's party	32
Socialist party	27
Christian Historical Union	9
Liberal party	8
	77
1951–1952	
Catholic People's party	32
Socialist party	27
Christian Historical Union	9
Liberal party	8
	77
1952–1956	
Catholic People's party	30
Socialist party	30
Antirevolutionary party	12
Christian Historical Union	9
	81
1956–1958	
Catholic People's party	49
Socialist party	50
Antirevolutionary party	15
Christian Historical Union	13
	127
1959–1963	
Catholic People's party	49
Antirevolutionary party	14
Christian Historical Union	12
Liberal party	19
	84
1963–1965	
Catholic People's party	50
Antirevolutionary party	13
Christian Historical Union	13
Liberal party	16
	92

Table 3.2 Continued

Governing Coalition	Seats (Lower Chamber)
1965–1966	
Catholic People's party	50
Socialist party	43
Antirevolutionary party	13
	106

SOURCES: Numerous country monographs and *Keesing's Contemporary Archives*.
NOTE: The 1956 and 1966 caretaker governments are omitted.

requirement of seventy-six) controlled eighty-six seats. The smallest party held twelve seats. Thus no party could be removed. The 1971 cabinet controlled eighty-two seats; the smallest cabinet party had eight seats. The 1973 cabinet had a firm majority of only fifty-six and the ambiguous support of two religious parties. These parties had ministers in the government, but the parliamentary parties refused to endorse their participation. The 1977 government had only two parties—the Christian Democratic Appeal and the Liberals—and a majority of only a single vote in the decisive Lower Chamber. The government formed in September 1981 has been the only one with an unnecessary party. It consisted of the Christian Democrats, Socialists, and Democrats-66. It fell apart in October—just five weeks after it took office—was reformed, and collapsed definitively in May 1982. New elections were followed by another minimum-winning government of the Christian Democrats and Liberals.

The Israeli and Dutch systems changed because changed levels of electoral support and mergers undermined the conviction that the dominant party could not be dislodged. The Israeli Labor party's share of the vote fell from 46.7 percent in 1969 to 24.6 percent in 1977. At the same time, Herut, the major opposition party of the right, became the Likud through a series of mergers with smaller parties and saw its share of the vote rise from 14 percent in 1961 to 33.4 percent in 1977. A plausible alternative to a Labor-led government thus emerged.

Party Leaders and Coalitions

A similar process took place in the Netherlands, where the Catholic party vote declined from 32 percent in the 1950s to 26.5 percent in 1967 and 17.7 percent in 1972. The party's small Protestant allies also experienced a steady decline, losing about 40 percent of their share of the vote between 1948 and 1972. The decline in the religious, and especially Catholic, vote made plausible a socialist strategy of presenting itself as an alternative to a Catholic-led government. And, indeed, from the late 1960s the socialists pursued a policy of polarization precisely with the aim of presenting voters with such a bi-polar choice. If anything, the merger of the religious parties as the Christian Democratic Appeal in the late 1970s, rather than restoring the lost dominance, reinforced the bipolar choice and confirmed the socialist strategy.

The two Israeli governments in the postdomination era show the same reduction in size. In the first case, the 1977 Begin government controlled sixty-three seats and contained no unnecessary parties. The second case, the 1981 Begin government, repeated this pattern. In sum, when competitive systems change from dominated to undominated, they regularly produce minimum-winning governments.

A minimum-winning government would contain no excess parties, and the withdrawal of one party would bring down the government. This situation permits of a kind of blackmail of the dominant party (and all others in the government) by a single dissatisfied party; for a party can threaten to leave the government at will, and thus compel the dominant party to choose between making concessions or renegotiating the entire government agreement. The leaders of the dominant party can avoid this dilemma if they can form a government that includes one or more unnecessary parties, none of which can bring down the government by itself. This is by definition an oversized government.

Such a strategy is possible in a dominated-competitive system, given the dominant party's typically central ideological position, because a crisis that would cause one party to leave the government would not be likely to cause a second to do the same. And a single party that does withdraw gains little thereby, since the dissident party does not have the power to do real damage so long as it is expendable. As events that force two parties on opposite sides of the dominant party to leave the government simultaneously are rare, oversized governments not only reduce the power of each member save the dominant party, but provide the dominant party with an insurance policy against unanticipated events that cause one partner to leave the government. Given these benefits, it is clearly in the dominant party leaders' interest to create oversized governments, if this can be done without making undue policy concessions.

Oversized governments do not necessarily cost the dominant party more than minimum-winning coalitions; indeed, they can cost it less in policy concessions. The formateurs can use the dominant party's central position to effect a balance of power during negotiations and within the government that regularly yields policy outcomes satisfactory to the party. If the dominant party has partners on opposite sides of it on the same dimension (for example, left-right or secular-nonsecular), then these flank parties tend to balance each other out, as neither can get what it wants without the dominant party's support. And since the system cannot function for long without majority government and the dominant party is indispensable to a majority government, the result is not much removed from what would occur in a government consisting only of the dominant party. This is especially the case, because it is almost definitionally true that the two flank parties will seldom find an issue on which they can agree sufficiently to form a strong alliance against the dominant party.

A flank party must normally subordinate its policy differences with the dominant party or remain in opposition, because the dominant party has the option of governing with other flank parties. The corollary is that the dominant party has little incentive to abandon its policy preferences. We should expect, therefore, that the dominant party formateurs will not be willing to compromise explicitly their party's preferences. It does not follow, however, that the formateurs will compel a flank party to compromise explicitly its preferences. Since dominance insures that policy outcomes will usually be satisfactory, the dominant party formateurs need not compel explicit compromises in government formation. Moreover, since such compromises will be difficult for flank party leaders to sell to their followers and will in consequence reduce the probability of oversized governments, the dominant party formateurs will generally not want to insist on such compromises in government formation.

Clearly, the necessity of a majority government mandates the inclusion of parties with tangential and convergent preferences. But the dominant party leaders should have few objections to divergent-implicit relationships, for such relationships will permit the enlargement of the coalition. And the enlarged coalition will actually enhance the dominant party's control over final outcomes. As well, it will remove the prospect of blackmail that is inherent in minimum-winning governments. The inference, therefore, is that the limit of tolerance in dominated-competitive systems will be provided by divergent-implicit relationships. All parties at and below this limit will be included in the government. All parties that insist that the formateurs' party explicitly compromise one or more of its relevant preferences will be excluded. Again, I will assume that when two or more parties meet the limit of tolerance but refuse to serve together, the formateurs' party will always prefer to govern with the party or parties which provide the larger majority.

In general, the authority of the dominant party increases as the number of majority-relevant democratic parties in the system increases—and especially as flank parties appear on each side of the dominant party on each dimension—and as the polarization of the system is moderated and the autonomy of leaders is thereby increased. The minimum requirement of change from an undominated to a dominated system is the existence of more than three majority-relevant parties. With only three parties, one party can assume that in the future unbridgeable differences between the first and second will permit it to participate on comparatively more favorable terms. In the meantime, it can enjoy the benefits of being the sole party in opposition.

The relationship between the number of parties and the appearance and authority of a dominant party is indicated by the Belgian experience. Until 1972, the party system consisted of three relevant democratic parties: the Christian Socials, the Socialists, and the Liberals, with the Christian Socials located between the Socialists and the Liberals on the left-right dimension, but unflanked by relevant parties on the secular-nonsecular and communal dimensions. The acquisition of relevant status in 1972 by the Francophone Democratic Front, the Flemish People's party, and the Walloon/Brussels Rally and the gradual dissolution of the three original parties provided the Flemish Christian party with multiple flank parties on the left-right and communal dimensions. By its size and position, the Flemish Christian party, which came into existence as a separate party in 1973, was indispensable to a majority government.[7] With the exceptions of the 1974 government and the series of 1981 caretaker administrations that preceded the introduction of emergency rule, Belgian governments have been oversized.

The 1974 government, consisting of the Flemish Christian Socials, Walloon Christian Socials, Flemish and Walloon Liberals, and Walloon/Brussels Rally, contained no superfluous parties, but still demonstrated the basic logic of a dominated system. The Socialist party was willing to participate in a Flemish Christian government, but not one that included the liberal parties. The Flemish Christians negotiated with the socialists and liberals and found that the socialists demanded explicit compromises on religious education and communal government issues. The Flemish Christians were willing to accept an implicit compromise on these issues; they were willing to accept a period of "government study"—the classic form of the implicit compromise. But they would not grant the socialists explicit concessions. The liberals were willing to settle for a period of study; and so the Flemish Christians chose to govern with the two liberal parties. This pattern was repeated in negotiations with the Flemish People's party, the Francophone Front, and the Rally, with the last-mentioned entering the government on implicit compromise terms. Thus, while the Flemish Christians were unable to construct an oversized government, they were able to manipulate the other parties and demonstrate to those who made unyielding demands that they could govern without them.[8]

From 1973 to the end of 1980, Belgium had six politically responsible governments. Five of these, the 1974 government being the exception, were oversized.[9] During this time the party system became more and more polarized.[10] In 1981, a series of caretaker and politically weak governments were formed until elections were called for November 1981. The Martens government, formed in December 1981 and consisting of the two Christian Social and Liberal parties, is a minimum-winning government premised on the granting by parliament of emergency authority to bypass parliament on critical economic questions.[11] The explanation for such a nonparliamentary government must go well beyond the scope of the theory presented here. Belgium demonstrates that growing polarization and the concomitant loss of leadership autonomy inhibit the construction of oversized governments. But it also demonstrates that in dominated-competitive systems, the tendency toward oversized governments remains strong until very late in the process of polarization.

Undominated-Competitive Democracies

In the undominated variant of the competitive system, the formateurs' party is no longer an essential component of a majority government. It is now possible for potential members to form a winning government that excludes the party. And, even when temporary policy differences preclude this, it is possible for the parties to calculate that the formateurship will be transferred to another party in the future and that they will then be able to participate on more favorable terms. These are no more than definitional consequences of an undominated system. But they greatly alter behavior: parties are no longer systematically compelled to subordinate the policy differences they have with the formateurs' party in order to entertain government participation. In consequence, potential members can now negotiate with the formateurs much more as equals than they could in a dominated system.

It will be recalled that one of the assumptions of traditional coalition theory has been that an overriding objective of politicians forming governments is the desire to form winning or majority governments. The limited relevance of this assumption should now be apparent: it is only in undominated-competitive systems that one finds the need for majorities that is absent in consensual systems; the ability to create them that is absent in conflictual systems; and the urgency that is missing in dominated-competitive systems, where dominance makes creation of majority governments virtually assured and shifts formateurs' attention from creating majorities to creating oversized governments. In sum, it is only in undominated-competitive systems that the majority consideration assumes the decisiveness that traditional theories assign it.

In undominated-competitive systems, the limit of tolerance will be a function of the need to create majority governments and will therefore be variable within the limit of dissonance that must be tolerated in order to create a minimum-winning government. Bearing in mind the assumption that party leaders always strive to minimize policy compromises, several inferences about the formateurs' behavior in undominated-competitive systems can be drawn. 1) The formateurs will first seek to construct a majority based solely on tangential and convergent preference relationships. 2) The scarcity of such relationships will normally require that the formateurs move up the scale of relationships in search of a majority. 3) The opportunity to change the party of the formateurs or await the appearance of a more compatible one will drastically reduce the incentive that exists for potential members to accept implicit compromises. In consequence, even divergent-implicit relationships will often be insufficient to provide the formateurs with a majority. 4) In the absence of a sufficient supply of such relationships, the formateurs will include in the government the party or parties with whom their party has a relationship that requires it to make the fewest explicit compromises in order to create a minimum-member majority. 5) Governments will always be minimum-compromise and minimum-member majorities. They will be minimum-member in the sense that they will contain no superfluous parties, not in the sense that they will be based on the smallest number of parties required to create a majority. Thus, if the formateurs can make a majority by conceding one explicit compromise to two parties or two compromises to one party, the preference for minimizing concessions will lead them to form a government with the two parties.

The inference that governments will be minimum-winning can be confirmed empirically. We have six cases of undominated-competitive systems: Germany, since about 1961; the Netherlands, from 1967 to the present; Israel, since 1977; Belgium, before 1973; and Iceland and Ireland, for the entire postwar period. The crucial tests are the Netherlands, Israel, and Iceland, since Germany, Ireland, and Belgium, while always producing minimum-winning governments, have had three party systems during their undominated periods. We have already seen that the Dutch and Israeli cases conform closely to the expectations of minimum-winning governments. The Icelandic cases do also: of the thirteen postwar governments, excluding caretakers, only two have deviated from minimum-winning status.[12] If we aggregate the universe of cases from all undominated-competitive systems, we find, as table 3.3 shows, that of forty-three governments, forty have been minimum-winning. And as table 3.3 also demonstrates, of the twenty-seven cases of government formation in dominated-competitive systems, twenty-five conform to our expectation of an oversized status.

Table 3.3 Governments in Undominated- and Dominated-Competitive Democracies

	Undominated		
Country	Minority	Minimum-Winning	Oversized
Germany (1960–1981)	0	9	0
Belgium (1945–1973)	0	13	0
Iceland (1945–1981)	2	11	0
Netherlands (1967–1982)	0	5	1
Israel (1977–1981)	0	2	0
Total	2	40	1

	Dominated		
Country	Minority	Minimum-Winning	Oversized
Israel (1950–1974)	0	0	12
Netherlands (1945–1966)	0	1	7
Belgium (1973–1980)	0	1	5
Germany (1950s)	0	0	1
Total	0	2	25

SOURCES: The country analyses in part two; numerous country monographs; *Keesing's Contemporary Archives;* Klaus von Beyme, *Die parlamentarischen Regierungssysteme in Europa* (Munich: Piper, 1973).

The hypothesis for outcomes in undominated-competitive systems is essentially true by definition. It can fail only if a formateur chooses to create a government by making *more* than the minimum number of concessions required to create a minimum-winning government or chooses to create a government that is not minimum-winning. Making the minimum number of concessions to obtain one's goals is almost a universal law of political behavior. And we know from table 3.3 that governments in undominated-competitive systems are almost always (forty out of forty-three cases) minimum-winning. The hypothesis, then, simply combines an empirical fact (minimum-winning governments) with a universal law of political behavior (minimize concessions). Like any tautology, therefore, it can only rarely be incorrect and does not require an empirical test.

Minority and Majority Governments

We have seen that the occurrence of oversized and minimum-winning governments in competitive systems conforms closely to the expectations of the analysis. It is now possible to abstract the general theory and obtain a further test by way of the distribution of minority and majority governments.

Government formation is just one arena of interparty cooperation. The occurrence of cooperation in any arena is a function of the need and ability to cooperate in the arena. By need, I mean the level of effort that would otherwise be necessary outside the arena to overcome the centrifugal tensions and related leadership constraints that are inherent in a system of a particular type. By ability, I mean the opportunities for, and constraints on, interparty cooperation provided generally by the characteristics of the system. We may say that need increases as polarization increases or the strength of consensus-building mechanisms and norms decreases. Contrarily, ability decreases as polarization increases or the strength of consensus-building mechanisms and norms decreases. Albeit quite abstractly, these terms can be used to summarize the essential theoretical argument insofar as it concerns system-level variables.

The need for cooperation in the governmental arena should be lower in consensual systems than in competitive systems. In contrast, the ability of parties to cooperate outside this arena should be higher in consensual systems. The inference to be drawn is that minority governments should occur relatively more frequently in consensual systems than they do in competitive systems.

As both systems lack consensus-building mechanisms and norms, the distinction between competitive and conflictual systems is in the latter's absence of established legitimacy. This has important consequences for need and ability: need is increased while ability is diminished. Of decisive importance, of course, is ability. And we should therefore expect that conflictual systems will experience minority governments relatively more frequently than do competitive systems.

Table 3.4 Minority and Majority Governments in Multiparty Democracies

Country	Minority	Majority
Consensual		
Norway	9	2
Sweden	5	3
Denmark	16	4
Competitive		
Iceland	2	11
Israel*	0	15
Netherlands†	0	14
Belgium	0	19
Germany	0	10
Conflictual		
IV French Republic	10	16
Weimar Republic	7	3
Italy	19	19
Finland‡	8	12

SOURCES: The country analyses in part two; numerous monographs; *Keesing's Contemporary Archives;* von Beyme, *Die parlamentarischen Regierungssysteme in Europa.*
NOTE: This table does not include single-party majority and caretaker governments. A new government is counted as having been formed (a) whenever the party composition of the cabinet changes by entrance or withdrawal of a party; (b) whenever a government's resignation is submitted for nontechnical reasons; (c) in the wake of parliamentary elections. See appendix A, "Identifying Parties and Governments," for a detailed discussion of the definitions. The postwar period used is 1945–1981, except as noted.
  * 1950–1982.
  † 1945–1982.
  ‡ 1945–1966. After 1966, Finland is classified as an unconsolidated democracy. The transition is discussed in chapter 7.

To invert the logic of the argument: competitive systems experience comparatively moderate levels of need and ability. The absence of consensus-building mechanisms and norms means that the need for majorities in the governmental arena is greater than in consensual systems. The presence of legitimacy means that the ability to create majority governments exists at a higher level than in conflictual systems. We should, therefore, expect that majority governments will occur with greater frequency in competitive systems than in consensual and conflictual systems. The data in table 3.4 reveal that

Party Leaders and Coalitions

the inferences are empirically sustained. Indeed, the confirmation could hardly be stronger.

It is a fairly simple matter to test the hypotheses about outcomes in each of the system types. But the theory itself—the assumptions from which the hypotheses were deduced—cannot be tested directly, because such a test would require access to the private decision-making records of parties. Nonetheless, we can have some confidence in the theory, if 1) it is logically compelling and consistent with our general knowledge of political behavior; 2) it produces hypotheses that are logically necessary; 3) these hypotheses receive strong empirical support; and 4) we are able to test the hypotheses and explain specific outcomes without recourse to causes that are outside the theory. The first two requirements are a part of theory building and should now have been met. The third and fourth requirements must be met by empirical tests.

The hypotheses have been tested against the outcomes of sixty-seven government formations in Norway, Sweden, Denmark, Finland, Italy, the Netherlands, and Israel. The methodological underpinnings of the tests—the scope of the theory, selection of cases, operational definitions, procedures, and so forth—are detailed in appendix A. The next three chapters include the tests from Israel (a competitive democracy), Denmark (a consensual democracy), and Finland (a conflictual democracy).

Part Two

Governing Coalitions in Four Types of Democracies

CHAPTER FOUR

Israel

Origins of the Party System

The essential components of the modern Israeli party system were established by the mobilizational conflicts within the Zionist movement and the Yishuv, the Jewish community in Palestine, during the decades before statehood. Because the institutions of multipartism based on proportional representation and parliamentary government were established during these decades, the lack of formal independence before 1948 does not preclude the application of a mobilization and cleavage-formation model to assign profiles to parties.

There are, however, several important respects in which the Israeli party system's development differed from the development of Continental party systems. In the first place, the prestatehood community was basically born democratic. The Zionist movement was led from its inception by European Jews who had been schooled for the most part in the traditions of turn-of-the-century liberalism and socialism and who came to Palestine committed to the establishment of a democratic state. Thus, the liberal democratic format and universal suffrage were never the burning issues in the Yishuv that they were in contemporary Europe.[1]

A second distinctive feature of Israeli development was that, while the evolving patterns of competition within the Yishuv were decisive for the formation of the party system, these patterns were heavily influenced by the ideologies that successive waves of immigrants brought with them from Europe and by conflicts within the international Zionist movement, especially the World Zionist Organization (WZO), which provided virtually all of the financial support on which Yishuv development was contingent.[2]

The third distinctive feature of the Israeli experience was that most of the men and women who came to Palestine from Europe were, almost by definition given the inspiration which brought them, already politically mobilized. Party competition focused less on bringing them into political activity than in mobilizing them to emigrate in the first place and then, only secondarily, to support a particular party once they arrived. I say secondarily, because the decision to emigrate was normally inspired, in the early years, not simply by a desire to escape oppression in Europe, but as well by a particular vision of the type of Jewish homeland that should be created in Palestine.[3] The ideological commitment that motivated emigration to Palestine normally led to a particular pattern of subsequent voting behavior.

European Jews who wished to emigrate on the more narrowly pragmatic grounds of socioeconomic improvement generally did not go to Palestine. Rather, they chose to migrate out of the Jewish communities of Europe through assimilation or emigration to the United States. Indeed, between 1881 and 1914, over 2 million European Jews emigrated to the United States, whereas the entire Jewish community of Palestine numbered only about 84,000 as late as 1921, when the United States imposed limits on immigration from Europe.[4] It was not until after 1921 that Jews inclined to migrate on narrowly socioeconomic grounds began to choose Palestine in significant numbers. And it was not until after World War II that nonideological immigrants, mainly from other Middle Eastern countries, began to arrive in large numbers. By that time, party institutions were already well established, and the new waves of immigrants were not reflected in the appearance of new parties. Rather, the new immigrants were distributed proportionally among the old parties.[5]

As a theological expectation, the idea of a Jewish return to Palestine stretches back to the fall of Jerusalem to the Romans in A.D. 66.[6] As a political ideology, Zionism originated in the last quarter of the nineteenth century from the failure of emancipation to lead to assimilation on a broad scale in Central Europe and intensified anti-Semitism in Central and Eastern Europe after 1873. The availability of the United States meant that Zionism as a motivating force had to tap wellsprings of action other than simple economic improvement. These were the visions of a Jewish homeland as a religious community, as a socialist community, and as a refuge from European oppression.[7]

For much of the history of the Zionist movement, a majority of religious Jews condemned it, because they believed that the establishment of the state would come through messianic intervention rather than the efforts of common men. The arguments of religious Zionists did not, at least in the beginning, convince many religious Jews that Zionism was not a denial of the divine power that was expected to return them to the Holy Land.[8] Nonetheless, religious Zionists created a following, and in 1902 the Mizrachi—with the objective of creating a religious majority in Palestine—became the first party to organize as a distinct unit within the World Zionist Organization, which had been established in 1897 to bring into existence a "Jewish Homeland, openly recognized, legally secured."[9] Eventually, most religious Jews came to accept Zionism, and four religious parties existed by the time of independence. Two of these parties, Poalei Agudah and Agudah Yisrael, initially came into being in opposition to Zionism. More important, however, was the fact that all four came to share a commitment to the creation of a Jewish community whose people lived according to religious law.[10]

The second ideology, that which became dominant

among those who came to Palestine, was of a Jewish homeland built on socialist principles. This ideology blended the socialist images of a perfect society that were current in Eastern and Central Europe at the end of the nineteenth century and Jewish nationalism. From the outset, the socialist Zionists who came to Palestine applied doctrines of class warfare and were indifferent or actually hostile to religion.[11]

The third vision of a Jewish homeland was supported by a majority of Zionists outside of Palestine, but did not draw the most zealous adherents to Palestine. Instead, it was supported mainly by Western European and American middle-class Jews who contributed financially but declined to emigrate. Those who adhered to this ideology wanted to build a secular, bourgeois state and society modeled on the liberal democracies of Western Europe and saw a national homeland as the solution to the problems of European Jewry.[12]

The groups and parties active in the Zionist movement competed for control of it on the basis of a system of proportional representation that was also used in the representative institutions of the Yishuv and subsequently for elections to the Knesset. The key to control of the movement was in Palestine, for members of the Yishuv possessed a double-weighted vote in World Zionist Organization elections and the extra moral authority of individuals actually pioneering the Zionist faith.[13] In consequence, the leaders of the Yishuv also became the leaders of the WZO.

At least in the first and most crucial period, that of the Second Aliyah (1904–1914), when the first major wave of state builders arrived and when the pattern for future years was set, more socialist and religious Zionists went to Palestine than did so-called General Zionists, as adherents of the third, bourgeois, vision were called.[14] The characteristic institutions of the Yishuv were the creations of socialists and religionists, although in WZO elections the General Zionists consistently won about twice as many votes abroad as they did in Palestine.[15]

Religious Zionists never had more than very limited success in persuading their European cobelievers that Zionism was not a denial of religious belief. The inability of the religionists to mobilize more immigrants consistently limited their parties to about 15 percent of the Yishuv electorate and conceded primacy in the Yishuv to labor Zionists.[16] The primacy of anticlerical, socialist Zionism in the Yishuv in the 1920s and 1930s was viewed by religious Zionists as a perversion of the unity of nationhood and religion in Judaism. When the Fifth Congress of the World Zionist Organization gave majority support to secular education, a segment of the religious Mizrachi party broke away in protest. This breakaway served as the precipitant for the creation of the Agudah Organization.[17] The Agudah became unambiguously opposed to Zionism because of the perceived perversion of Judaism.[18] Within the Yishuv, the ultra-orthodox affiliated with the Agudah, whereas religious Jews who were not prepared to break with Zionism and wished to continue to advance the position of religion within the movement remained in the Mizrachi. It was not until the catastrophe of the 1930s in Europe that the ultra-orthodox began to accept the need for a Zionist state as a refuge for Jews. By that time, it was too late for most of Agudah's supporters in Central and Eastern Europe to escape to Palestine. They were condemned to suffer the horrors of the Holocaust; and the Agudah party was destined to remain a minority party even within the religious community in the Yishuv.[19]

The socialist Zionists within the Second Aliyah divided into two parties in Palestine. The largest single group in the Second Aliyah was Poalei Zion (Workers of Zion), which developed from scattered groups in Russia, Lithuania, and Poland. The second socialist party was Hapoel Hazair (Young Worker), which developed in opposition to Poalei Zion and objected to the latter's constant emphasis on class struggle in an environment in which it did not always seem relevant.[20]

In 1920, 22,000 of the eligible 28,000 voters participated in the first elections of the Asefat Hanivhasim, the Assembly of Delegates of the Yishuv.[21] Achdut Haavodah, a party created by Poalei Zion in 1919 and excluding Hapoel Hazair, received more votes than any other party. In the same year, it also received more votes than all other labor groups combined in elections for the newly created Histadrut, the General Federation of Jewish Workers. The Histadrut consolidated many of the economic, welfare, and cultural functions that had previously been performed by the individual labor parties.[22] The Histadrut became the most important organization in the Yishuv; control of it was decisive in consolidating the dominance of labor, for the middle-class parties had no comparable competing organization.[23]

In the early years of the 1920s, notwithstanding their progress in Palestine, the labor parties remained quite weak in the international movement. All of the labor parties together garnered only 8 percent of the delegate votes in the elections to the World Zionist Congress in 1921.[24] Labor's weakness resulted in part from its failure in the past to mobilize support in WZO elections, because it had up to then received unchallenged financial support from the WZO. The vast amounts of money the WZO sent to the Yishuv had gone mainly to labor organizations because they were the most active organizations.[25]

The immigrants of the Third Aliyah, immediately after the First World War, were similar in attitudes and backgrounds to those of the Second Aliyah. But those of the Fourth Aliyah (1924–26) were not. The Fourth Aliyah, embracing about 70,000 immigrants in just three years, brought to Palestine chiefly middle-class Jews who left Poland because of the so-called "Grabski Laws," named after the Polish government of the day and intended to push Jews out of broad sections of the Polish economy.[26] Thus encouraged to leave, and with the American door now closed, many went to Palestine. For the first time, labor was confronted with a major bourgeois political challenge. Previously, labor had received most of the World Zionist Organization's resources simply because it provided the bulk of the immigrants. The Fourth Aliyah immigration changed that and compelled better organization on all sides.[27]

In 1927, a sharp economic downturn struck the Yishuv. In that year, some 40 percent of the wage earners of Tel

Aviv were unemployed.²⁸ These economic circumstances and the arrival of a wave of immigrants with competing economic values led the WZO to adopt an increasingly critical attitude toward labor's economic enterprises, almost all of which required constant subsidies.²⁹ The threat to labor's position was compounded by the creation of a Jewish Agency that would receive support from all interested Jews—Zionists and non-Zionists, in Europe and in America—for the development of the Jewish community. The creation of the agency was a requirement of the League of Nation's original mandate. When created, the agency included influential American businessmen who were very much committed to capitalist development and were intensely critical of labor's activities.³⁰ All of these factors produced a "new insistence by the various committees of the World Zionist Organization on profitability and accountability, neither of which were strong points of the labor-dominated enterprises."³¹

Another motivation for political organization was added by control over immigration. "As pressure developed for entry into Palestine because of the deteriorating situation in Europe and the reluctance of other countries to admit Jews, immigration certificates became a prize."³² The British mandatory authorities controlled the number of immigrants that would be admitted within various classifications (capitalist, laborer, etc.). But it was the Jewish Agency that distributed the certificates. Since these were distributed according to party strength, party mobilization became imperative.

As the pressures of middle-class immigration and competition within the WZO and Jewish Agency and Assembly of Delegates mounted, and as the conflicts that had earlier separated them faded in importance, Hapoel Hazair and Achdut Haavodah agreed to merge in 1930 to form Mapai.³³

Mapai would come to dominate Israeli politics for the next four decades. In 1933, Mapai and the smaller labor parties campaigned vigorously at home and abroad in the WZO elections and managed to gain 44 percent of the delegate vote for labor candidates. Labor won four places on the executive in that year, and in 1935 the leader of Mapai, David Ben-Gurion, became its chairman as well as president of the executive committee of the Jewish Agency.[34]

The creation of Mapai had not resulted in the unification of the labor movement. Hashomer Hazair, a socialist party created in the mid-1920s by immigrants of the Third Aliyah, remained outside Mapai. Initially, Hashomer Hazair had viewed collective settlements as the only true model of a future socialist society. It was this vision that precipitated its founding and led to early conflicts with Hapoel Hazair and Achdut Haavodah. The economic crises of the 1920s and the Russian Revolution undercut this commitment, and the party gradually sought the support of urban workers and adopted a revolutionary Marxist doctrine. It suffered a series of subsequent splits, as some members rejected Zionism and returned to the Soviet Union or joined the Palestine Communist party. Nonetheless, a core of the party survived in the Yishuv, and the party acquired the character of a hard-line Marxist, pro-Soviet party.[35]

The General Zionists, unable to compete effectively with labor Zionism in Palestine because of the pattern of immigration and their ideological unwillingness to create the sorts of social and economic institutions—such as the Histadrut—that sustained labor immigrants in an inhospitable environment, declined rapidly before the Fourth Aliyah and became absorbed in internal conflicts. By the time of the Second World Conference of the WZO in 1935, the General Zionists had split at home and abroad. The split was precipitated primarily by disagreements over cooperation with labor. The faction that became known as "General Zionist-A" favored continued investment in labor enterprises. The "General Zionist-B" faction opposed such investment.[36]

The split within the General Zionist movement and the General Zionists' lack of well-developed institutions within Palestine meant that the secular Zionist middle class was without a cohesive party and provided the opportunity for the rise of the Revisionist party. The Revisionists did in fact develop initially within the European structures of general Zionism and found their greatest support among the middle-class Polish Jews who emigrated in the Fourth Aliyah.[37]

Revisionism's leader was Vladimir Jabotinsky, who organized a Jewish Legion during the First World War and then an illegal Jewish Defense Force in Palestine in 1920 in response to Arab riots. For the latter, Jabotinsky was imprisoned by the British. Upon his release, he became a member of the Zionist executive, but came into growing conflict with the labor parties over their passive acceptance of Britain's diminishing commitment to a homeland that embraced the entire mandate. In 1935, the Revisionist party left the WZO over this issue and established a competitive international organization, the New Zionist Organization. The Revisionists emphasized a homeland as a refuge, militant defense of the idea of a homeland embracing the entire mandate territory, uncompromising relations with the British and Arabs, and opposition to socialist economic development. Revisionism supplied what the General Zionists had failed to supply: a bourgeois party with a coherent ideology, an organizational presence in the Yishuv, and a willingness to challenge labor on the entire range of issues then on the political agenda.[38]

Labor and revisionism offered conflicting policies on all of the issues that were decisive in the 1930s: on relations with the British and Arabs, on the acceptability of partition, on the end goal of the homeland. The bitterness of the conflict grew as the situation of European Jewry became more desperate and Arab militancy mounted. Labor leaders responded to Arab violence in the 1930s with a policy known as "havlaga," or self-restraint, which narrowly defined self-defense and generally precluded offensive military action against Arab bases. Whereas labor leaders took it as axiomatic that there existed no fundamental conflict of interest between Jews and Arabs and that a policy of accommodation would eventually persuade the Arabs of this, the Revisionists proceeded from the assumption that such acceptance could be won only by a "wall of iron."[39]

The 1937 Peel Commission Report, which recommended partition and signaled the end of the British commitment, sharpened the conflict between Mapai and the Revisionists. Mapai accepted the proposed partition while the Revisionists rejected it unconditionally.[40] The British commitment to a Jewish national homeland came to an end with the White Paper of 1939. The paper proposed to limit Jewish immigration to 75,000 over the next decade and immediately prohibited the purchase of Arab land by Jews.[41] The onset of the Second World War limited the relevance of the white paper, but the future of Palestine in British eyes was now unambiguously revealed. The white paper and the war compelled the parties to make choices that further embittered relations between Mapai and the Revisionists. Mapai opposed the paper, but sided with the British in the war. The Irgun, the military wing of revisionism, divided, with the majority fighting alongside the British until 1944 and then fighting against the British. The minority, the Lechi (or "Stern Gang"), fought the British from the outset. In 1944, the two military wings of revisionism reunited in the struggle against the British. Mapai and the other labor parties, however, never fought against the British and, in fact, found their forces actually in conflict with Revisionist forces during and after the war.[42]

At the end of the war, Britain turned the question of Palestine over to the United Nations, which voted for partition in 1947. Mapai accepted the partition. The other two labor parties did not. The first of these was the old pro-Soviet, left-socialist Hashomer Hazair, which insisted that a binational (Jewish-Arab) state be created. The second was Achdut Haavodah, which had been recreated by a faction that had broken away from Mapai in 1944. The break was caused by Achdut Haavodah's greater commitment to socialism—thus the readoption of the name Achdut Haavodah—and by its insistence on a Jewish state that embraced the entire mandate. For this, it was often referred to as "Herut cum socialism," Herut being the postindependence party of revisionism. In 1948, their shared perception that they were more socialist than Mapai and their shared opposition (although for very different reasons) to the partition boundaries led Achdut Haavodah and Hashomer Hazair to merge and form Mapam. Achdut Haavodah had absorbed the old Poalei Zion in 1946.

As it happened, the partition and boundary questions per se were not sources of enduring conflict among the socialist parties. The borders of Israel were settled by the War of Independence, and these were accepted by all of the socialist parties. The underlying attitudes toward the Arabs and foreign powers, however, were of enduring importance in differentiating the socialist parties and sparking conflict among them.[43]

The borders were not accepted by Herut, the postwar party of the Revisionist movement. Herut united the Revisionists and their two military wings, Lechi and Irgun, into a single party that would carry the capitalist, revanchist banner of revisionism in the new state. Herut continued to demand Jewish sovereignty over the original mandate territory.[44]

The two General Zionist parties, A and B, attempted a short-lived reunification in 1946–47. When the effort failed, the A faction established the Progressive party, while the B faction retained the name General Zionist party. The two parties accepted the postwar boundaries. Neither was motivated by foreign policy questions. Rather, each was concerned almost exclusively with economic policy. They were distinguished by the Progressives' more centrist position on socioeconomic questions.[45]

The religious parties provided the final component of the party system with which Israel entered statehood. Both the Agudahs and the Mizrachis had split into middle- and working-class factions and then parties in the 1920s, with the former retaining the parent name and the latter taking the names Poalei Agudah Yisrael and Hapoel Mizrachi. The orthodox workers combined religious Zionism and socialism. With the ultra-orthodox Agudahs' acceptance of the State of Israel, the four religious parties were able to form the United Religious Front to contest the first Knesset election, held in 1949. The front was short-lived because of the Agudahs' more extreme demands for the adoption of religious laws and because of socioeconomic differences among the four component parties. In 1951, the four parties ran separate electoral lists. For the purposes of understanding government formation in the 1950s, the two Agudahs can be treated as a single party. Indeed, between 1954 and 1960, they functioned as a single party. The Mizrachis, too, can be discussed together for the period after 1951, because their preferences were also identical. The two united in the National Religious party in 1955.[46]

To summarize, then, Mapai acquired socioeconomic, foreign, and religious policy profiles. Mapam, the product of the merger of Achdut Haavodah and Hashomer Hazair, acquired socioeconomic, foreign, and religious policy profiles. Each of the two component parties had acquired the three profiles before the merger. The nonsocialist parties, Herut, the General Zionists, and the Progressives, all of which had grown out of the bourgeois, secular general Zionism tradition, brought with them socioeconomic and religious policy profiles. Herut, as the postindependence embodiment of revisionism, had a foreign policy profile as well.

When the four religious parties were united as the Torah Front, their internal divisions prevented them from articulating more than their religious policy profile. When the two Mizrachi parties united as the National Religious party, they did so under the domination of the workers' wing, and the NRP has consequently been both orthodox and socialist-leaning. When united, the Agudahs suffered the conflict between their socialist and nonsocialist factions and limited themselves entirely to ultra-orthodox concerns. In effect, they could articulate only a religious profile. The contradictions between their socioeconomic interests contributed to the dissolution of the Agudah bloc in 1961. This contradiction was reinforced by the nonsocialist faction's more extreme orthodoxy. The workers' faction had material interests that would benefit by greater cooperation with governments, and these material interests led it to moderate its orthodoxy.[47]

The Governments, 1950–1975

The 1950 Mapai–Religious Front–Progressive–Sephardim Government

On October 15, 1950, Prime Minister David Ben-Gurion submitted his government's resignation to the President of Israel, Chaim Weizman. The resignation arose from the refusal of the United Religious Front to accept proposed cabinet changes unless accompanied by policy concessions. Under attack from the right, left, and religious as a result of the inefficiencies and inequities of its rationing policies, Mapai wanted to make cabinet changes to alleviate the criticism. Ben-Gurion wanted to establish a new Ministry of Trade and Industry to take responsibility for rationing and shift the Mapai Minister of Supply, Dov Joseph, who was the main target of attack, to a less vulnerable position. In order to maintain the existing balance of power in the cabinet, Mapai wanted the new Trade and Industry post to go to a businessman (which would mollify the right), but one who was nonpartisan and not a member of the Knesset. A number of lesser personnel changes were also intended.[48] The Religious Front made several concessions the price of its acceptance of these changes. It demanded that it receive the new Trade and Industry portfolio. It also demanded policy concessions. When the front refused to accept an ultimatum from Ben-Gurion that it accept the changes without qualification, Ben-Gurion submitted the government's resignation. President Weizman then asked Ben-Gurion to form a new government.[49]

Immediately after receiving this commission, Ben-Gurion asked Mapam and General Zionist leaders to discuss the formation of a new government with him. Both parties, however, had fundamental conflicts with Mapai that were not amenable to implicit compromises. Mapam demanded that the next government abandon Mapai's policy of support for the United States' position in the Korean War, and substitute a pro-Soviet foreign policy for Mapai's pro-Western policy. Neither Mapai nor Mapam was willing to agree to disagree on these issues.[50] The General Zionists, for their part, demanded of Mapai that the next government dismantle the state regulation of imports, production, prices, and sales. The controls constituted the heart of Mapai's economic policy; neither party was willing to set the issue aside.[51]

The Religious Front dropped its nonpolicy demand, possession of the Trade and Industry portfolio, when Mapai agreed to the appointment of an orthodox businessman as Director General of the ministry.[52] The front's policy demands were threefold: guarantees of continued orthodox control over religious schools; a ban on the importation of nonkosher meats; and a new Sabbath law.[53]

At independence, Israel had carried over from the Yishuv years a decentralized education system supported by public funds, with autonomous branches (called "trends") controlled by the political parties. Parents could send their children to one of the four recognized trends: general (middle class) secular, labor, or religious (Mizrachi or Agudah). The rivalry among the parties to attract children to their trend was intense, because the party with the greatest success was presumed to benefit politically in the future. The religious parties were especially concerned to maintain control of the schools that had once belonged to them now that the schools were nominally under the control of the Minister of Education.

Mapai was ambivalent about the entire education system. On the one hand, a part of the party wanted to abolish the trends and establish a unified school system. On the other hand, part of the party, including many who would have otherwise preferred a unified system, were loath to surrender the benefits of labor schools. The upshot was that the party had no policy. It agreed within itself to disagree and was willing to accept continued religious control of religious schools. But it opposed religious attempts to expand religious influence in education.[54]

So when the Religious Front demanded a Deputy Minister of Education as a guarantee of the continued autonomy of religious schools, Mapai saw such a demand as a matter of an expanded religious role in education and would not accept it. To some extent, the conflict appears to have been a case of each party attributing to the other a policy which it did not in fact have, since each was committed to perpetuation of the status quo. Notwithstanding the issue having been central to the fall of the previous government, the two parties were able to resolve it administratively by agreeing to establish divisions within the Ministry of Education for each of the trends. Such a solution was apparently sufficient to convince each side that the status quo was secure.[55]

The second issue between the Religious Front and Mapai was the front's insistence that meat imports, for which the state appropriated foreign exchange, conform to religious dietary laws. The front wanted an end to the importation of nonkosher meats, which Mapai would not accept because such meats were less expensive and because a ban would restrict consumer choice. In the event, both sides agreed to disagree. They reaffirmed an agreement dating from the days of the provisional government that gave the Ministers of Supply and Religious Affairs joint authority over meat imports. Given an orthodox Minister of Religious Affairs, such an arrangement would satisfy the front—if it were abided by—because it would give that minister a veto. In fact, there was no expectation that the arrangement would be abided by. Mapai-dominated governments had repeatedly brushed the agreement aside in the past, and Mapai gave no indication that it would not do so in the future. Reaffirmation of the ineffectual agreement was, then, a way by which both sides could temporarily set the issue aside without abandoning their preferences.[56]

The final orthodox demand was for a Sabbath observance law that would ban interurban public transportation on the Sabbath and religious holidays. Mapai would not commit itself to such a law. Again, the parties agreed to disagree: they decided to establish a ministerial committee to study the issue. No limit was placed on the amount of time the committee could take (it could take forever); and the committee was not actually charged with drafting legislation. Until the committee reported, the status quo would remain unaltered and the front would refrain from introducing legislation in the Knesset on its own.[57]

When Mapai proposed the ministerial shuffle at the end of the last government, the Progressives and Sephardim party supported the proposed changes. Except that the Progressives shared Mapai's objections to the demands of the Religious Front, the Progressives and Sephardim did not use the occasion of the reformation to advance policy demands. The Sephardim, a small (four seats) party that had roots in the prestatehood period, was not a policy-oriented party. Its commitment was to a Sephardic "presence."[58] Following the second Knesset election (1951), the party was absorbed by the General Zionists.

Two other parties existed at this time. The first of these was Herut, the statehood party of revisionism. Herut had a whole range of conflicts with Mapai. The two most fundamental were Herut's demand for legislation declaring Jordanian-occupied sectors of Jerusalem to be part of the state of Israel and its insistence, along with the General Zionists', that state regulation of imports, sales, production, and prices be dismantled. The demand for a declaration of sovereignty over all of Jerusalem reflected Herut's revisionist origins and was totally unacceptable to Mapai, which was inclined toward an accommodationist policy toward the Arabs. Neither party expressed an interest in an implicit compromise.[59]

The final party in the system was the Communist party, or Maki (Miflaga Communistit Yisraelit). The obstacles to Mapai-Maki cooperation were and remained during the latter's entire existence absolute. The parties were in conflict on economic policy, on relations with the Arabs, and on relations with the Soviet Union. Maki always remained well beyond the pale of the democratic parties and was never considered for government membership even in principle.[60]

With the democratic parties, Herut, the General Zionists and Mapam, Mapai's relations were divergent-explicit. With the Progressives and Sephardim they were convergent. With the Religious Front they were divergent-implicit. The government actually formed consisted of Mapai, the Progressives, Sephardim, and Religious Front. This outcome conforms to the hypothesis that the limit of tolerance in dominated-competitive systems is the divergent-implicit relationship.

The 1951 Mapai–Hapoel Mizrachi–Poalei Agudah Yisrael–Agudah Yisrael Government

Early in 1951, the leaders of the Religious Front were in need of an issue that would preserve the unity of the front, which was then on the verge of dissolution because of conflicts among its orthodox and ultra-orthodox factions. Front leaders seized on the issue of immigrant education, an issue of immense concern to all of the front factions. In March 1950, after much negotiation, the front and Mapai had agreed that all schools in Yemenite camps (almost entirely orthodox) would remain orthodox. In other immigrant camps, parents would choose between a religious and a secular school. This agreement ratified the dominant position of the orthodox in certain parts of Israeli society and formalized once again an understanding between Mapai and the front that the status quo would be preserved.[61]

The issue could be reopened in 1951, however, because during the preceding year, the government had begun to move immigrants out of their old temporary camps and into semipermanent work settlements, known as *ma'abarot*. With the Yemenites moving into *ma'abarot*, the Minister of Education and Mapai considered the old agreement with the front to be at an end and applied to *ma'abarot* Yemenites the same standards applied elsewhere: parents were given a choice of schools. Such a choice would result in an exodus of thousands of children to secular schools or, for economic reasons, to Histadrut-run, Mapai-oriented religious schools. So the front insisted that the old agreement be applied to the *ma'abarot*.[62] Negotiations followed within the government, but no understanding could be reached. In February, a Knesset vote on Mapai's education proposals led to the fall of the government when the front voted with the opposition. After futile efforts to form a new government, new elections were scheduled for July 30.[63]

Following the elections, Ben-Gurion, representing Mapai, held talks with all of the parties except Maki and Herut. The main issue among the secular parties was whether to negotiate reparations with West Germany. Mapai favored the negotiations. Mapam and Herut opposed them. Mapam, a coalition of the pro-Soviet Hashomer Hazair and the neutralist Achdut Haavodah, viewed such talks as an effort by Mapai to align Israel with the West. Mapai and Mapam were in disagreement also over policy toward the American involvement in Korea, which Mapai supported. None of the parties was willing to budge on these issues. None expressed a willingness to defer them.[64]

Herut was additionally in conflict with Mapai over relations with the Arab countries. Herut continued to insist on a declaration of Israeli sovereignty over all of Jerusalem. More broadly, it wanted a policy of confrontation and insisted that a precondition of peace must be "recognized Jewish sovereignty over an undivided Land of Israel, and [withdrawal of all] Arab military forces 'from the historical territory of Eretz Yisrael east and west of the Jordan.' "[65]

The General Zionists' past calls for decontrol of the economy were supplemented by demands for nationalization of labor exchanges and of medical care. The preference for nationalization stemmed from a desire to weaken the power of the Histadrut. The Histadrut was not simply a trade union. It was also the largest single employer in the country. Two major sources of its power were its control of labor exchanges and its health insurance program. There was no chance that Mapai would accept the General Zionists' demands. But the two parties were able to reach an agreement to "study" these issues before their talks collapsed on another issue.[66] That issue was state control of the economy. Mapai would not abandon the controls, and the General Zionists would not join the government if the controls remained in place. Herut shared the General Zionists' opposition to the controls.[67]

The Progressives had economic policies that were comparable to the General Zionists', but announced that they were willing to leave these issues unresolved. However, they made their own participation contingent on the participation of the General Zionists, who were their main competitors for the votes of moderate nonsocialists. Having fallen from five Knesset seats to four while the General Zionists rose from seven to twenty in the last election, the Progressives were unwilling to assume government responsibility unless their competitors did the same.[68] This decision, because it was based on nonpolicy calculations, cannot be explained by the theory.

The matter of *ma'abarot* schools had precipitated the fall of the last government, but it was not resolved in the formation of this one. Indeed, none of the points of conflict between Mapai and the Religious Front were resolved. The front dissolved after the past government's collapse. The four groups that had originally formed the front now functioned as separate parties. Their policies, however, were nearly identical. Beyond a favorable resolution of the *ma'abarot* dispute, the four parties concentrated their campaigns and negotiating efforts on preserving a separate religious trend in the national education system (Mapai, Herut, and the Progressives now wanted a single, unified school system; the religious parties and Mapam opposed it); guarantees of continued rabbinic jurisdiction in matters of personal status (marriage, divorce, alimony); and a new ban on the importation of nonkosher meats. The two Agudah parties additionally wanted orthodox women to be exempted from national service.[69]

The briefest summary of the outcome is that Mapai and the orthodox parties agreed once again to ignore their differences. In formal terms, this agreement was expressed by an understanding that a one-year moratorium would be placed on the resolution of all education issues, including the original question of *ma'abarot* schools. A moratorium was likewise agreed to on the resolution of questions of rabbinic jurisdiction and conscription. The final hurdle, what to do about imports of nonkosher meats, was surmounted by yet another reaffirmation of the old (still-ineffectual) provisional government agreement.[70]

So Mapai was again able to reach implicit compromises with the orthodox parties. With Mapam, the General Zionists, and Herut, its differences remained explicit. The Progressives declined participation on nonpolicy grounds. The outcome, a government of Mapai and the four orthodox parties, fits the hypothesis that the limit of tolerance will be the implicit compromise. The orthodox parties were willing to make such compromises because Mapai had the choice, if forced to make real concessions, of making them to anticlerical parties. If it were willing to compromise its economic policies with the General Zionists, it could create a coalition in which it would be free to pursue its foreign and anticlerical policies. Even, as in this case, when Mapai could not create an oversized government, it could use its dominant, pivotal position to impose implicit compromises on the orthodox parties. For those parties knew that, if pressed too hard, Mapai could always find allies elsewhere.

The 1952 Mapai–Hapoel Mizrachi–General Zionist–Progressive Government

The government that had taken office in 1951 had placed a one-year moratorium on two bitterly disputed issues: reform of the school system and the liability of orthodox women for national service. As the anniversary of the government approached, the parties positioned themselves for a showdown on these issues. The Israel Defense Service Law provided exemptions for women who objected to military service on conscientious or religious grounds. Mapai and the other secular parties wanted women who did not claim the exemption to be subject to compulsory noncombat military services and for the period of this service to be extended from the usual twelve to twenty-four months. The orthodox parties opposed this revision, but it passed the Knesset in February 1950. Since orthodox women were not affected by it, the orthodox parties did not object strenuously to it.[71]

Soon a new problem presented itself: the wording of the law was such that a woman could easily escape all service by claiming to be a member of an orthodox branch of Judaism. To overcome this, Mapai proposed, and the other secular parties endorsed, conscription of orthodox women for nonmilitary service. The religious parties were divided in their response to Mapai's proposal. The Mizrachi parties favored the proposal. The Agudahs opposed it. With the termination of the one-year moratorium, Mapai was determined to bring its reform proposal to a vote in the Knesset, where it was assured of a majority.[72]

The moratorium was also about to expire on the question of education reform. Only three parties were committed to preserving the four trends. They were Mapam and the Agudahs. Within Mapai, the balance in favor of unification had shifted decisively even before the formation of the last government, and Mapai was determined to take Knesset action on this issue also when the moratorium expired. The General Zionists, Progressives, and Herut were also committed to unification. Indeed, before their negotiations broke off prior to the formation of the previous government, Mapai and the General Zionists had already reached agreement on school unification. So Mapai's intentions for the postmoratorium period were unambiguous.[73]

As the year was drawing to a close, the Agudahs began exerting pressure within the cabinet for an extension of the moratorium on school and conscription reform. When Mapai refused to budge, the Agudahs resigned on September 18, 1951. In the negotiations for a new government, the two Agudah parties demanded an unconditional declaration by Mapai that the status quo on conscription and education would be preserved. Mapai would not yield from its commitment to introduce the reforms of education and conscription. Neither would the Agudahs yield in their opposition to these reforms. And so the relationship was divergent-explicit. Each side refused to join with the other on such a basis. Indeed, the Agudahs would refuse to join any government until the conscription law was reversed.[74] In 1961, the labor wing, Poalei Agudah, broke from the parent party and established itself as a separate party. It was then willing to join a Mapai government. The parent Agudah party refused to join any government until 1977, when it was able to extract a pledge to restore the exemption for orthodox women from a Likud (Herut) government.

Unlike the Agudahs, the Mizrachis were not opposed to nonmilitary service for orthodox women. But they flatly rejected the Mapai interpretation of the past government's agreement on education. According to Mapai, the parties had agreed to unify the school system at the end of the moratorium. The Mizrachis viewed the moratorium as a postponement of a decision and insisted that it had always demanded two trends, one secular and one religious. Mapai and the Mizrachis agreed yet again to disagree: they established a committee to examine the question. The agreement among the three parties stated: "If at the conclusion, the Mizrachis will not concur with the new program [of national education], they shall be free to leave the coalition, without this being considered a breach of the coalition agreement."[75]

The Mizrachis made two other prominent demands when this government was being formed. The first, to which Mapai did not object, was for the establishment of separate units for orthodox men in the state's paramilitary youth organization.[76] The second was for an orthodox veto when decisions were made about which industries would be allowed to operate on the Sabbath. The latter was unacceptable to Mapai; the parties agreed that the next government would "consider" the issue. One each issue, then, Mapai and the Mizrachis either agreed from the outset or agreed to disagree.[77]

It was in its bargaining relationship with the General Zionists that Mapai offered important concessions. Contemporary observers and subsequent scholars have considered Mapai's agreement to accelerate the decontrol of the economy as one of Mapai's most important concessions to the General Zionists. From the perspective of the theory of government formation, however, this concession was a minor one; it did not engage a conflict of directional principles. For, by the time this government was being negotiated, Mapai had already come to the conclusion that the perilous state of the Israeli economy required a change of policy direction. "By 1952, Mapai came to see [Israel's economic] salvation only through massive imports of capital from any available source and through utilization and encouragement of any enterprise that could and did make work."[78] Mapai's change of economic course had already committed it to decontrol of the economy before the new government was negotiated. The General Zionists extracted not a change of policy direction but an acceleration of a policy to which Mapai was already committed.

Much more important, and involving an explicit compromise on Mapai's part, was Mapai's acceptance of the General Zionists' demand for a reduction in income tax rates for middle-income taxpayers. This reduction was clearly extracted against Mapai's will. The General Zionists, too, made explicit concessions in dropping their demand for the nationalization of labor exchanges and the health service of the Histadrut. In effect, the General Zionists had to accept the continuation of the Histadrut as the nation's largest employer.[79]

Mapai's concessions were not limited to the economic realm. It committed itself to the depoliticization of the civil service—the removal of party considerations from hiring and promotion and the introduction of impartial personnel policies. Since the old system of cronyism overwhelmingly worked in Mapai's favor, this, too, was an important concession. As well, Mapai agreed to the postponement of municipal elections for a period of two years. This was a substantial gain for the General Zionists, who at the time controlled many municipal governments.[80]

The Progressives were easier for Mapai to deal with. They made only two major demands: unification of the school system (which Mapai supported, of course); and that the government not commit itself to the introduction of a 10 percent electoral clause, a requirement that parties gain at least 10 percent of the national poll before they were eligible for Knesset seats. Both Mapai and the General Zionists were in favor of such a clause. Receiving only about 4 percent of the national vote, the Progressives would have been eliminated. In the event, Mapai and the Progressives agreed to paper over the matter. A specific percentage was dropped, and the government program simply declared that the government would formulate proposals "with the intent of amending the electoral law in order to avoid further fragmentation of the nation's political spectrum," which was to say, the parties would make no common commitments.[81]

At this point, the possibility of a coalition between Mapam and Mapai was probably at its low point. Mapam continued to demand a pro-Soviet policy and an end to support for the American involvement in Korea. It opposed ratification of the reparations treaty with West Germany (successfully negotiated by the outgoing government). It opposed unification of the school system. And it now opposed Mapai's policies of decontrol of the economy and of encouraging foreign investment. It proposed, instead, an economic policy premised on strict regulation and reliance only on domestically generated investment capital. Neither party expressed a willingness to set any of these conflicts aside. Of the major issues of the day, Mapai and Mapam were in agreement on only one: both endorsed national service for orthodox women.[82]

Herut, too, supported conscription of orthodox women. It was in conflict with Mapai, however, over—above all—reparations from West Germany. It continued to emphasize its demand for sovereignty over Jerusalem and the Arab military evacuation of the West Bank of the Jordan as a precondition of a peace settlement.[83] Again, neither party expressed an interest in making any of these divergent preferences divergent-implicit.[84]

In summary, then, Mapai had divergent-explicit relationships with the Agudahs, Mapam, and Herut. With the Mizrachis it had divergent-implicit relationships. With the Progressives it had a convergent relationship on policy issues. But on the question of electoral reform, a more straightforward conflict of political interests that falls outside the framework of the theory, the two parties had a divergent-implicit relationship. For the Progressives, the electoral reform question was clearly the decisive one, because their survival hung in the balance. There seems to be little doubt that the Progressives meant it when they insisted that dropping reform was the irreducible quid pro quo of their participation. Because there is no place in the theory for such a nonpolicy issue, the theory cannot account for the participation of the Progressives in the government.

The case of the General Zionist–Mapai relationship is somewhat comparable. The General Zionists extracted a number of important nonpolicy concessions from Mapai: postponement of municipal elections and civil service reform. The latter can be partially explained by understanding that Ben-Gurion and his immediate followers in Mapai were committed to a policy of rationalizing the state bureaucracy. Even so, the policy aroused intense opposition within the party. That the Mapai leadership would accept such concessions is the best evidence that it concluded that the cooperation of the General Zionists could not otherwise be obtained. So we must presume that the General Zionists made these demands part of the irreducible set of conditions on which their participation was contingent. These conditions, like the Progressives' insistence on no electoral reform, cannot be accounted for by the theory.[85]

The government, of course, consisted of Mapai, the General Zionists, the Progressives, and the Mizrachis. Only the inclusion of the last-mentioned can be accounted for by the theory. The Mizrachis' inclusion was premised on divergent-implicit relations. The theory does perform satisfactorily in predicting the presence of Mapam and Herut and the Agudahs in the opposition.

Why did Mapai make the policy concessions to the General Zionists? Perhaps because Mapai's dominance was severely constrained at the time by the configuration of bargaining relations. It had insuperable differences with all parties save the Mizrachis, General Zionists, and Progressives. Governing with the Mizrachis alone, Mapai would have only the slimmest possible majority (60 of 120 Knesset seats) and would become a prisoner to the Mizrachis' constant demands in defense of orthodoxy. A government with the General Zionists, however, would raise the government's strength to 83 seats and make the Mizrachis dispensable. Likewise, a government that included the Progressives as well (4 seats) would raise the total to 87 seats, and make either the Mizrachis *or* the General Zionists dispensable. Moreover, the Hapoel Mizrachis' and General Zionists' respective worker and capitalist orientations would tend to balance each other and reinforce Mapai's centrism.[86]

The analysis can be extended further. Both of the nonpolicy concessions Mapai made to the General Zionists were to be delivered across time. To that extent, they could be canceled and thereby served to induce continued General Zionist cooperation once the General Zionists were in the government.[87] Given that the only policy concession Mapai actually granted to the General Zionists was the agreement to reduce income taxes, and given the way in which General Zionist participation would enhance Mapai's overall authority, Mapai's leaders may have concluded that the price was not too high under the circumstances.[88]

The 1953 Mapai–Mizrachi–Hapoel Mizrachi– General Zionist–Progressive Government

This case is more straightforward than most in Israel insofar as it turned on a single issue. The issue was symbolic; but underlying the symbolism was a more concrete dispute over the values that schools would attempt to inculcate in students. On May 1, 1953, a workers' holiday in Israel, the Red flag was displayed and the "Internationale" sung in a number of state schools that belonged to the labor trend. This event was to provoke a bitter conflict between the socialist and nonsocialist parties and bring down the incumbent government.[89]

In anticipation of the pending passage of the State Education Law, which would dissolve the trends and establish a unified national school system, a step agreed upon by the members of the coalition, the General Zionists immediately protested the use of the schools for party purposes. They insisted that the matter be discussed in the cabinet and, then, that the government ban future occurrences in all schools which were about to enter the unified system.[90] In a manner similar to conflicts over prayer and religious instruction in schools, the matter quickly became the most bitterly disputed of the day.

Mapai's central committee endorsed the demonstrations of class consciousness and adopted the view that the new education law should be amended to permit such demonstrations. The four General Zionist ministers resigned, contending that the Mapai central committee's decision amounted to a breach of the agreement designed to create a national school system.[91] Acting for Mapai, Ben-Gurion initiated negotiations with other parties. The discussions with Mapam collapsed because Mapam demanded the preservation of the labor trend in education and abandonment of the Western-oriented foreign policy. Among other things, this would have meant canceling the reparations agreement with West Germany. None of these demands were acceptable to Mapai. Neither party was interestd in deferring them.[92] The Agudahs were willing to join a government on two conditions: deferral of a final decision on the unification of the trends; and abolition of the conscription of orthodox women. These were no more acceptable to Mapai now than they had been at the formation of the previous government.[93]

Predictably, Herut was adamantly opposed to displays of working-class consciousness in public schools. It naturally opposed the revisions of the Education Act (which it otherwise supported) that were proposed by the Mapai central committee. Otherwise, Herut brought forward the conflicts that had divided it and Mapai when the outgoing government was formed just six months earlier: above all, acceptance of reparations from West Germany.[94]

After a ten-day period of discussion, it became clear that Mapai had three options: form a government of Mapai, the

Mizrachis, and the Progressives, which would provide a minimum-winning majority of sixty-four seats; call new elections; or induce the General Zionists to return to the government. Mapai was able to do the last-mentioned by offering the General Zionists an agreement to disagree and threatening new elections. In effect, the Mapai central committee contrived for both Mapai and the General Zionists to step back from the dispute by declaring that it would not take a final position on the issue until the party council met in five or six months' time. It proposed that both parties set the matter aside until that time. The General Zionists, anxious to avoid a new election, and anxious to remain in government, found this acceptable.[95]

The General Zionists returned to the government on this basis, and Mapai was able to maintain the four-party coalition. Mapai's relations with the other government parties remained as they had been when the previous government was created five months earlier: divergent-implicit with the Mizrachis convergent with the Progressives. With the General Zionists, of course, they were now divergent-implicit because of the settlement of the single issue that existed between the two parties when the new government was formed. With Herut, Mapam, and the Agudahs, the relationships remained divergent-explicit. So the outcome—the return of the General Zionists to the government on the basis of an implicit compromise, and the continued membership of the Progressives and NRP on the basis of convergent and divergent-implicit relationships, and the continuation of the Agudahs, Herut, and Mapam in opposition—conforms to the expectations of the theory.

Why did Mapai offer the General Zionists the opportunity to return to the government, and why did the General Zionists accept it? In the view of Ben-Gurion and the Mapai Knesset delegation, both of whom leaned on the Mapai central committee to postpone the matter, the value of the General Zionists was as a counterweight in the government to the Mizrachis. If the "flag dispute" could be deferred, Mapai had little to lose by having the General Zionists in the government. No other Mapai concessions were involved. The evolution of Mapai's economic preferences even before the formation of the previous government meant that the policies of the two parties were no longer far apart. The one real concession the General Zionists had demanded, tax cuts for middle-income taxpayers, had already been accepted by Mapai when the previous government was formed. The General Zionists' anticlericalism reinforced Mapai's anticlericalism and provided a useful balance against the Mizrachis. Likewise, the Hapoel Mizrachis' worker orientation nicely reinforced Mapai's orientation in the event of future conflicts with the General Zionists over economic policy. Finally, the General Zionists' lack of strong foreign policy views gave Mapai largely a free hand in that area.[96]

Why did the General Zionists accept Mapai's offer? Insofar as we can glean motivations from the comments of the party leaders and contemporary observers, their acceptance of the offer was motivated by the fact that the alternatives were perceived to be even less desirable. These alternatives were early elections followed by a similar compromise; or early elections followed by a return to opposition. Moreover, even if the General Zionists did attempt to exert maximum pressure on Mapai by refusing the implicit compromise, they could not force Mapai out of government. Mapai could form a majority government with the Mizrachis and Progressives. Or worse still, it could be compelled to form a government with the orthodox and the left-wing socialist party, Mapam. In the final analysis, Mapai could always govern without the General Zionists.[97]

The new government served until January 26, 1954, when Ben-Gurion submitted his personal, and according to Israeli law therefore the cabinet's resignation. Ben-Gurion resigned for reasons of health. Mapai appointed Moshe Sharett to succeed Ben-Gurion, and the four-party coalition continued. Since the change was strictly one of personnel, the first Sharett government is treated as a continuation of the previous coalition.[98] It served from January 26, 1954, until June 29, 1955. Sharett submitted the government's resignation when the General Zionists abstained on a Herut-sponsored motion of no-confidence. The motion grew out of the so-called Kastner case.⁹⁹ Sharett then formed a caretaker government that served through the Knesset elections held the following month and the subsequent government negotiations.

The 1955 Mapai–Achdut Haavodah–Mapam–National Religious Party–Progressive Government

Following the general election of July 26, Mapai conducted government negotiations for three months. A new government was not installed until November 2. Again, the education system provided the primary focus of the NRP's concerns. It wanted a legal provision that would permit schools to be transferred from the secular to the religious trend, or vice versa, on the vote of a majority of the parents of the schools' students. This was acceptable to Mapai, because it saw the proposal as neutral. Mapai also agreed to the preservation of a religious trend comparable to the one established in the recently unified primary system in the proposed state secondary system.¹⁰⁰

The NRP also wanted, and Mapai accepted without objection, the establishment of an orthodox trend in Gadna, a paramilitary youth organization. Mapai had accepted this in principle in 1952; it now agreed to implement this previous agreement.¹⁰¹ The NRP advanced one other basic demand in the 1955 negotiations. It wanted an enabling act to allow local authorities to decide whether pig breeding would be permitted. Mapai had agreed several years earlier that the matter should be decided locally; so granting the enabling act, a subject of only marginal concern to Mapai in the first place, was compatible with Mapai's own principles. All of the demands the NRP advanced in 1955, then, were tangential to Mapai's own preferences.¹⁰²

"The major thrust of the Progressives [in the 1955 campaign and negotiations] was in the area of national health care, specifically for nationalization of existing sick funds and hospitals."¹⁰³ The single largest health insurance scheme was that run by the Histadrut. Health insurance was one of its principal inducements for members, and the Progressives' proposal was above all aimed at weakening the position of the Histadrut in the national economy. It was inconceivable that Mapai would willingly agree to major changes in this sensitive area, and the outcome was a classic agreement to disagree: the two parties agreed that the next government would "consider" a state insurance program as an alternative to existing collective and private plans.[104]

Unlike the NRP, the Agudah bloc—formed by reunification of the two Agudah parties—was unwilling to accept the maintenance of the secular-orthodox balance in public policy. Once again it insisted that the exemption of orthodox women from national service was the quid pro quo it required for its participation in a government. Once again Mapai was unwilling to compromise the issue. Neither party expressed an interest in making the disagreement implicit.[105] The Agudahs remained in opposition.

The General Zionists, too, were in the opposition when the government took office. The General Zionists refused even in principle to consider participation with Mapai in the aftermath of the election, which reduced their Knesset fraction from twenty-three to thirteen seats. Younger party activists blamed participation in previous coalitions for this drop. The electoral defeat produced such intense factional struggle that the leadership was compelled to withdraw the party from coalition discussions entirely apart from any policy questions. This conflict within the party and the uncertainty about the course the party would pursue were the primary reasons for the slow pace of the negotiations in 1955. Ben-Gurion, who had returned from retirement to resume leadership of Mapai, was anxious to give the General Zionists ample opportunity to join the negotiations, because he wanted the largest coalition policy that differences would allow.[106]

When previous coalitions had been formed, Mapam had regularly demanded that the next government abandon the pro-Western foreign policy orientation (e.g., no reparations from Germany, an end to support of American policy in Korea) and move Israel into alignment with the Soviet Union. This policy became increasingly untenable, however, as the Soviet Union adopted a progressively more anti-Zionist foreign policy and anti-Semitic domestic policy. By 1953–54, the tension between Mapam's policy preferences and the Soviet Union's anti-Zionism and anti-Semitism could no longer be contained. In 1953, a showdown between the party's left and center-right occurred. The outcome was the dismissal from the party of the still-pro-Soviet faction under the leadership of Moshe Sneh.[107] The party suffered a subsequent reduction at the end of 1954, when a minority faction left because the practice of democratic centralism had reduced its role to a marginal one. This faction was essentially Achdut Haavodah, the party which had united with Hashomer Hazair to form Mapam in 1948. The departing faction readopted the name Achdut Haavodah, and the rump party retained the name Mapam.[108]

By 1955, then, both Achdut Haavodah and what remained of Mapam had abandoned their pro-Soviet line. And they had, under the pressure of Israel's economic weakness, as well dropped their earlier demands for an economic policy based on the use of only local capital and expanded state enterprises. These demands withered because of the manifest dependence of Israel on private and public foreign grants, loans, and investment. In view of the economic difficulties that Israel was already experiencing, proposals which were based on economic self-reliance had lost all credibility.[109] The process of modifying economic policy preferences occurred in tandem with the modification of Mapam's foreign policy preferences and reinforced the conflict with the Sneh faction in 1953 and 1954. The upshot of it all was that when the two component parties—Achdut Haavodah and Hashomer Hazair (the new Mapam)—emerged from their old alliance at the end of 1954, their economic preferences, too, had been diluted. So diluted, in fact, that they played no role in negotiations with Mapai.

As it happened, in 1955, "the two leftist parties presented Mapai with demands so reasonable as to be impossible to resist."[110] The two parties placed their policy demands jointly, and the basic elements were that no foreign military bases would be established on Israeli soil and that no foreign security pacts would be entered into. This focus on foreign policy reflected the much-stepped-up level of violence in the Arab-Israeli conflict in 1955. Mapai readily agreed to these and agreed as well to a request for a reduction in the scope of the military government along the border with Jordan.[111] "Since the foreign policy demands of the leftists were actually generally identical to Mapai's own program, it was not difficult for Mapai to grant these concessions."[112]

This brings us to the final party in the system, Herut. As it had in the past and as it would continue to do until the 1967 war, Herut demanded that the next government work to establish the claim of Israeli sovereignty to all of the original mandate, including what had become the Kingdom of Jordan.[113] The demand appeared somewhat ritualized at times, because Herut never made clear how it expected Israel to gain or regain this territory. Nevertheless, the demand was genuine: during all the years before the 1967 war, no policy was of greater importance to Herut. Herut virtually made defense of the claim its *raison d'être*. This disagreement between Mapai and Herut about acceptance or rejection of the existing borders provided the most fundamental conflict between the parties during these years.[114] Herut's demand for maintenance of the claim was exactly the opposite of Mapai's constant effort to win international recognition of the 1948 armistice borders. For Herut, maintenance of the claim was deemed essential because of the party's faith that future opportunities would arise that would allow Israel to act on the claim. Failure to make the claim, Herut always warned Israelis, would mean that "if we succeed in driving the enemy out of the areas he has conquered, we shall be reminded that we ourselves admitted these areas were foreign soil."[115]

To this Herut also added the demands it had regularly made in the past: nationalization of health care; a ban on new state enterprises; and compulsory arbitration of labor disputes.[116] It also added two demands that reflected recent Israeli circumstances. In the first place, Herut insisted that no diplomatic relations be established with Germany. Until the announcement of the Halstein Doctrine in September 1955, and a subsequent West German pledge to the Arabs that it would not recognize Israel in exchange for their recognition of only West Germany, Mapai governments had been gradually moving toward diplomatic relations with West Germany.[117]

The second demand that reflected immediate conditions was Herut's insistence that the government abandon Mapai's policy of police action against escalating Arab terrorist attacks, and respond by seizing the Gaza Strip.[118] Not surprisingly, neither Mapai nor Herut expressed the least interest in transforming these differences into implicit differences for the sake of government cooperation. Indeed, no negotiations were even considered.[119]

Let us pull the case together. Mapai had divergent-explicit relations with Herut and the Agudah bloc. The General Zionists removed themselves from possible government membership on nonpolicy grounds. With Achdut Haavodah and Mapam, Mapai had convergent relations. With the NRP, Mapai had only tangential preference relations. With the Progressives, Mapai's relationship was divergent-implicit on the basis of the agreement to "consider" a national health insurance scheme. The theory predicts the limit of tolerance will be provided by the implicit compromise. Accordingly, we would expect the formation of a government consisting of Mapai, Achdut Haavodah, Mapam, the NRP, and the Progressive party. This was indeed the government that took office on November 2.

The 1958 Mapai–Achdut Haavodah–Mapam–NRP–Progressive Government

On December 31, 1957, Ben-Gurion submitted the cabinet's resignation in protest of a breach of cabinet collective responsibility by Mapam and Achdut Haavodah. Two weeks earlier, Ben-Gurion had sought cabinet approval of negotiations with West Germany aimed at the purchase of strategic materials and armaments. The negotiations were approved, but only over the strenuous objections of Achdut Haavodah and Mapam.[120] Achdut Haavodah then published in its party organ,

La-Merhav, a report of the cabinet decision and a warning that Mapai's refusal to cancel the cabinet decision could jeopardize the coalition.[121] As a result of the disclosure, Ben-Gurion canceled the negotiations and demanded the resignation of the Achdut Haavodah ministers. When they refused to resign, he submitted the cabinet's resignation.

The negotiations that ensued were almost exclusively among Mapai, Achdut Haavodah, and Mapam. The NRP and the Progressives were willing to return to the government on the same terms negotiated when the last coalition was formed.[122] The General Zionists remained in internal turmoil because of their 1955 election setback and the ensuing factional struggle; they were unwilling to join any government. The Agudahs continued to demand an end to the program of national service for orthodox women. Herut, too, continued with its long-standing demands of sovereignty over the entire original mandate and so forth. As well, it was unalterably opposed to the purchasing of strategic materials and armaments from Germany. Mapai leaders never considered negotiations with Herut.[123]

The government was reformed after one week of negotiations. It was reformed on the basis of an implicit compromise. Mapai, Achdut Haavodah, and Mapam agreed that the latter two parties had the right to abstain on all Knesset votes that pertained to relations with Germany.[124] So Mapai now formed a government based on implicit compromises with Mapam, Achdut Haavodah, and the Progressives (the government would "consider" a national health scheme). With the NRP it continued to have tangential preferences.

The 1958 Mapai–Achdut Haavodah–Mapam–Progressive Government

The National Religious party ministers withdrew from the government on June 22, 1958, because of a conflict with Mapai (and the other coalition members) that engaged one of the most sensitive questions in Israeli politics: Who is a Jew? In March, the government had instructed registration officials that henceforth they were to accept the veracity of information about nationality and religion supplied by registrants. Thus, no proof was to be required of any individual declaring himself to be a Jew. Likewise, no proof was to be required when both parents declared a child to be a Jew.[125]

"Who is a Jew?" has been a subject of intense controversy between the orthodox and the secular in Israel because it pits traditional tenets of Zionism against orthodox interpretations of Jewish law.[126] Religious affiliation is of great importance for purposes of immigration, because a Jew is eligible for immediate citizenship, and in matters of civil status.[127] Mapai's liberal understanding of Jewish identity was reflected in the government's instruction to registration officers. The orthodox parties, however, defined as Jewish an individual whose mother had been Jewish or who had formally converted to Judaism. By such a definition, the son of a Jewish man and non-Jewish woman was not a Jew unless he converted, even if he had been raised in the religion.[128]

When the conflict first surfaced in March, a cabinet committee was formed to study it. In June, against the advice of the orthodox, the cabinet voted to reaffirm its earlier decision to classify as Jewish anyone who declared himself to be Jewish or who was so declared by his parents. The reaffirmation immediately provoked a threat from the NRP that it would withdraw its ministers. Mapai countered this threat with a willingness to let the NRP ministers abstain on relevant Knesset votes. The NRP rejected the offer and withdrew from the government on June 22.[129] A week of negotiations followed, with Mapai leaders reiterating the offer of a right to abstain on relevant Knesset votes and the NRP insisting on its definition of who is a Jew.

When Mapai refused to budge, the NRP decided to remain outside the government.[130] The reformed government consisted of Mapai, Achdut Haavodah, Mapam, and the Progressives. It remained oversized even after the withdrawal of the NRP and continued on the basis of previously arranged implicit compromises that were reaffirmed. All other bargaining relationships also remained the same.

The 1959 Mapai—Achdut Haavodah—Mapam—NRP—Progressive Government

The coalition carried on until July 1959, when it resigned following renewed conflicts about relations with Germany. The government's resignation was provoked when Mapam and Achdut Haavodah voted against (rather than abstain on) a government-sponsored motion authorizing the sale of small arms to Germany.[131] Because Knesset elections were already scheduled for November, a caretaker administration took office. The elections occurred on November 3.

In the campaign the Agudah bloc demanded exemption of orthodox women from national service; a ban on the sale of pork; restrictions on postmortems (a violation of orthodox law); abolition of work permits for Jews on the Sabbath; and a new Sabbath law restricting commercial and industrial activity and public transportation on the Sabbath. In the subsequent negotiations, Mapai offered an implicit compromise: the next government would form a committee to study the issues. The Agudahs demanded explicit concessions and withdrew from the negotiations when Mapai would not make them.[132]

The NRP's position was more flexible. The NRP wanted a reexamination of the "Who is a Jew?" question, a ban on postmortems, and a new Sabbath law. Unlike the Agudah bloc, the NRP accepted Mapai's offer of a ministerial committee to study the issues. The NRP also demanded extension of the arrangement existing in the state elementary schools, with their special religious units, to the proposed system of state secondary schools. The establishment of a state system of compulsory secondary education had been a principal focus of Mapai's election campaign. The NRP agreed with Mapai's proposal for a single secondary school system, but wanted it to provide each student with a choice of a secular or religious curriculum. Mapai had agreed to such an arrangement in 1955, and that agreement was—now that the actual establishment of the system was approaching—now reaffirmed.[133]

In 1959, with little actually having been done to implement the 1955 agreement to "consider" a state health insurance scheme, the Progressives again campaigned for a national health program and again settled for less. In 1959, interestingly, Ben-Gurion actually gave his personal approval to a plan that would provide uninsured citizens with state insurance. Under pressure from his own party, however, Ben-Gurion was compelled to retract his approval. The Progressives had to settle for a cabinet committee that would attempt to find a "proper solution" to the problem of health insurance.[134] "As usual, the ministerial committee was a guarantee of at least temporary oblivion for the Progressives' demands on health care."[135]

In 1959, Mapam campaigned for an end to military administration of the Arab territories. Mapai and Mapam agreed that the next government ought to "review" the matter.[136] Otherwise, the main thrust of the campaigns of Mapam and Achdut Haavodah in 1959 were directed at the issue that had brought down the last political government and at the related question of the scope of cabinet responsibility. The government had fallen when Mapam and Achdut Haavodah had opposed a government (that is, Mapai) proposal approving arms sales to Germany. Along with educational reform (not opposed by any party), Mapai made enforcement of collective cabinet responsibility the focus of its 1959 campaign. Since it always controlled a majority of cabinet votes, collective responsibility was a means by which Mapai could reinforce its dominance.[137]

Mapam and Achdut Haavodah refused to embrace arms sales to Germany or collective responsibility. Ultimately, the three parties agreed that collective responsibility would apply only to the matters agreed upon in advance and that it would not apply to questions involving the military government of Arab territories and Israeli-German relations or youth movements in public schools. As regards the final point: Mapam was seeking the right to organize the schoolchildren of leftist parents. This was something to which Mapai was opposed. Across the board on the contentious issues, then, Mapai, Mapam, and Achdut Haavodah agreed to disagree.[138]

The General Zionists announced during the campaign that they would not participate in any government that included Mapam and Achdut Haavodah and demanded that the next government abolish foreign currency controls, nationalize health insurance and hospitals, and reduce the income tax on middle-income taxpayers. Mapai offered to leave all of these unresolved and for cabinet study. When the General Zionists rejected the offer, Mapai's leaders decided to govern with the more flexible Mapam and Achdut Haavodah and left the General Zionists in opposition.[139]

Once again, Herut insisted that the next government lay claim to sovereignty over all of the original mandate and nationalize health insurance and care. It embraced the General Zionists' call for an end to currency controls and, above all, categorically rejected arms sales to Germany. Neither Mapai nor Herut was interested in even preliminary negotiations, and Herut remained in opposition.[140]

The government formed consisted of Mapai, the NRP, Mapam, Achdut Haavodah, and the Progressives. With each partner, Mapai had a divergent-implicit relationship. With each party in opposition, it had a divergent-explicit relationship.

The 1961 Mapai–NRP–Achdut Haavodah–Poalei Agudah Government

The coalition formed in November 1959 came to an end when Ben-Gurion submitted its resignation in the wake of bitter criticism of him by the smaller coalition parties. This criticism grew out of Ben-Gurion's general handling of the "Lavon affair"—a security debacle in the mid-1950s which involved the then Mapai Defense Minister Pinchas Lavon—and in particular his rejection of a cabinet committee report on the affair which exonerated Lavon of misconduct. Following the resignation of the government, a month of futile negotiations ensued. All of the parties that had been members of the outgoing government demanded that Mapai replace Ben-Gurion as Prime Minister. When Mapai refused, a caretaker government was formed and new Knesset elections were called.[141]

The electoral outcome was of no particular significance for the subsequent government formation. These negotiations began as they had left off before the election: a blocking coalition of Mapam, Achdut Haavodah, the Liberals (the General Zionists and the Progressives), and the NRP had formed against Mapai. In effect, they were challenging Mapai's dominance. They insisted that Mapai could no longer receive a majority of the cabinet portfolios and that Mapai replace Ben-Gurion. They also demanded that the Knesset's control over the military be enhanced. This was essentially an attempt to transfer some influence from an institution in which they were weak—the cabinet—to one in which their influence was greater—the legislature. For several weeks Mapai refused to accommodate the demands of the coalition, and a standoff occurred. Thereafter, the anti-Mapai coalition collapsed.[142] Mapai's dominance, if somewhat tarnished by its very public internal conflicts about the Lavon affair and Ben-Gurion's personal attacks on some of the members of his former government, was preserved. Most important, Mapai was unyielding in its insistence that it retain a majority of cabinet positions. It also refused to replace Ben-Gurion, although there were many in Mapai who would have been pleased to see him depart. The decision to stand by Ben-Gurion was apparently motivated at least as much by the conviction among Mapai leaders that they must not reward the anti-Mapai coalition as it was by personal loyalty to Ben-Gurion.[143]

The demands the NRP expressed in the 1961 campaign were along the same lines they had been in the past. It called for a Sabbath law that would ban entertainment and public transportation on the Sabbath, a new law restricting pig raising, and a law restricting postmortems. In 1961, the NRP was successful in extracting an explicit concession from Mapai: Mapai agreed to support legislation that would ban entertainment (but not public transportation) on the Sabbath.[144] Mapai also agreed to support legislation that would restrict pig breeding largely to the Arab-Christian area around Nazareth. To this, Mapai did not actually object, because local ordinances had already had the effect of restricting the breeding to this area.

Mapai made a second explicit concession to the NRP when it agreed to a law placing relatively weak restrictions on postmortems. Mapai had been opposed to any such restrictions.[145]

These same concessions were made to gain the support of Poalei Agudah Yisrael (Pagi). Pagi constituted the socialist wing in the Agudah bloc and had broken with the bloc prior to the 1961 election. It advanced the same demands as the NRP. As well, and above all, it demanded that the state provide a higher level of funding for Agudah schools. This demand was motivated by Pagi's competition with the Agudah party. Although primary for Pagi, the increase in the level of funding was an inconsequential issue for Mapai. Pagi's small size—two Knesset seats—did not entitle it to a full portfolio. Nonetheless, it did receive a deputy ministerial position and pledged itself to support the government's program.[146] So it is treated here as a coalition member.

The parent Agudah party advanced all of the policy preferences that Pagi and the NRP advanced, but it was less accommodating. It demanded the inclusion of public transportation in the proposed Sabbath law, wanted pig breeding entirely banned, opposed all postmortems, and continued to insist that orthodox women be excluded from national service. It refused compromises and remained in opposition.[147]

Achdut Haavodah and Mapam campaigned and bargained for an end to military government in the Arab territories. Mapai refused to give such an undertaking, but did offer to set the issue aside by recognizing the right to a free Knesset vote on the matter. Achdut Haavodah accepted the implicit compromise. Mapam refused.[148] For the first time since the Moshe Sneh era, the two leftist parties emphasized economic and wage policy conflicts with Mapai in the campaign and subsequent negotiations. Both demanded that no more state industries be transferred to private hands, that there be no increases in indirect taxes, and that income tax rates on lower incomes be reduced. Mapai was opposed to every one of these preferences, but was compelled to accept all of them to get Achdut Haavodah to enter the government.[149] Mapam withdrew from the negotiations earlier because of Mapai's refusal to end the military government of the Arab territories.[150]

The General Zionists and the Progressives merged to form the Liberal party just before the 1961 election. The new party's negotiations with Mapai were complicated by the bitter personal attacks arising out of the Lavon affair that Ben-Gurion had made against the leader of the Progressives, Pinchas Rosen, and by a series of overtures that the leader of Herut, Menachim Begin, had made to the Liberals to join with Herut in a single, nonsocialist block. The attacks on Rosen alienated many ex-Progressives and made them less willing than they had been in the past to lobby for participation in the new government. The overtures from Begin made many of the former General Zionists more interested in cooperation with Herut than in government participation. The upshot was that the Liberals were unwilling to join in a Mapai government unless they were able to do so on their own terms.[151] They were not. The Liberals reiterated the old policy of the Progressives and General Zionists of a national health scheme to replace the Histadrut's program and made this the irreducible condition of their collaboration. Mapai's offer of another implicit compromise was insufficient, and so the Liberals remained in opposition.[152] All of the traditional conflicts between Mapai and Herut were unchanged, and no negotiations occurred between them.[153]

The outcome was a coalition of Mapai, Achdut Haavodah, the NRP, and Pagi. It was not an outcome anticipated by the theory, in the first place, because Mapai was compelled to make explicit policy concessions to each of the parties that joined the government; in the second place, because the government was essentially a minimum-winning government. I say "essentially" because as it controlled only sixty-eight seats, only Pagi with its two seats was an expendable partner. The NRP and Achdut Haavodah were indispensable to a majority.

Why did the theory fail in this case? There appear to be several reasons. First, relations among Mapai and the past government members had been seriously damaged—embittered—by Ben-Gurion's unpredictable behavior and his attacks on party leaders related to the Lavon affair. The depth of this embitterment was demonstrated by the unprecedented anti-Mapai and anti-Ben-Gurion coalition that formed after the election. This bitterness affected all party leaders. It appears to have been decisive in weakening the position of the ex-Progressive wing of the Liberals and Mapam's reluctance to do business with a Mapai still led by Ben-Gurion. Herut's overtures to the right wing of the Liberals were also important. By reducing the Liberals' interest in a return to government, they raised the price Mapai would have to pay to get the Liberals in a government. Moreover, once it was apparent that the Liberals were unlikely to enter the government, Achdut Haavodah and Mapam could raise the price of their own participation, because they no longer felt compelled to participate to balance the influence of a nonsocialist party. And when Mapam and the Liberals had both made it apparent that they were not going to participate, Achdut Haavodah and the NRP could feel free to demand explicit concessions. Mapai then had no choice but to be forthcoming with them, because the two parties were then indispensable to a functional majority. In effect, the government was formed, and the expectation of the theory violated, because Mapai temporarily lost its dominance. And this temporary loss of dominance was above all due to the conflicts that were engendered by the debate over the Lavon affair.

    The new government served until June 26, 1963. At that time, Ben-Gurion resigned the premiership because the factional conflict within Mapai that the Lavon affair had engendered had undermined his leadership position. He was succeeded as Prime Minister by Levi Eshkol.[154] The resignation of the government that, according to Israeli law, had to accompany the Prime Minister's resignation was purely technical. The decision to substitute Eshkol for Ben-Gurion took place within Mapai and did not result in renewed negotiations among the parties. When Mapai selected Eshkol, the old coalition was immediately reformed on the basis of the outgoing government's coalition agreement.[155] Consequently, Eshkol's first government is treated as a continuation of the previous government.

Eshkol's second government is treated in the same manner. On December 14, 1964, Eshkol resigned to compel a showdown with Ben-Gurion, who had been lobbying within Mapai for Eshkol's removal and for an investigation of the 1954 Lavon affair and the 1960 ministerial investigation of it. The Mapai central committee reaffirmed Eshkol's leadership of the party and government and rebuffed Ben-Gurion's leadership challenge. On December 22, Eshkol reestablished the government on the basis of the existing coalition agreement. No policy negotiations occurred. All parties returned by prearrangement to the government and to the same ministries.[156] Consequently, the formation of this technically new government is also omitted. It served until after the sixth Knesset election, held on November 2, 1965.

The 1965 Alignment—Mapam—NRP—Pagi—Liberal Government

In 1964 and 1965, Mapai and Achdut Haavodah joined to create a new labor party known as the Alignment. In 1965, they ran together on a single Knesset list. The Alignment thus became Mapai's successor as the dominant party in Israeli politics. It was not, however, simply an enlarged Mapai. Its preferences reflected the compromises that had been necessary to bring Mapai and Achdut Haavodah together. They also reflected a change that was occurring within Mapai at the same time as, and partly as a result of, the merger of Mapai and Achdut Haavodah. This change was the departure of Ben-Gurion and the fairly conservative group of secondary leaders who surrounded him. Together they created yet another new party, this one known, according to its acronym, as Rafi.[157]

After the Mapai central committee rejected Ben-Gurion's demand for a reopening of the Lavon affair and reaffirmed Levi Eshkol's leadership in December 1963, Ben-Gurion took his challenge to the party conference. In February 1964, the conference endorsed Eshkol's leadership and rejected Ben-Gurion's attempt to regain it by a margin of 60 to 40 percent. It was clear that Ben-Gurion and his followers, a group of young technocrats known as "Young Mapai," had lost control of the organization to an older generation of party men ("Old Mapai") who were committed to ending the Lavon affair, preserving the social functions of the party and the Histadrut, and cooperating more closely with Achdut Haavodah. The closing of the Lavon affair, the fall of Ben-Gurion's faction to minority status within Mapai, and Mapai's movement toward Achdut Haavodah all contributed to the creation of Rafi.[158]

Rafi gained a disappointing ten Knesset seats in 1965. Ben-Gurion had taken most of Mapai's most charismatic leaders with him, but he lacked Mapai's organizational machinery. With its poor showing in 1965, Rafi was stillborn, and most of its leading figures, excluding Ben-Gurion, who retired, began to return to Mapai. Eventually, Rafi joined the Alignment as one of its several factions.[159]

Rafi's attempts to create a distinct policy identity in 1965 notwithstanding, it was essentially a party of notables. It was not a result of the kinds of societal cleavages that I have employed to understand the origins of other parties. Consequently, an attempt to explain its absence from the 1965 government in terms of the theory would be off the mark. The party remained outside the 1965 government because of the organizational and personal struggles that led to its creation and embittered relations between its leaders and the leaders of Old Mapai.[160] Policy issues were of secondary importance in the creation of Rafi and even less important in its role as an opposition party after 1965.[161]

In order to bring about a union with Achdut Haavodah, Mapai had been required to reverse a number of preferences that it had maintained or had been moving toward when still under the leadership of Ben-Gurion's faction. The most important of these involved the military government of Arab territories. Achdut Haavodah wanted an end to military government, and acceptance of an end to it was part of the price Old Mapai had to pay to create the Alignment. It likewise had to abandon the idea, not yet at the level of articulated policy, of introducing legislation that would limit the right to strike and other legislation that would tie wage increases to productivity as well as the cost-of-living index rather than to the index alone.[162]

These changes were important, because when Mapam emphasized these issues in its 1965 campaign, it found itself taking positions that were now compatible with those of the Alignment. Mapam wanted an end to military government, and it opposed limiting the right to strike and tying wage increases to productivity. Because of the departure of Ben-Gurion's faction and the compromises the creation of the Alignment entailed, Mapam found its preferences convergent with those of the formateurs' party for the first time since 1955.[163]

The creation of the Alignment was not the only party-system change that preceded the 1965 election. The former Progressives split from the Liberal party they had created with the General Zionists and formed their own party, the Independent Liberals. The creation of the Independent Liberals was precipitated by the movement of the ex–General Zionists toward an alliance with Herut.[164] The Independent Liberals again demanded a national health insurance scheme. And again, they accepted "the need to compromise their proposal to a level where they received only such symbolic outputs as cabinet investigations and other vague commitments." In 1965, the Independent Liberals accepted the Alignment's offer of another implicit compromise: the next government would establish a National Hospital Authority, which would examine the "eventual" nationalization of health care.[165]

Herut and the former General Zionists united prior to the 1965 election and campaigned together as the Gahal list. The policies of Gahal reflected Herut's longstanding concern with foreign policy and the General Zionists' economic orientation. Gahal consequently combined Herut's irredentist foreign policy demands with the General Zionists' demands for economic liberalization and the transference to the state of the Histadrut's health insurance program. Gahal maintained the old calls for compulsory arbitration of labor disputes in vital industries and services and also campaigned for an end to preferential tax treatment for Histadrut and collective enterprises. It also wanted an end to export subsidies. Once again, the programs of Herut and the General Zionists directly challenged the core of labor's foreign and domestic policies. As Mapai had been unwilling to negotiate with Herut in the past, the Alignment was now unwilling to negotiate with Gahal. And Gahal, for its part, indicated no interest in such negotiations.[166]

The promise of a new Sabbath law, which the NRP extracted from Mapai when the 1961 government was formed, was never acted on by the government, because draft proposals of a law aroused strong opposition within Mapai, Achdut Haavodah, and Mapam. In 1965, therefore, the NRP again campaigned for a new Sabbath law as the price of its entry into another coalition. The Alignment in 1965, however, was in less need of the NRP's cooperation than Mapai had been four years earlier. The Alignment would only offer another implicit compromise: the next government would present to the Knesset legislation reaffirming the right of local governments to regulate Sabbath activities.[167]

Such a right was already established and most regulation of Sabbath activity was already the result of local laws, so the offered legislation would have no real impact. It did, however, offer the NRP a face-saver which made it easier for NRP leaders to contend that they had not abandoned their commitment to greater legal restrictions on Sabbath activity. After a month of debate, the NRP accepted the offer. As an inducement, the Alignment agreed that the existing Sabbath restrictions which applied to state and private industries would be extended to kibbutzim-owned enterprises which employed hired labor. This extension was proposed and supported by the Alignment, because the Alignment viewed the restrictions as protections of the social rights of workers rather than religious observances. The NRP, of course, could interpret them otherwise. They, too, smoothed the way for the NRP's acceptance of the Alignment's implicit compromise of the Sabbath law conflict.[168]

Poalei Agudah Yisrael advanced demands for a Sabbath law, but was mainly concerned to gain an increase in the level of state financial support for its schools. The Alignment's agreement to such an increase was sufficient to commit Pagi to support the new government. Agudah Yisrael, too, demanded a new Sabbath law. It also continued to insist that the quid pro quo for its participation must be the exclusion of orthodox women from national service. Neither it nor the Alignment expressed an interest in deferring the issue, and the Agudahs again remained in opposition.[169]

When the Alignment formed the new coalition, then, it had a convergent-preference relationship with Mapam; a divergent-implicit relationship with the NRP and the Independent Liberals; and a tangential relationship with Pagi. With Gahal and the Agudahs the relationship was divergent-explicit. The Alignment-Rafi relationship cannot be classified in these terms. With the exception of the peculiar Alignment-Rafi relationship, the other relationships lead to an outcome the theory anticipates: a government of the Alignment, NRP, Independent Liberals, Mapam, and Pagi.

The new government remained in office until June 5, 1967, when an emergency war cabinet was formed in anticipation of the Six-Day War. It included representatives from every party except the Arab and Jewish Communist parties. The war cabinet remained in office beyond the end of the War of Attrition in August 1970. At that time Gahal withdrew in protest of the government's decision to accept the Rogers Peace Plan for the termination of the War of Attrition. The other parties remained in the government, which did not resign, but continued to serve through the Yom Kippur War of October 1973. When the war cabinet was formed in 1967, when Golda Meir replaced Levi Eshkol as Prime Minister in 1969, when the government continued after the 1969 election and after the withdrawal of Gahal in 1970, no negotiations as such occurred among the parties. On each occasion the parties agreed to maintain the coalition, in view of the international situation, without regard to policy conflicts.[170] Because these were crisis governments, they fall outside the scope of the theory. The next government formed under noncrisis circumstances did not appear until after the December 1973 election.

During these intervening years, important changes in the party system took place. In 1968, Mapam and most of Rafi joined with the Alignment and formed the Labor Alignment. The Rafi minority that did not join the Labor Alignment formed the State List for the 1969 election. In 1973, the State List and Gahal, together with another small splinter group, the Free Center, formed the Likud. The formation of Likud did not result in a change in the profiles or even the policy preferences of Gahal. The ex-Herut and ex–General Zionists who created Gahal remained overwhelmingly the dominant factions in the new Likud.

The March 1974 Labor–NRP–Independent Liberal Government
The June 1974 Labor–Independent Liberal–Citizen's Rights Movement Government
The October 1974 Labor–NRP–Independent Liberal Government

The election of the eighth Knesset was originally scheduled for October 1973, but did not actually occur until December 31, 1973, because of the outbreak of the Yom Kippur War on October 6. The Meir government's failure to anticipate the Arab attack until a few hours before it occurred and its failure to order a full mobilization when it did learn that war was imminent rather than policy principles as such provided the main focuses of the election campaign after the war. Blame for the intelligence and security failures of the Meir government was assigned by voters to the Labor party. Labor and its affiliated Arab lists lost six seats in December 1973, falling from sixty to fifty-four. Likud rose to thirty-nine.[171] Because of the consolidation of the party system, the dominant party no longer had democratic socialist parties on its left as Mapai and the original Alignment had. Only two moderate nonsocialist parties remained on its right: the Independent Liberal party, with only four seats, and the still-smaller Citizen's Rights movement, with only three seats. Labor remained the dominant party, however, because the communist parties' hold on five seats and the existence of several independents in the Knesset whose votes could not be relied on meant that Labor was indispensable to a majority government. But just barely so. The governments formed in 1974 would be the last formed by a dominant party in Israel.

Among the democratic parties, Labor had available the following relevant parties as potential partners: the Independent Liberals, the National Religious party, the Agudahs, the Citizen's Rights movement, and Likud. Since Likud and the Agudahs would maintain preference relationships with Labor that were divergent-explicit, Labor's dominance would rest on its ability to exploit the conflicts among the Independent Liberals and Citizen's Rights movement and the National Religious party. With any two of these parties it could construct a majority government. The story of the three government formations of 1974 is essentially the story of Labor asserting and demonstrating its dominance in the face of electoral losses and attacks on its handling of the war that led many to believe prematurely that it was no longer dominant.[172]

Virtually every policy conflict that had existed between Gahal and the Alignment in the 1960s continued to exist between Likud and the Labor Alignment in 1973 and 1974. Likud, of course, concentrated its postwar campaign against Labor on the Meir government's conduct of the war. Nonetheless, beneath the rhetorical and symbolic struggle, real policy differences were evident. Likud once again stressed nationalization of health insurance and care, compulsory arbitration of labor disputes, and an end to exchange controls and export subsidies. It also called for the privatization of Histadrut-controlled enterprises.[173]

After the 1967 Six-Day War, the Herut faction (the dominant faction) in Gahal abandoned its claim of Israeli sovereignty over all of the original mandate territory. The acquisition during the 1967 war of the West Bank (Judea and Samaria in the language of Likud), the Gaza Strip, and the Sinai refocused Herut's attention. It, and therefore Likud, now accepted Jordanian sovereignty over Jordan, minus the West Bank. It demanded that the West Bank be treated as an integral part of Israel, not subject to return, or partial return, as part of a larger peace settlement. It also insisted on the unrestricted right of Jews to establish settlements there.[174]

The Alignment, in contrast, did not identify the West Bank as an integral part of Israel, was willing in principle to consider the return of at least a part of the territory to Jordan as a part of a comprehensive accord, and wanted settlements restricted to those that would enhance Israel's security and claims to defensible borders.[175]

In both socioeconomic and foreign policy, then, Likud and Labor were as much in conflict as their predecessors had been. Only the content of the foreign policy questions had changed. Once again, neither party expressed an interest in negotiations, and the relations were all left divergent-explicit.[176]

Labor's relationships with the Agudahs—running as a single list in 1973—were also divergent-explicit. The Agudahs continued to insist that orthodox women must be exempted from national service. They also insisted that only orthodox conversions performed abroad should be sufficient to qualify an individual as a bona fide member of the Jewish faith. That is, they did not want Reformed and Conservative conversions acknowledged. These two demands were sufficient to insure that no cooperation with Labor would occur. Labor was, as usual, willing to offer the Agudahs the opportunity to defer the questions. The Agudahs declined, the relationship remained divergent-explicit, and the Agudahs remained in opposition.[177]

In the NRP's view, the status of the West Bank was a religious question: acquisition of the territory was part of the biblical fulfillment of the Jewish people. The territory, therefore, should be treated as an integral part of Israel with respect to possible peace negotiations and Jewish settlements.[178] Like the Agudahs, the NRP insisted that henceforth only orthodox conversions performed abroad should constitute satisfactory evidence of membership in the Jewish faith.[179] The willingness of the NRP to set aside these issues changed several times in 1974 according to changes in the Labor party and Labor's relations with other parties. This shifting NRP attitude was the main cause of the changing composition of the 1974 governments. It is a matter to which we will return.

The Independent Liberals, with only a socioeconomic policy profile, campaigned as they and their predecessors had for several decades for a nationalization of health insurance and care. It certainly had other preferences, but within its profile, this was always the centerpiece of the small party's campaign. Outside the realm of the concrete profile preferences, the party also campaigned for a moderate approach (compatible with Labor's) toward possible territorial concessions and advertised itself to its professional and entrepreneurial middle-class constituency as an important restraining force against the collectivist inclinations of Labor and the antisecularist demands of the religious parties.[180]

The Citizen's Rights movement was led by an intensely anticlerical civil rights activist, Shulamit Aloni, who had previously been a Labor member of the Knesset, but came into increasing conflict with Golda Meir and other leaders of the dominant Mapai faction because of her (Aloni's) insistence that Labor should terminate the repeated cooperation with the religious parties and pursue a policy of radical secularization. Aloni's views could become the basis for a new party because of growing conflict between secularists and antisecularists in Israel after 1967. The NRP's interpretation of the West Bank question in biblical terms was one source of this conflict, but probably not the most important. More significant, probably, were a number of court cases that involved mixed marriages, the children of mixed marriages, their status in Israeli society, and the rabbinate's control of marriage and divorce. These provoked widespread controversy. And this controversy was reinforced by what secularists judged to be NRP and Agudah attacks on the status quo in religious matters.[181]

Socioeconomically, the Citizen's Rights movement was a party of the progressive, nonsocialist middle class. Anticlericalism rather than socioeconomic affairs, however, provided the party's *raison d'être*. It campaigned for a complete separation of church and state and the establishment of civil marriage and divorce. It surprised contemporary observers by gaining three seats in 1973, enough to make it a relevant party.[182]

The first government of 1974 was formed by Golda Meir on March 19. The delay in the formation of the government was the result of the NRP's reluctance to implicitly compromise its demands with respect to orthodox conversions and the West Bank. Eventually, the NRP did accept implicit compromises on these issues: the conversion question would be left unresolved for a year, and the parties would reach no conclusions on West Bank settlement policy and the status of the West Bank.[183] Meir also eventually reached an agreement with the Liberals to disagree on nationalization of health insurance.[184] The Liberals, like the NRP, initially read the election returns as proof that the position of Labor had been seriously weakened and were consequently much less inclined to compromise than they had previously been. The Citizen's Rights movement refused to participate in any government that included the NRP. Consequently, when the NRP reduced its demands—which the CRM would not do—the CRM remained outside the government.[185]

The outcome, then, conforms to our expectations: the government consisted of coalition partners with whom Labor was able to arrange divergent-implicit relationships. Parties whose relationship with Labor was divergent-explicit remained in opposition.

Meir's government was the briefest in Israeli history. It resigned on April 11, 1974, a month and a day after its formation. The government's resignation was triggered by the findings of a commission of inquiry established in November to examine the previous government's conduct of the war. The commission's conclusions, implicitly condemning the decisions of Meir as Prime Minister and Moshe Dayan as Defense Minister, forced their resignations and thereby the resignation of the government.[186]

Labor replaced Meir as party leader and Prime Minister designate with Yitzhak Rabin. Rabin attempted to reform the three-party coalition on the basis of the previous agreements. This was acceptable to the Independent Liberals. But the NRP now reverted to its earlier demand that Labor grant it explicit concessions on the status of the West Bank, settlements, and orthodox conversions. This Rabin refused to do.[187] When the NRP remained adamant, Rabin turned to the Citizen's Rights movement, which agreed to form a government with Labor and the Independent Liberals and defer all issues involving state-church relations for three months. Rabin's move to form a government with the CRM and fix a three-month deadline on the church-state questions was an unconcealed attempt to coerce the NRP into abandoning its insistence on explicit concessions.[188]

The Labor–CRM–Independent Liberal coalition was formed on June 4. It conformed to the expectation of the theory insofar as it was based only on divergent-implicit relationships. The outcome did not conform, however, insofar as it was a minimum-winning government. It controlled only sixty-two Knesset seats and included no unnecessary parties. The previous government—which Rabin was trying to restore—had been oversized. It had controlled sixty-nine Knesset seats, and the Independent Liberals had been superfluous.

Rabin's manipulation of the CRM-NRP conflict worked. In October, the NRP agreed to return to the government on the basis of implicit compromises on all issues. The Independent Liberals were willing to continue on the basis of the original agreement with Meir. The NRP rejoined the government; as a result, the CRM departed.[189] The government regained its larger sixty-nine-seat majority and its oversized status. It remained in office until December 1976.

Summary

Between 1950 and October 1974, we have thirteen cases of government formation in Israel. Excluding those instances in which a party removed itself from possible membership in a government for nonpolicy reasons, we were able to predict the composition of the government and the opposition in eleven of the thirteen cases. We failed in 1952, when the General Zionists were included in the government. We predicted that the policy relationship with Mapai would leave the General Zionists in opposition. We also failed to predict the outcome of the 1961 government formation. In that case, we would have expected all three of the parties that joined Mapai in government to remain in opposition. I will return to these cases below.

Across the thirteen cases, we have eighty-six relationships between the party of the formateurs and the other relevant parties in the legislature. These eighty-six relationships include the relationships in which a potential member refused to join a government for reasons unrelated to policy preferences. There were four such relationships. In 1955 and twice in 1958, the General Zionists were led by their electoral defeat of 1955 to remain in opposition regardless of their policy relationships wich Mapai. Similarly, Rafi's position of opposition in 1965 must be explained in terms of the personal antagonisms that existed between the leaders of Mapai and Rafi.

We have three more relationships which were based on a mixture of policy and nonpolicy considerations but in which the latter were decisive. In 1952, the General Zionists and Progressives joined a Mapai coalition, but did so only because they gained concessions from Mapai on nonpolicy questions. The General Zionists made their participation contingent on postponement of municipal elections for two years and civil service reform. The Progressives made their participation contingent on an agreement not to introduce electoral reform. What is important here is not that the two parties advanced such demands, which is common enough, but that they clearly would not have been willing to participate without Mapai's acceptance of them.

In 1961, the Liberals had a policy relationship with Mapai (divergent-explicit), but it was the personal enmity aroused by the Lavon affair rather than a commitment to their preferences which kept the Liberals in opposition. All of the evidence is that the Liberals would otherwise have been willing to accept Mapai's offer of an agreement to disagree and would have joined the government. A satisfactory explanation, therefore, must be couched in terms of the Lavon affair rather than the policy relationship per se.

After subtracting the seven instances in which parties refused to negotiate for nonpolicy reasons or made their final decision contingent on nonpolicy calculations, we have seventy-nine bargaining relationships remaining. In these seventy-nine relationships, behavior was based exclusively on policy preferences. Seventy-six of the seventy-nine relationships led to placements in the government and opposition that conform to the hypothesis for the dominated-competitive system. The four instances in which the hypothesis is not sustained have already been mentioned. They occurred in the 1952 and 1961 formations. In 1952, Mapai included the General Zionists in the government even at the price of explicit policy concessions. This case we have already counted as a failure because of the decisive importance the General Zionists attached to nonpolicy concessions. In 1961, Mapai again made explicit concessions; this time to gain the participation of the NRP, Achdut Haavodah, and Pagi.

In sum, when we subtract the cases in which a party removes itself from possible membership on nonpolicy grounds, the cases in which policy is decisive but the theory nonetheless fails to predict the outcome, and the cases in which the theory predicts correctly but does not provide a satisfactory explanation, we find that we have seventy-six of the original eighty-six relationships (or 88 percent) remaining. These seventy-six relationships the theory is able to predict *and* explain. It is successful in these cases in the sense that the placement in government or opposition is what we would expect on the basis of the relationship type, and this relationship has been defined by the participants entirely in terms of policy preferences.

CHAPTER FIVE

Denmark

Origins of the Party System

Under the pressure of the wave of revolutions and unrest that swept Europe in 1848 and at the urging of a group of urban liberals known as the National Liberals, the King of Denmark, Frederik VII, was persuaded in 1849 to grant a constitution that guaranteed religious freedom, freedom of speech, and the general liberty of the individual. The constitution vested legislative power in a Rigsdag consisting of two chambers, the Folketing and the Landsting, the latter being elected indirectly and on a more restricted franchise in order to insure its conservative character.

The Folketing franchise was among the most liberal in Europe at the time. Members were directly elected in single-member constituencies by all men of thirty years and over who were economically independent and without a criminal record. This initially enfranchised about 73 percent of the men over thirty, and the proportion gradually increased until, in practice at the end of the century, all men had the vote. Women had the vote from 1918.[1] It was not until 1901, however, that the secret ballot replaced public voting; and not until 1915 that single-member constituencies gave way to proportional representation.

The National Liberals were nationalists in the sense that they emphasized the place of a strong military in Danish foreign policy and were among the Danes most willing to go to war with Prussia to retain Slesvig-Holstein. They were liberals in the sense that they pushed for the removal of guilds and other barriers to free internal and external trade. They were also liberals of the classical mold in their demand for constitutional government. By 1860, they had largely achieved their economic as well as constitutional objective and therafter became defenders of the status quo in Danish politics.[2]

With the loss of Slesvig-Holstein in the 1864 Dano-Prussian War, the National Liberals were discredited as a governing force. In search of new allies, the King turned to Denmark's small class of great landowners, then about four hundred families. The landowners had previously stood aloof from politics, but were now anxious to participate in order to block the participation of the much larger class of independent, middle-class farmers.[3] The landed elite, with the support of the now rather reactionary National Liberals, drove through the Rigsdag constitutional changes that narrowed the upper-house franchise. This change insured the upper classes' hold on the Landsting and thus their control of Danish governments for the balance of the century. The alliance of the urban and rural elites was symptomatic of the increasingly class-based nature of Danish politics and, in its constitutional aspect, provided the framework for a series of crises that were to be the main feature of Danish politics for the next forty-five years.

The initial basis for the alliance of the landed and urban elites was provided by their shared tax-exempt status and by the demand of middle-class farmers, who were heavily taxed, that a national income tax be adopted. For middle-class farmers the question of taxation became closely tied to the demand for parliamentary government—that is, a government responsible to a Folketing majority. Until the principle of parliamentary government was established, the King's ministers would be able to continue to ignore the Folketing—in which the farmers were represented—and survive on the support of the upper house, which was solidly in the hands of the upper-class rural and urban conservatives.

In 1872, the independent farmers and their middle-class urban allies achieved a majority in the Folketing, and for the next thirty years repeatedly sought to obstruct financial legislation and coupled this obstruction with demands for parliamentary reform. They were referred to broadly as the *Venstre*, the Left, or the Liberals. The conservative governments would routinely enact provisional budgets by decree and dissolve the Folketing. The Left would generally return somewhat strengthened after each election. In response, in 1876, a conservative Prime Minister, J. B. Estrup, established the United Right, consisting of landowners and erstwhile National Liberals and some independents. This was largely a defensive move and was intended to resist demands for democratization and to support military expenditures. The United Right was the first party in the sense that it established a true national organizational structure down to the local level.[4]

Initially, Denmark's military posture and foreign policy became lines of cleavage in the battle over parliamentary government because expenditures for fortifications around Copenhagen were among the principal items in the budgets the conservative governments enacted by decree. The farmers first opposed the fortifications because of their dubious constitutional validity. They later came to oppose the basic premise of the Right's foreign policy. That premise was that, because it was beyond the capability of any government to provide for the defense of the entire nation, all efforts should be concentrated on defending Copenhagen. In the event of war, according to such a strategy, the rest of the country would be conceded while an all-out effort was made to hold Copenhagen. Simultaneously, attempts would be made to gain diplomatic and military assistance from a third country.[5]

The farmers objected to this strategy on several counts. In the first place, they did not live in Copenhagen, and so it was of little value to them. Second, it was expensive, and the tax burden fell disproportionately on them. Third, the obvious foreign threat was Germany, and Denmark surely could not mount an effective resistance to a German attack. Fourth, any foreign assistance would have to come from Britain or France, and each had demonstrated in 1864 that it would not aid the Danes in a conflict with Germany. The farmers' final objection was that the Danish military had traditionally been the preserve of the landed elite and was a symbol and potential instrument of the landed elites' power in society. As an alternative foreign and military strategy, the Left proposed to recognize the futility of Denmark's situation, pursue a course of absolute and passive neutrality, and maintain only a militia across the country rather than a modern military around Copenhagen.[6]

Until the end of the century, conservative governments were able to manipulate divisions within the Left and thereby compensate for the gradual electoral decline the Right experienced as the Left, and especially the Social Democratic party, mobilized new voters. But another conservative government became impossible after the 1901 election, which so reduced the Right's Folketing minority that the King had no choice but to turn to the Left to form the next government. Although the King would attempt to challenge it one last time in the spring of 1920, the change of 1901 essentially marked the establishment of the principle of parliamentary government: henceforth, governments would be based on the Folketing majority. In Danish history, this turning point became known as the "Change of System."[7]

As the Left and Right were struggling over the constitutional and foreign policy questions in the last quarter of the nineteenth century, other lines of cleavage were becoming increasingly apparent in Danish society. The most important of these, already alluded to, was the class cleavage—in the countryside and in the city. Danish land reforms at the end of the eighteenth century and the commercialization of agriculture in the first half of the nineteenth century had created three distinct rural classes by the second half of the nineteenth century. The first of these was the comparatively very small class of large landowners of aristocratic lineage who supported the United Right. The second class was the much larger class of independent, relatively prosperous middle-class farmers. The third and still-larger group was the class of smallholders, whose land was insufficient to support them, and the landless rural proletariat. In 1894, slightly more than half of all holdings belonged to members of the smallholders class. Both the smallholders and the rural workers were compelled to seek part- and full-time work on middle-class farms and in town to support themselves.[8]

As the farmers were determined to free themselves from the vestigial influences of the landed elite, they were equally determined not to lose the use of the smallholders and rural workers. With the commercialization of agriculture, farmers came to treat their laborers not simply as a subordinate class, but frequently as little more than slaves. Whereas early in the century it had been common for workers to be housed and fed as junior members of the family, in the second half it became common for them to be housed with or in conditions comparable to those provided for farm animals.[9]

State efforts to help smallholders to buy land for themselves—sponsored by the old elites and urban liberals who feared socialism—were carefully controlled by the representatives of the rural middle class. The Smallholdings Act of 1899, for instance, which introduced the principle of state loans to smallholders, restricted the plots that could be purchased to a size not sufficient for the owners to live off of exclusively. They were, however, too large for the owner to take a full-time job in addition to running his smallholding. In this way, farmers in need of inexpensive labor were still assured of a plentiful supply.[10] Likewise, when in 1903 the farmers finally achieved their long-standing goal of tax reform, they devised a new system which placed a disproportionate burden on the smallholders.[11]

It was not until the second renewal of the Smallholdings Act in 1909 that it became possible for rural workers to purchase plots sufficient to provide full-time employment. This change was a reflection of changes in the party system itself. By the first years of the twentieth century, the Rigsdag contained four distinct groups that were evolving into the four main parties in modern Denmark. The first of these was the Right, consisting of representatives of the rural and industrial elite, but receiving support also from wealthier independent farmers, middle-class businessmen, higher civil servants, and urban professionals. The Right was committed to three goals: delaying the democratization of the upper house; minimizing state intervention in the economy, although it did support limited social reforms to reduce the appeal of the Social Democrats; and mobilizing popular support for defense expenditures. In 1915, the Right would change its name to the Conservative party.

The second group, called the Reform Liberals, represented middle-class farmers and had the largest Folketing delegation in the first decade of the century. The Reform Liberals would become known simply as the Liberals, or occasionally the Agrarian Liberals, following the expulsion in 1903 of the Radicals. Once the parliamentary principle was established and they had realized a series of longstanding programmatic demands during the first decade of the century, the Agrarian Liberals increasingly became defenders of the status quo in Danish society and concerned themselves almost exclusively with socioeconomic and agricultural issues.

The third group, the Radical Liberals, broke with the Agrarian Liberals in 1903.[12] The split was precipitated by the Radicals' greater commitment to social reforms—in particular their commitment to the interests of the smallholders vis-à-vis the middle-class farmers—and by their opposition to the parent party's greater willingness to negotiate defense questions with the Right. The Agrarian Liberals, having won their parliamentary point, largely dropped their opposition to a modern Danish military. Those Liberals who continued to object on other grounds gravitated toward the Radical Liberals. The Radicals' principal antagonist on the defense question was the Right, which maintained the preference of its National Liberal predecessor for a modern military posture.

The final Rigsdag group in the early years of the century was the Social Democratic party, established nominally in 1871 and gradually made into a modern national party over the next quarter of a century. The party was born reformist and committed to the parliamentary road to power.[13] In contrast to its counterparts in Norway and Sweden, it never needed to call into play implicit or explicit threats of violence to obtain its goals. Its moderation was probably due to the comparative ease of access that the liberal franchise afforded the industrial working class in Denmark and to the availability of bourgeois parties with which it could cooperate. After the creation of the Radical Liberals, the two parties shared out seats until the introduction of proportional representation in 1915, with the Social Democrats agreeing not to compete against the Radicals in rural Jutland, where the Agrarian Liberals were especially strong. In 1909, the Radicals formed their first government and, from 1913 to 1924, provided most governments and were supported by the Social Democrats. From 1929 to the outbreak of World War II, the Social Democrats and Radicals governed together.

The Social Democrats shared the Radicals' opposition to the Right's military policy. Indeed, until the 1930s, the Social Democrats were more extreme in their opposition to a Danish military than were the Radicals. Whereas the Radicals carried forward the traditional Left demand for only a national militia, the Social Democrats' preferences in this area were motivated not only by the concerns that led the bourgeois Left to oppose a modern military, but by opposition deriving from classical socialist views of warfare among capitalist states.[14]

It is paradoxical that a country with a party sometimes referred to as the Agrarian Liberal party would not have a consumer-producer cleavage. The paradox is reinforced when we note that as late as the early 1960s, 78 percent of farm owners voted for the Agrarian Liberals and 73 percent of blue-collar workers voted for the Social Democratic party.[15] There can be no doubt that the Agrarian Liberal party is the party of middle-class farmers and that it attends carefully to the interests of Danish agriculture. But the party's electoral support can more readily be explained by historical patterns of party competition than by a consumer-producer cleavage.

The Agrarian Liberals were able to capture the vote of the independent farm-owning class because no other party offered this class a credible alternative in the formative years of the party system. The Radical Liberals identified themselves in rural areas as advocates of the interests of smallholders *against* the interests of the agrarian middle class. The Social Democrats, too, acted as a working-class party and, as well, never made a sustained effort to challenge the Agrarian Liberals in their Jutland stronghold. Indeed, in this competition the Social Democrats deferred to the Radicals until the introduction of proportional representation. And the Conservatives were, of course, historically the party of the independent farmers' arch-antagonist, the large landowner. In consequence, middle-class farmers remained, largely by default, the preserve of the Agrarian Liberals, who themselves never made a serious effort to compete with the other parties for the urban and especially working-class vote.[16]

The absence of the intense consumer-producer conflict that appeared elsewhere in Scandinavia has been due to the historical prosperity and efficiency of Danish agriculture and to the vital role it played in inducing industrialization and later sustaining the export-oriented manufacturing sector. In the most critical years of the party system's development, 1900 to 1914, total net agricultural production rose by 57 percent. At the same time, the prices Danish farmers received rose more than the prices they paid, and their net real income more than doubled.[17] As elsewhere, industrialization was in part a function of the demand agriculture generated for various types of machinery and consumption goods. But in the absence of other circumstances, such industrialization in a small country would come up against the balance-of-payments constraints with which all Scandinavian countries—including Denmark—have had to struggle. And it was here that Danish agriculture played its most vital mitigating role in the economy through its booming exports, particularly so in view of the sharp improvement in the terms of trade that such exports enjoyed after 1890. By its international competitiveness, the sector played a central role as the earner of the foreign exchange that was vital to the modernization of Danish manufacturing. This was a role that agriculture in Norway, Sweden, and especially Finland was incapable of playing.[18] In contrast to agriculture in the other Nordic countries, Danish agriculture did not until the 1960s require public subsidization. And when subsidization was required, it was not to maintain a sector that could not otherwise be price-competitive in international markets, but was due to overproduction throughout Europe.[19] Nor has it needed protection from foreign competitors by means of high tariff barriers that have artificially raised the price of food for urban consumers.

The competitiveness of Danish agriculture has been due to many factors—soil, climate, producer organization among them—but especially to the agricultural reforms of the late eighteenth and early twentieth centuries. These reforms resulted in a severely rationalized sector composed largely of middle-sized farms and very few marginal units. The starkest contrast is with Finland, where postwar agrarian reform produced thousands of tiny units which could only provide farmers with a living if heavily subsidized and which could never compete on the international market.

The four parties—Radicals, Liberals, Social Democrats, and Conservatives—are continuously represented in the Rigsdag in the twenty-year period of government formation that we will examine. I will discuss the parties that were formed during that twenty-year period when I examine the government formations. Two others parties that were also formed in the early years of the party system and were sporadically represented during the years of government formation merit a brief mention here.

The first of these is the Danish Communist party, which was formed in 1919 as an amalgamation of far left groups that wished to adhere to the Third International. In the usual fashion, the party sought to defend working-class interests, and was antidemocratic and pro-Soviet.[20] The last party established during the early period was the Justice party, or *Retsforbund*. It, too, was formed in 1919 by a collection of groups advocating the adoption of a single tax on property-value increases and the abolition of all other forms of taxation. In this, it drew its inspiration from the American economist Henry George. As well, the party demanded complete economic freedom.[21]

In sum, the democratic parties developed the following profiles: Agrarian Liberals, socioeconomic; Conservatives, socioeconomic and foreign policy; Radical Liberals, socioeconomic and foreign policy; Social Democrats, socioeconomic and foreign policy; Justice party, socioeconomic. The Communist party, of course, acquired socioeconomic and foreign policy profiles and, as well, an antidemocratic posture.

The Governments, 1955–1975

Since the constitutional changes of 1953, Denmark has been governed by a single-house legislature, the Folketing, elected every fourth year. As there were 175 party seats after the 1953 election, the majority requirement in the mid-fifties was 88. Additionally, representatives from Greenland and the Faeroe Islands participated in the Folketing. Since these were territorial rather than party representatives and did not vote on party-divisive questions, they are not counted in the majority requirement. The following parties were represented after the 1953 election: the Social Democrats (74 seats), Radical Liberals (14), Liberals (42), Conservatives (30), the Communist party (8), the Justice party (6), and the Slesvig party (1).[22]

The Slesvig party, which disappeared from the Folketing at the 1964 election, never had more than a single seat and never obtained majority-relevance. The Justice party disappeared from the legislature as a result of the 1960 election; it remained unrepresented until 1973. The inclusion and exclusion of the party from government cannot be understood in terms of the theory of government formation because, strictly speaking, it has not been a party at all: it has not enforced party discipline in parliamentary voting. The Danish Communist party, more a sect than a party in terms of its significance in Danish politics, disappeared from the Folketing at the 1960 election. The party has never been a candidate for inclusion in any government. Its dubious commitment to the constitutional order is sufficient to explain this isolation.

The 1955 Social Democratic Government

In the wake of then Prime Minister Hans Hedtoft's death in January 1955, the Social Democrats selected H. C. Hansen as Hedtoft's successor. Hansen immediately opened government negotiations with the other parties. At this juncture, two issues overshadowed all others in Danish politics. The first was an economic one: how to respond to an anticipated half-billion-kroner and growing balance-of-payments deficit. The policies of the Social Democrats and Radicals were the same, but incompatible with those of the Liberals and Conservatives. The latter two parties wanted an end to state support for home construction; a decoupling of the wage and price indices; a freeze on several new but not implemented social programs; and higher indirect taxes to dampen domestic consumption.[23]

The Social Democrats and Radicals, too, advocated higher indirect taxes. But they wanted the costs of these increases rebated for low-income families by means of greater cash assistance and child grants. Moreover, they both proposed a forced loan on all taxable incomes in excess of 4,000 kroner. The Conservatives and Liberals were opposed to the increased assistance and the forced loan. The Social Democrats and Radicals in turn rejected the decoupling of the wage and price indices and the termination of support for home construction.[24] These differences were explicit ones, because the Liberals and Conservatives made their policies the price of their cooperation.[25]

Foreign policy provided the second issue: whether to approve the Paris agreements on German rearmament and entry into NATO. The Social Democrats and Conservatives were in favor of approval. The Radicals, the third party with a relevant profile, were opposed. The Radicals wanted a referendum on the question. Since the major powers had already committed themselves to German rearmament and membership, any referendum would effectively have been about continued Danish membership in the alliance. The Radicals were long-standing opponents of Danish participation in NATO. By requesting a referendum, they were offering the Social Democrats the opportunity to take the question out of the party system and were proposing an implicit compromise.[26] The Social Democrats demurred.

The Social Democrats, then, had divergent relationships with all of the other parties. As we would expect, the government that emerged from the negotiations was a minority Social Democratic administration. It remained in office until after the 1957 elections.

The 1957 Social Democratic–Radical–Justice Party Government

"A twelve day orgy in tactics, negotiations and compromise" is the way Herbert Tingsten characterized the formation of the 1957 government.[27] It was among the more unlikely coalitions in postwar Danish politics. Its unlikeliness derived from the compromises it entailed. The Social Democrats now accepted an implicit compromise with the Radicals on NATO membership. Much more peculiar was the inclusion of the Justice party in the government, for the Justice leaders could not promise the Social Democrats that they would enforce parliamentary discipline. Moreover, the Justice negotiator, Viggo Starcke, abandoned almost all of his party's policies in negotiating entry into the coalition.

On May 23, 1957, when serious negotiations were first initiated between the Social Democrats and the Radicals, the Prime Minister and Social Democratic leader, H. C. Hansen, stated that his party would insist that the next government declare that foreign policy would remain unchanged.[28] That is, the Radicals would have to accept NATO membership. The Radical leaders responded that they could accept this if their party was allowed to remain passive in certain situations. The "certain situations" were parliamentary votes related to NATO and the military budget. In other words, the "Radicals had clearly indicated that they were no longer going to let NATO policy be a barrier to cabinet participation," but were looking to the Social Democrats for an implicit compromise to ease the abandonment of their long-standing opposition to NATO.[29] The Justice party, also opposed to NATO, but with no foreign policy profile, joined the negotiations later in the day and simply accepted membership. These reversals occurred "despite the refusal of the entire Radical parliamentary group and about half of the Justice parliamentary group to support the alliance policies of the previous Social Democratic government."[30]

The Radicals' willingness to implicitly compromise the NATO question now, as earlier, derived from their recognition that membership was an accomplished fact and that continued opposition would only isolate them in government negotiations. The implicit compromise gave them an opportunity to accept membership without approving it. By 1957, the need to do so was well understood within the party.[31] For their part, the Social Democrats were now ready to accept a compromise they had previously rejected because, unlike a referendum, allowing the Radicals to abstain imposed no costs.[32]

Beyond NATO membership, the main issue at the time this government was formed was again the balance-of-payments deficit, which was now reaching crisis proportions. All parties except the Justice party agreed that import demand had to be rapidly reduced and saving and investment rapidly increased. The question of how to obtain these goals separated the Social Democrats and Radicals from the Liberals and Conservatives and all parties from the Justice party. The Social Democratic proposals were formulated by Viggo Kampmann, the Finance Minister in the outgoing government and, along with Hansen, the primary Social Democratic negotiator. On the basis of the Kampmann formulations, the Social Democrats wanted a 27-million-dollar loan from the International Monetary Fund; a 150-million-kroner reduction in state expenditures; a 150-million-kroner increase in indirect taxes, designed to stem the demand for consumer imports; the establishment of a tax exemption for the first 500 kroner in interest income for individuals with incomes below 15,000 kroner; an increase in the marginal tax rates for individuals in upper-income brackets; an increase in the capital gains tax; and negotiations among the government, unions, and employers to avoid the cost-of-living increases that would otherwise come due in July as a result of the above measures—in effect, a negotiated incomes policy. The final piece of the Social Democratic package called for the continued use of exchange controls.[33]

The Radicals shared all of these preferences and added several that were essentially elaborations of the Social Democratic proposals: the use of state guarantees in place of state loans for private residential construction; an increase in the rate of interest charged on state loans for public housing; an increase in public housing rents; an increase in the employers' contribution to the unemployment fund of 15 million kroner per year. All of these were in line with the Social Democrats' plans for reduced state spending.[34]

While the Liberals and Conservatives could endorse several of the Social Democratic proposals, their preferences were in direct conflict with the Social Democrats' on several points. Specifically, they wanted tax exemptions on *all* interest income, and they wanted the exemptions available to taxpayers in *all* brackets; no increase in capital gains taxes; no increase in the marginal income tax rate for individuals in upper brackets—instead, the introduction of a flat, proportional rate on all incomes; and no government intervention in the labor market—that is, no attempt to negotiate an incomes agreement.[35]

The Justice party had no policy to deal with the balance-of-payments deficit. It did, however, have an economic program, and this was in conflict with Social Democratic preferences at virtually every point. In the first place, the party had for many years campaigned for the removal of all restrictions on currency exchange. It had also demanded the removal of all tariffs and import regulations. As well, it called for radical reductions in the income tax. It proposed, instead, that the state's primary source of revenue should be the *grundskyld;* that is, a tax on the increase in value of land and property. The enactment of such a system of taxation had been the party's *raison d'être* since its inception. The Social Democratic party had been for many years opposed to the adoption of the *grundskyld.* And it is plain that the Justice party's other preferences were diametrically opposed to those of the Social Democrats.[36]

In sum, the Social Democrats had a divergent-implicit relationship with the Radicals on NATO membership; a convergent relationship with the Radicals on economic policy; a divergent relationship with the Liberals and Conservatives on economic policy; and a divergent relationship with the Justice party on economic policy.

As it happened, the Social Democratic and Justice party negotiators managed to transform some of their relationships from divergent-explicit to divergent-implicit by pledging the government to study the introduction of a "voluntary" *grundskyld* and the eventual removal of barriers to free imports. But on the establishment of free currency exchange and a general reduction in income taxes, the relationship remained divergent-explicit: the Justice party simply capitulated without any face-saving devices.[37] So, overall, the Social Democratic–Justice relationship must be classified as divergent-explicit.

The final outcome was a coalition of the Social Democrats, Radicals, and Justice party. This is an outcome that clearly violates the expectations of the theory, which would have had us expect that the Social Democrats would be unwilling to arrange the implicit relationships that were made with the Radicals and Justice party and that these parties would themselves have been unwilling to accept such relationships. The motivations of the Radicals and Social Democrats in arranging the implicit compromise on the NATO question have already been considered.

Strictly speaking, we should not expect the theory of government formation to account for the Social Democratic–Justice relationship at all, because lacking parliamentary discipline, the Justice party does not fit the definition of a party. Until this government was formed, the leaders of other parties dismissed the Justice party as an irresponsible oddity.[38] This made sense given the party's peculiar policies and lack of discipline. The sudden change of attitude by the Social Democrats was the result of a fear that, if the Justice party were not in government with them, it would join with the Liberals and Conservatives to form a government.[39]

If the outcome does not conform to our expectations, it remains the case that it does ultimately provide some indirect support for the general model of behavior: the decision to join the government so divided the Justice party that it disappeared from Danish politics at the next election. The decision to join was motivated by the personal desire of the party's principal leader, Viggo Starcke, to serve in a government before he retired. This decision provoked bitter divisions within the party and Starcke was intensely criticized for it. Contemporary observers drew a direct connection between the conflicts the decision provoked and the party's loss of all its Folketing seats at the next election.[40]

The 1960 Social Democratic–Radical–Justice Party and Social Democratic–Radical Governments

When H.C. Hansen died on February 19, 1960, Viggo Kampmann was elected party leader and Prime Minister designate. Kampmann held talks with the leaders of the other coalition parties, and afterward each party group in the Folketing voted to continue the coalition.[41] The policy questions that surrounded this government formation were the same as those that existed six months later when Kampmann formed his second government in the wake of Folketing elections. Consequently, the two governments can be discussed together.

It is worth emphasizing that NATO and related questions were not significant issues when Kampmann formed his first government. In January 1960, the five parties had succeeded in negotiating a long-term defense policy agreement that projected future expenditures and established principles of cooperation with the other alliance members in the areas of nuclear weapons and Baltic defense.[42] Only the soon-to-disappear Danish Communist party opposed this.

It was equally the case that the other major foreign policy decision in Danish politics in 1960 was not an issue: whether to join the European Free Trade Association. Membership was supported or accepted by all parties. Likewise, all parties supported the tariff reductions that were formulated by a Folketing committee in 1960 and were a requirement of membership. Only the Liberals did not endorse membership in the final Folketing vote. The party abstained because it preferred further tariff reductions and membership in the European Economic Community.[43]

Three issues were central to Danish politics throughout 1960: tax reform, housing policy, and the balance of payments. The tax debate was framed by proposals advanced by the coalition government and by the Liberals and Conservatives. The governing parties proposed general reductions in income taxes that would preserve the progressive rate schedule for lower and upper incomes and introduce a flat proportional rate of 32 percent for middle-income taxpayers. The Liberals and Conservatives, with some differences of detail between them, proposed the abolition of progressive rates and the introduction of a flat 18 percent proportional rate on all incomes.[44]

The governing parties proposed to offset the revenues lost in reducing income taxes by taxing profits from the sale of real estate as normal income and by adding a surtax. The objective was not simply to make good a part of the lost revenue; it was also to put pressure on escalating property prices that were rapidly raising the price of housing.[45] The Liberals and Conservatives were opposed to the increased property taxes on the ground that they would distort the investment market. Instead, they proposed to make up the lost revenue by canceling the Minister of Housing's authority to issue low-interest loans for public housing construction. The Social Democrats and Liberals attacked this as a threat to low-income families and the construction industry.[46]

The third point of debate among the parties involved the impact that the taxation and housing proposals would have on the balance of payments. The Social Democrats and Radicals contended that the Liberal and Conservative proposals would result in an insufficiently large budget surplus and would therefore generate a level of domestic demand for imports that would in turn put downward pressure on the value of the krone. The Liberals and Conservatives countered that their proposals would avoid this by increasing private investment to a level the government's proposals could not obtain. At heart, the issue was a strategic one: could balance-of-payments difficulties best be met by allowing the markets to make investment and consumption decisions? Or would they best be met by allowing the state to make these decisions?

The Justice party, to the extent that it concerned itself with these matters, apparently found the tax, spending, and balance-of-payments policies of the Social Democrats and Radicals in line with its own preferences. All the evidence, however, shows that these questions were somewhat peripheral for the party at this time. The party was consumed by internal conflicts and well on the way to extinction in the Folketing. Within half a year it would lose all of its seats. It was, therefore, of no significance at all when Kampmann formed his second government later in the year. Indeed, even in the making of the first Kampmann government the party was essentially irrelevant. The preferences that had been identifiably products of the Justice party in 1957 no longer really existed after the capitulations of that year. Not having met the definition of a party to begin with and now without clear policy preferences, it would be pointless to try to classify a relationship between Justice and the Social Democrats in 1960. Several members of the Justice Folketing group continued to participate in the government when Kampmann reconstituted the coalition in 1960.[47]

Two parties appeared in the Folketing for the first time as a result of the 1960 elections. The first of these was the Socialist People's party (SPP), founded by Aksel Larsen, the erstwhile general secretary of the Communist party. During the 1950s, Larsen had grown increasingly disenchanted with the "steel hard militant sect" character of the Communist party and its slavish support of the Soviet Union. After the experience of the Twentieth Congress of the Communist Party, he openly called for the Danish party to "free itself from the tradition that [it] automatically support everything that comes from the socialist countries" and called for the transformation of the party into a mass-democratic party of the working class.[48] In 1958, the central committee of the party expelled Larsen and his minority of followers, whereupon he set out to create the SPP. The new party must be assigned profiles in the areas of socio-economic and foreign policy, the latter having been half of the matter that precipitated the expulsion of the Larsenites from the Communist party. The other half was Larsen's commitment to a parliamentary path.[49] In the 1960 elections, the SPP acquired eleven Folketing seats and eliminated the representatives of the Communist party.

The party was born opposed to Danish membership in NATO, and the demand for withdrawal formed the foreign policy centerpiece of its 1960 electoral campaign. In consequence, when Kampmann formed his second government, the Social Democrats and the SPP were in conflict on this point. The two parties also had divergent preferences on the economic questions: the SPP campaigned on demands for nationalization of large parts of the Danish economy, including the construction materials industry, private phone companies, and life insurance companies. As well, the party wanted the government to take over the National Bank, the semi-autonomous central bank. In the classic conflict between a socialist and a social democratic party, the former advocated state ownership and the latter advocated state control.[50]

The second party to enter the Folketing at the 1960 election was the Independence party *(Uafhaengige)*. The party was founded in 1953 as an outgrowth of a leadership struggle in the Liberal party. As Prime Minister of a minority Liberal government that had come to office in 1945, Knud Kristensen had worked openly for the incorporation of South Slesvig despite his government's formal position of opposition to a change in the status of the territory. After the 1947 election brought in a Social Democratic government, Kristensen continued as leader of the Liberal party and continued to advocate the incorporation of South Sleswig. In January 1949, he resigned his Folketing seat to express his opposition to the accepted Slesvig policy, and in September he stepped down as party leader. In September 1953, he became head of a new party born in opposition to Slesvig policy and the 1953 constitution. Opposition to the constitution and accepted Slesvig policy eventually faded, but concern for Danish foreign policy generally did not. As a result, the party must be assigned a foreign policy profile as well as the usual socioeconomic profile.[51]

The demands for a return to the old two-chamber legislature and strong support for the Danish minority in South Slesvig that had been the focal points of the party's earliest efforts had receded in importance by 1960. They had been superseded by then by strong support for NATO membership, a complete state withdrawal from the housing market, and income tax reductions in line with those proposed by the Liberals and Conservatives.[52] Only on NATO membership did the Social Democrats and Independents have convergent preferences in 1960. The Independents were opposed to the Social Democrats' use of a tax increase to slow the rise of real estate prices, were opposed to state loan guarantees for home construction, and wanted the removal of rent control.[53]

In sum, then, when Kampmann formed his first government, the Social Democrats had convergent relationships on all issues only with the Radical Liberals. The relationships with the Liberals and Conservatives were, on one or more issues, divergent. Again, when Kampmann formed his second government, it was with only the Radicals that the Social Democrats had entirely convergent preferences. With the Socialist People's party the preferences were divergent on NATO membership and economic policy (nationalization and the status of the central bank); with the Liberals and Conservatives they were divergent on taxation, housing, and the balance of payments; with the Independents they were divergent on taxation and housing. In both instances, the government that emerged was a Social Democratic–Liberal coalition. The first included ministers from the Justice Folketing group. Both governments, then, conform to the expectations of the theory.

The second Kampmann government controlled eighty-eight Folketing seats, while a majority required control of eighty-nine seats. Kampmann acquired the eighty-ninth seat by offering a Greenland representative, Mikael Gam, the position of Minister of Greenland Affairs. By calling on an independent who had previously abstained in party votes, Kampmann was able to gain a majority. More telling is that Kampmann gave every indication that he would be unwilling to make the compromises required to bring a third party into government to gain a majority, had Gam's vote been unavailable.[54]

The 1962 Social Democratic–Radical Government

In September 1962, Kampmann resigned because of failing health. The Social Democratic Folketing group selected J. O. Krag to succeed Kampmann and lead the negotiations for a new government. Because extensive negotiations did occur, the change was more than a technical one of Prime Minister, and the next government is counted as a new one. Four issues dominated party conflict: NATO membership, possible membership in the European Economic Community, a tax agreement that had recently been negotiated among the four old parties, and the government's price-control policies.

The Socialist People's party continued to make opposition to NATO membership a primary focus and, as well, had now positioned itself as the main opponent of Danish membership in the EEC. At this time, Danish politicians expected Great Britain's application for EEC membership to be accepted, and the Danish government was actively involved in negotiations to follow Britain, Denmark's largest trading partner, into the community. Membership was supported by the Social Democrats. It was also supported by the Radicals, Liberals, and Conservatives.[55]

In June 1962, the Social Democrats, Radicals, Liberals, and Conservatives had negotiated a rather complex economic package designed to bolster the krone, reduce domestic consumption, and increase investment. Among other things, the package included the introduction of a wholesale tax of 9 percent, a reduction of land and income taxes, an increase in pensions and child maintenance payments, a commitment to a 500-million-kroner budget surplus for the current fiscal year, a 25 percent increase in the controlled rents on the pre-1939 housing stock, and the exclusion of the various tax increases from the price index used to calculate wage increases.[56] This agreement was opposed by the Socialist People's party, which instead proposed tax increases on tobacco and alcohol, cancellation of the rent increase and wholesale tax, and an increase in low-interest state construction loans.[57] The package was equally opposed by the Independents, who called for a complete state withdrawal from housing and construction, cancellation of the wholesale tax, and cancellation of the child assistance and pension increases.[58] In the summer of 1962, the Social Democrats proposed that the four-party economic agreement be supplemented by a grant of authority to the Monopoly Control Authority *(monopoltilsynet)* to investigate price increases and fix prices and profits. The Radicals found the basic principle acceptable. The Liberals, Conservatives, and Independents opposed any such grant of authority. The Socialist People's party wanted instead an across-the-board wage and profits freeze, a proposal rejected by all other parties.[59]

On balance, then, it was again the case that the party of the formateurs, the Social Democrats, had convergent preferences only with the Radicals. With the Socialist People's party, it had divergent relationships on NATO and EEC membership, on the four-party economic package, and on price controls. With the Liberals and Conservatives, the party had convergent relationships on the EEC and NATO and the four-party agreement, but divergent relationships on price controls. With the Independents, the Social Democrats had divergent relationships on the four-party agreement and price controls.

When the government was formed, it again consisted of the Social Democrats and Radicals, as we would anticipate. And, as his predecessor had done, Krag secured a parliamentary majority of a single vote by including Mikael Gam in the cabinet. Again, the more significant point is that all the evidence indicates that had Gam's vote not been available, Krag would not have made concessions to bring a third party into the government.[60]

The 1964 Social Democratic Government

The Social Democratic–Radical coalition lasted until the September 1964 Folketing election. In the wake of the election the Social Democratic party again had the formateurship, and Krag took the lead on behalf of the Social Democrats in negotiations to form a new government. The conflicts among the parties were straightforward, and Krag devoted less than two days to discussions with the other parties. At the end of the talks he formed a minority Social Democratic cabinet.

The Socialist People's party continued to challenge the Social Democrats to reverse their support for NATO membership. There is no evidence of interest in either party in an implicit compromise of the sort that the Social Democrats had arranged with the Radicals in 1957.[61] France having rejected the British application for admission into the EEC, Danish membership in the community was no longer on the agenda when this government was formed.

On the issue that the Social Democrats had sought to make the centerpiece of their party's campaign, the establishment of a pay-as-you-earn income-tax system, the Socialist People's party was in agreement with the Social Democrats.[62] Indeed, the Socialist People's party was the only other party to support this policy. The Social Democrats' former coalition partners, the Radicals, were now in disagreement with the Social Democrats about taxation-at-source and their own proposal for the use of a retail sales tax.[63] The Liberals, Conservatives, and Independents, too, opposed taxation-at-source and campaigned for the termination of the double taxation of real estate profits that the Social Democrats had implemented in 1960. The three parties also wanted rent control ended for units built before 1939.[64] Both of these policies were contrary to Social Democratic policy.

In each case of a divergent policy, neither of the parties indicated a willingness to make the differences implicit. This is noteworthy, because none of the policy questions required immediate action. The establishment of a system of taxation-at-source, for instance, would have required at least two years of preparation, even if a majority favorable to it had existed in the Folketing. No such majority existed; so it was going to be postponed regardless of the government formed. The Radicals' proposal of a retail sales tax was likewise going to be deferred for lack of a legislative majority.

The outcome fits the theory. In the absence of convergent policies, the government was limited to the Social Democrats.

The 1966 Social Democratic Government

The cabinet Krag formed in 1964 remained in office until the winter of 1966, when Krag dissolved the Folketing and scheduled an election for November. The dissolution was precipitated by the inability of the four old parties to reach an agreement on a package of tax reforms. Anticipating that a campaign fought over the question of taxation-at-source would have a favorable outcome for his party, Krag allowed the negotiations among the four parties to proceed for only a few days before deciding to go to the country.[65] The election was a serious setback for the Social Democrats. Their Folketing group fell from seventy-six to sixty-nine members. The real winner was the Socialist People's party, which doubled its fraction from ten to twenty members. The Liberals and Conservatives lost three and two seats respectively. The Radicals, in spite of having risen from nineteen to twenty-three seats, lost their majority-relevance for the first time in decades. The Social Democrats retained the formateurship.[66]

The election campaign and subsequent negotiations were conditioned by two major agreements that had been reached in the first months of 1966 and by the failure to reach a third agreement on taxation. The first of these was the so-called "Big Party Housing Agreement," concluded among the Social Democrats, Radicals, Liberals, and Conservatives in January 1966. One of the most comprehensive social policy agreements of the postwar era, it among other things established new mortgage and insurance arrangements and a state building fund, increased public housing construction, and provided for rent increases in rent-controlled units.[67]

The second agreement, reached in February, involved economic policy and included some tax increases and postponements and public spending cuts. Even though the Conservative and Socialist People's parties were unwilling to endorse this agreement, the agreement had the effect of largely removing economic policy from the arena of party conflict during the election campaign.[68]

The housing agreement had exactly the opposite result and provided the focus for the domestic policy side of the Socialist People's party's 1966 campaign. The party had refused to sign the accord and bitterly attacked the Social Democrats for the rent increases, which fell mainly on lower-income workers. The party quite explicitly made cancellation of the housing agreement a quid pro quo of cooperation after the election.[69]

Whereas in 1964 the Social Democrats had advocated the substitution of a retail sales tax for the wholesale tax, the party had subsequently come to propose the substitution of a value added tax. This proposal was one of the three key pieces of the Social Democratic tax reform package, and the People's party opposed it on grounds of alleged regressivity and was thus again in conflict with the Social Democratic party. The other two components of the Social Democratic tax package, the institution of taxation-at-source and the cancellation of a deduction that allowed taxpayers to set off the past year's tax payments against current taxable income, were supported by the People's party.[70] The final line of conflict between the two parties again involved NATO membership, as the Socialist party continued to insist on a Danish withdrawal.[71] Thus the two parties had divergent preferences on NATO, a value added tax, and housing policy.

The relationship is an especially interesting one, because for the first time in Danish history an election had produced an absolute socialist majority in the Folketing. Had the two parties been willing to govern together, they would have been able to establish a majority socialist government. We would anticipate, then, that the temptation for each party to make sufficient concessions to form such a government would be especially acute at this time.

And, indeed, the two party leaderships held extensive negotiations after the election. The negotiations were aimed at creating just such a government, but failed. For each party, true to the expectations of the theory, demanded that the other party adopt convergent preferences where its preferences had previously been divergent. Neither party was willing to compromise its preferences explicitly, or even implicitly. The parties preferred to end the negotiations by publishing a lengthy memorandum detailing all the points on which they agreed and all the points on which they disagreed. They attributed their inability to form a government specifically to NATO membership, housing policy, and the value added tax, the three issues on which they had divergent-explicit relations.[72] Thus, we find that in an instance in which practice would be most likely to deviate from the theory, the theory is sustained.

The other relationships were fairly simple. The Radicals opposed the Social Democratic proposal to introduce taxation-at-source, but supported the proposal to end the deduction of past taxes. The Liberals opposed taxation-at-source and wanted the deduction maintained. The Conservatives wanted the deduction maintained and wanted the introduction of voluntary taxation-at-source, a proposal that reflected the conflict of interest between salaried employees and employers within the party.[73] In sum, each of the three nonsocialist parties had at least one policy that was incompatible with the policies of the Social Democrats. Brief negotiations followed the elections, but none of the parties was willing to compromise.

The final party in the Folketing was a new party, the Liberal Center, which won four mandates in the November election.[74] It did not have majority-relevance and disappeared altogether in 1968. The Independence party lost all of its seats in the election. The outcome, a minority Social Democratic government, fits the theory. No convergent relationships existed, and none of the parties was willing to raise the limit of tolerance.

The 1968 Radical–Liberal–Conservative Government

The formation of this coalition will be easier to understand if we review the resolution of issues and the rise of new ones during the two years before it was formed. The removal of two issues—housing and taxation—was crucial to the formation of the coalition. In January 1966, the Social Democrats, Radicals, Liberals, and Conservatives had reached a comprehensive eight-year agreement on housing policy. The Socialist People's party remained outside the agreement and was intensely critical of it. But the signators to the agreement remained committed to its implementation, and for them it greatly reduced the importance of housing as a political issue.[75] Most important, it removed housing as a source of conflict among the Radicals, Liberals, and Conservatives.

In 1967, the Social Democrats and Socialist People's party negotiated a new housing accord on their own; this established a 1.3-billion-kroner state construction fund, drawing on a billion-kroner state deposit in the National Bank and a 300-million-kroner appropriation. Just as the 1966 agreement had removed divisions among the three bourgeois parties, this agreement united them—in opposition. They contended that it would be inflationary and would give the state new and unacceptable control over investment decisions and the property market.[76] All three parties demanded the cancellation of the agreement.

The second important development in 1967 was the resolution of the tax reform question. At the time of the election in November 1966, none of the parties had been in agreement on tax reform. In the spring of 1967, lengthy cross-party negotiations were held (with only the Liberals refusing to participate). The result was a comprehensive agreement on tax reform that largely conformed to the original Social Democratic preferences: the past-tax deduction would be abolished, taxation-at-source would be introduced from January 1, 1969, and a value added tax would be substituted for the wholesale tax. Both the Radicals and the Conservatives had read the 1966 election as a repudiation of their tax proposals and had dropped their objections in principle to these reforms even before negotiations were begun. By the autumn of 1967, even the Liberals, who had refused to participate in the tax negotiations, had come to accept the three reforms.[77] Thus, by the time of the next election, in January 1968, tax reform was no longer on the table; and most important, the three bourgeois parties were no longer divided by it.

The deterioration of the Danish economy is equally critical to an understanding of the 1968 government. In 1967, output growth became sluggish, inflation, unemployment, and interest rates rose, and the balance-of-payments deficit ballooned. By the end of the year, economic policy was once again at the top of the political agenda.[78] It was in this context that a devaluation of the British pound entered Danish politics in December 1967. To general surprise and broad opposition, the Social Democratic government responded with a 7.9 percent devaluation of the Danish krone. To sustain the anticipated effects of the devaluation, the government then introduced legislation to effect a freeze on profits, a ceiling on cost-of-living increases, and a 3 percent increase in income taxes for taxpayers in the upper brackets. When the proposals were put to a vote in the Folketing, the Socialist People's party joined with the Radicals, Liberals, and Conservatives in opposition and the Krag government lost the vote.[79] It immediately resigned and called elections for the following month—January 1968.

Two questions thus dominated Danish politics during the electoral campaign: the housing fund the socialist parties had created in 1967, and how to respond to the rapidly deteriorating economy and the situation created by the British devaluation and the subsequent Danish devaluation.

After the election, the Radicals received the formateurship. The party had campaigned on a program of reducing the money supply, a 500- to 600-million-kroner reduction in state expenditures, a tax reduction on unearned income, and voluntary restraint in labor market negotiations.[80] The Social Democrats had campaigned on the same program they had failed to get through the Folketing. In consequence, they had divergent-preference relationships with the Radicals on several points: in their advocacy of a freeze on profits and a ceiling on cost-of-living increases and their proposal for increased taxes on upper incomes to parallel the restraint on workers' incomes. As well, the Social Democrats campaigned against any further tightening of the money supply and opposed special tax treatment for savings and investment. Finally, because the Radicals were committed to the cancellation of the housing fund, the two parties were in conflict on that question as well.[81] The Socialist People's party's preferences paralleled those of the Social Democrats, except that the party opposed mandatory restraints on cost-of-living increases. In consequence, it, too, was in conflict with the Radicals on several programmatic points.[82]

The Liberals and Conservatives had campaigned on platforms virtually identical to the Radicals' on the economic questions and, as mentioned, shared the Radicals' commitment to cancellation of the housing fund.[83] On the principal issues, then, the three parties had convergent preferences. Negotiations among the three focused on how much defense spending would be cut—with the Radicals favoring larger cuts than the Liberals and Conservatives—and on the distribution of ministries among the parties.[84]

One new party made an appearance in the Folketing as a result of the 1968 election. The Left Socialist party, established by dissidents on the left of the Socialist People's party, gained four seats. The party proposed a program of extensive nationalization and, not surprisingly, was not a serious candidate for inclusion in the Radical government.[85] The Left Socialists lacked majority-relevance and disappeared at the next election.

The outcome, then, is a three-party coalition premised on convergent preferences. This conforms to the hypothesis for the consensual system.

The 1971 Social Democratic Government

The coalition government formed in 1968 remained in place until September 1971, at which time it decided to go to the country about fourteen months earlier than required by law, because it concluded that the rapidly declining economy would only make its electoral prospects worse as time passed. The upshot of the election was that the formateurship returned to the Social Democrats.

Two issues were paramount in the election campaign that preceded the formation of this government: membership in the EEC and how to respond to a balance-of-payments deficit that was beginning to assume crisis proportions. The question of EEC membership returned to center stage in Danish politics when Britain again applied for membership. The Social Democrats, Liberals, Radicals, and Conservatives again supported membership for Denmark. And once again the Socialist People's party opposed membership.[86]

The economic policy question was more complicated. In 1971, the Danish economy was again in severe difficulty, with a balance-of-payments deficit approaching 3.5 billion kroner in the twelve months prior to the election and with rapidly rising prices. On the monetary side, the coalition government's response had been one of tight money and record high interest rates. As well, in the spring and summer of 1971 the coalition had instituted a comprehensive and mandatory two-year incomes policy, increased capital gains taxes, instituted strict controls on communal spending, removed tax exemptions on shipping investment, and adjusted the price index to equal 100 for January 1971, which effectively prevented increases from setting in train previously negotiated cost-of-living increases.[87] When the coalition parties campaigned in September 1971, their basic premise was that however badly they had handled the economy in the past—a view widely shared by even their supporters—they now had in place the correct policies. Each of the three parties made a defense of these policies the centerpiece of its economic program.[88]

The Social Democrats had very different preferences. They rejected the incomes policy because, they argued, it would dampen wage increases for workers but have little impact on the incomes of salaried employees. In this, their view was shared by the Socialist People's party. Both socialist parties opposed the coalition's high-interest rates policy.[89] They argued that the government's efforts should be directed toward increasing production rather than reducing demand. Given that Denmark had difficulty attracting foreign capital, it was thus the government's responsibility to provide the necessary capital and direct its use. To this end, the Social Democrats proposed the creation of a National Capital Market Council that would include representatives from government, business, labor, and finance. The council would establish guidelines for and monitor the distribution of private bank credit. It would establish priorities and limit capital investment in low priority areas. The Socialist People's party advanced proposals that were comparable to this and differed only in details.[90]

As a complement to the council, the Social Democrats wanted to establish a state-owned investment bank. The Socialist People's party proposed the same thing.[91] Finally, the Social Democrats insisted that the government intervene in the foreign exchange market to support the krone against the German mark. The Socialist People's party had no well-articulated view on this question, but one must logically suppose they agreed. The Radicals also endorsed intervention. The Liberals and Conservatives wanted the krone to float.[92]

The Social Democrats, then, had divergent preference relationships with the Liberals, Radicals, and Conservatives on economic policy and with the Socialist People's party on EEC membership. The Socialist People's party continued, of course, to demand a withdrawal from NATO; but in 1971 this preference was conspicuous for its marginality in the party's campaign, which focused almost entirely on the EEC question. There is no indication that consideration was given on any side to concessions leading to a government based on divergent-implicit relationships. If this were to have occurred, it would have been most likely between the two socialist parties. Neither indicated an interest. And so, again, the outcome conforms to the expectations of the theory. In the absence of convergent relationships, a single-party government was formed.

The 1973 Liberal Government

The 1973 government was formed in the aftermath of the most destabilizing election in Danish history: the "protest election" of 1973. The party system exploded: no less than five previously unrepresented parties gained seats in the Folketing. Each of the five established parties suffered a major—in some cases, devastating—loss of seats. The Social Democratic fraction plunged from seventy to forty-six; the Conservatives' from thirty-one to sixteen. The Communist and Justice parties, which had last won seats in 1957, reappeared and won six and five respectively. Three newly created parties won among them forty-nine seats. The most well known of these was Mogens Glistrup's Progress party, which gained twenty-eight seats and overnight became the second largest party in the Folketing.[93]

The antecedents of this electoral earthquake can be inferred from the previous cases: rapidly rising prices, taxes and public expenditures accompanied by deteriorating foreign exchange reserves, and a faltering krone; and, as always, problems in the housing market. The difficulties were accompanied by a palpable sense that none of the five established parties was capable of dealing effectively with the problems that confronted Denmark. Danish politicians were well aware of this sentiment in the year preceding the election, as one opinion poll after another showed growing support for the new parties and declining confidence in the old.[94]

This knowledge had certain consequences for the ways in which issues were framed by the parties in 1973 and also for the government-formation outcome itself. One consequence was that the new leader of the Social Democrats, Anker Jorgensen, sought to give his party a clearer identity by moving it distinctly to the left. Jorgensen centered this move to the left on a new program of economic democracy. This quickly became one of the most debated political questions of the year, and it created important divisions. The basic programmatic elements of Jorgensen's economic democracy were (1) the establishment of a wage earners' fund, into which all employers would pay a tax equivalent to a percentage of the annual payroll. The tax would rise from .5 percent in 1974 to 5 percent in 1983. (2) The fund would be administered by a board appointed by the national trade union organization (LO) and the Minister of Labor. (3) Every wage earner would receive a share of the fund, and the first regular dividend would be paid out in 1982. The dividend would rise from 600 kroner in that year to 60,000 kroner in 1991. (4) Employer contributions would be tax deductible. (5) Publicly owned companies would make two-thirds of their contribution in the form of equity. (6) In companies employing more than fifty workers, the workers would have the right to elect two of the company's directors.[95]

Not surprisingly, the Radicals, Liberals, and Conservatives opposed this strenuously. They opposed the concentration of capital and economic power; the extraordinary power it would give the LO; the tax increases that would necessarily be required to make good the lost revenue; and the reduction in the state's ability to control the economy.[96] Among the parties, only the Socialist People's party had a convergent preference with the Social Democrats—for they favored establishment of such a program.[97]

The Social Democrats' response to the economic deterioration was a series of large tax increases enacted and proposed in the autumn of 1973 to reduce consumption. Taxes on cigarettes, beer, auto registrations, gasoline, and other items were raised. The Social Democrats also proposed advancement of value-added-tax payments for the agricultural and fisheries industries. They also wanted special taxes on shipping, insurance, and industrial property. In all, the increased taxes amounted to about 1.2 billion kroner.[98]

Although there were differences among them, the Liberals, Conservatives, and Radicals were united in a commitment to tax reductions, not increases. They also wanted substantial public spending cuts. Poul Hartling, the Liberal party leader and soon-to-be Prime Minister, talked about three billion kroner in reductions. The Liberals further proposed the removal of all housing industry regulations; the substitution of tax cuts for cost-of-living increases; and the cancellation of credit market restrictions. The Radicals and Conservatives focused mainly on tax reductions, but did endorse these additional Liberal points.[99]

The first of the new or returned Folketing parties was the Danish Communist party, back after thirteen years but still regarded as a pariah by the democratic parties. The second was the small Christian People's party, which won seven seats.[100] The third was the resurrected Justice party. The fourth was Mogens Glistrup's antitax, Progress party.[101] The Christian, Justice, and Progress parties rejected participation in a government of any composition.[102]

The final new party was the Center Democratic party. The party was established only in the months before the election by a group of right-wing Social Democrats who opposed Jorgensen's program of economic democracy and his tactical move to the left. Although supportive of NATO and the EEC, the party's origins were strictly in socioeconomic conflicts. The new party sought to create a following among middle-class suburbanites and developed policy preferences accordingly. It campaigned for a freeze on property taxes; a cancellation of the recently enacted tax increases on gasoline and auto registrations; a gradual removal of homes from taxation; and a general reduction in income taxes. There was nothing in the party's preferences that conflicted with Liberal preferences and much that was compatible.[103]

Let us now sum up the case. The Liberals had the formateurship and had divergent relationships with the Social Democrats and Socialist People's party. None of the three sought to make these differences implicit and form a government on that basis. With the Radicals, Conservatives, and Center Democrats the Liberals clearly had convergent preferences. We cannot speak of Liberal relationships with the Progress, Justice, and Christian People's parties, because each rejected participation in principle.

This leaves us expecting the Social Democrats and Socialist People's party to be in opposition and the Radicals, Conservatives, and Center Democrats in government with the Liberals. In fact, the prediction fails. The Liberals formed a government by themselves. A coalition of the four parties was indeed the outcome thought most likely by contemporary observers; and when the Liberals formed a government by themselves, the reaction among the media and other politicians was one of complete surprise. For discussions among the leaders of the four parties had proceeded smoothly and with the expectation that a four-party coalition would emerge.[104]

How, then, do we explain the unexpected outcome? The decision not to form the coalition was made by the leader of the Liberals, Poul Hartling. At the last moment Hartling unilaterally terminated the negotiations and presented the Folketing, almost as a *fait accompli,* a minority Liberal government. The Folketing (i.e., the two socialist parties, the Radicals, Conservatives, and Center Democrats) could either accept it or reject it. If they rejected it, they would have to assume responsibility for creating another government, and they would have to do it without the Liberals. Hartling could calculate that given the difficulties this would pose and the overwhelming desire to avoid another early election, the mainstream parties would be willing to support a purely Liberal government. Hartling apparently also calculated that the support the next government would require would be easier to elicit if the government consisted of only one center party rather than a block of parties of either the left or right. This, in any case, is the most compelling and widely accepted explanation of the outcome.[105] Most fundamentally, to be sure, the outcome was a result of the collapse of the old party system.

Summary

Between 1955 and 1974, ten governments were formed in Denmark. The theory is successful in predicting eight of these ten governments. The two cases of failure are the governments of 1957 and 1973. The theory predicted that in 1957 the Radicals and the Justice party would be in opposition. In fact, they joined the government. The theory anticipated that in 1973 the Radicals, Conservatives, and Center Democrats would join the government. In fact, they remained in opposition. I will return to these two cases below.

Among the ten governments, we have forty-five bargaining relationships. Of these forty-five relationships, thirty-seven lead to placements in the government or opposition that fit the theory. In three cases, the Justice, Progress, and Christian People's parties in 1973, the parties declined to participate in a government of any composition or policies. The other five cases of failure occurred in 1957 and 1973 and were referred to above.

A corollary of the hypothesis for consensual democracies is that party leaders should be unwilling to make implicit compromises. Of the thirty-one divergent relationships that we have examined, in only three cases did party leaders indicate a willingness to compromise implicitly. The first instance was in

1955, when the Radicals proposed, and the Social Democrats declined, to compromise their different policies toward NATO. The second instance occurred in 1957 and involved the same parties and the same issue. This time the Social Democrats accepted the compromise. The third occasion of implicit compromise was also in 1957 and involved the Social Democrats and the Justice party.

In testing the proposition that implicit compromises should not occur, the 1955, 1964, 1966, and 1971 outcomes are critical, because in each of these the government formed was a single-party minority government. If implicit compromises were to occur, they would have been most likely on these occasions, for larger governments would have required at least implicit compromises. Only in 1955, when the Social Democrats rebuffed the Radicals' offer, do we find some interest in an implicit compromise.

On balance, then, the Danish cases appear to provide quite satisfactory empirical support for the theory's predictive power. As well, they provide evidence of its explanatory power. There is no evidence of nonpolicy causation at work, save in 1957 and 1973, and when policies were decisive, they led to the expected results.

CHAPTER SIX

Finland

Origins of the Party System

When Finland was transferred from Sweden to Russia in 1809, the Diet of the Four Estates—the nobility, clergy, burghers, and peasantry—convened to acknowledge the authority of the Czar. The Estates did not meet again until 1863, when annual meetings were begun. It was with these regular meetings that the first lineages of the Finnish party system began to appear. Language and nationality provided the social bases for the early proto-parties that formed in the Estates during these years. The first of the early parties was the Finnish movement, which sought to make the majority language into an official and cultural language. In the 1870s, the movement acquired a majority position in the estates of the clergy and peasantry. In the late 1870s and early 1880s, a Swedish party came into being in reaction to the Finnish movement and, reflecting the Swedish language's position as the language of the small socioeconomic elite, assumed a majority position in the estates of the nobility and burghers.

Ethnolinguistic division remained the basic line of political conflict until the last years of the century. But the level of political participation remained quite low. Even after reforms in the 1860s extended the voting rights of burghers, less than 10 percent of the adult population was eligible to vote.[1] Indeed, little evidence of popular agitation for parliamentary reform and an extended suffrage appears until the final years of the century. Reflecting this, no parties in a modern sense yet existed. The parties that did exist were loose-knit groups formed around newspaper editors and individuals influential in the Estates. Agreement within the groups generally did not reach beyond ethnolinguistic questions.[2] Only at the end of the century, under the multiple pressures of Russification, industrialization, and the commercialization of agriculture did new cleavages and modern parties begin to take shape in Finland.

Until the end of the century, czarist governments had been content to permit Finland extensive internal autonomy. To strengthen a vulnerable flank, the Czar's government thereafter began a systematic campaign to incorporate Finland into the Russian Empire. The Russification campaign included attempts to merge the Finnish army into the Imperial Army, the use of the Russian language in the civil service and schools, the free entrance of Russians into the civil service, and a general strengthening of the powers of the Russian Governor-General.[3]

This threat to Finnish autonomy produced divisions over the best means and tactics by which to resist it. The Swedish party advocated a policy of passive resistance to Russification. The issue produced a split in the Finnish movement, with a new group, called the Young Finns, also endorsing passive resistance. The rump group, the Old Finns, preferred a policy of accommodation in the hope that the Czar would abandon Russification. In the long-term, these tactical differences would be of no significance, as all of these parties would come to endorse Finnish independence. Indeed, they would fight a bloody civil war that was, in their view, a war of national liberation. The split in the Finnish movement, however, would remain and eventually culminate in the establishment of two separate parties with more enduring differences.

Resistance to Russification gradually became inextricably linked to demands—supported by all parties—for home rule, abolition of the Estates, and extension of the franchise. The 1905 revolution in Russia provided the opportunity for a coup d'état in Helsinki. The constitutionalists, in cooperation with the tiny labor movement, seized power, elected a provisional government, and passed reform proposals to the Czar as a *fait accompli*.[4] At a stroke, the Estates was replaced by a unicameral legislature, the Eduskunta, elected on the basis of universal male and female suffrage. The beginning of modern party life in Finland dates from the changes caused by the electoral and parliamentary reforms of 1905–1906.

In the years preceding the reforms, there were already signs of party cohesion, but it was only the achievement of universal suffrage that turned the bourgeois groups into organizationally and programmatically modern parties around 1905–1908. The enfranchisement of the whole adult population from the 1907 election established the main components, with the exception of the Communist party, of the present-day Finnish party system. During the following decade, however, the possibility of parties leading political activity was still limited because the home government continued to be dominated by Russians. Especially during the world war, when the tempo of Russification and infringements of established Finnish rights increased, party activity was muted.

In May 1906, at a congress in Helsinki, the Swedish party was refounded. The new party, a continuation of the old Swedish party in the Estates, was to bring under one banner, irrespective of social classes, the entire Swedish-speaking population of Finland. In order to keep the party together, the concrete demands of the program were limited only to ethnolinguistic issues that were of importance to the entire language community. In fact, because Swedish Finns were a socioeconomic elite, and because the community's elite was in control of the party, the party came down squarely on the nonsocialist side of the socioeconomic cleavage. Indeed, until after the Second World War, the party would be the most right-wing party in Finland.[5]

In the earliest phase of party formation, the Finnish movement had united Finnish-speaking rural laborers with farmers and a part of the urban elite in the name of linguistic and cultural solidarity. The movement broke apart, however, as other conflicts arose. The first of these, as mentioned, was the response to Russification that split the Old and Young Finns. Of more enduring significance was the difference between these two groups on the socioeconomic cleavage. Although both belonged to the nonsocialist camp, the Young Finns were committed to a course of social liberalism, while the Old Finns were opposed to almost all state intervention. Ultimately, the Young Finns would become the Finnish Liberal party and the Old Finns the Conservative party. The second crack in Finnish solidarity occurred with the establishment in 1906–1908 of the Agrarian party. As was the case elsewhere in northern Europe, an agrarian party arose out of a sense that the original parties, urban-rural coalitions, were inherently incapable of adequately protecting agrarian interests.[6]

As Russification intensified after 1907, and especially as the Czar sought to withdraw the concessions to self-government that had been extracted from him in 1905, the bourgeois parties united behind the cause of national independence. As far as they were concerned, the Bolshevik seizure of power in Petrograd simply made independence all the more urgent. In December 1917, a nonsocialist government declared Finland's unilateral independence. At this time, the Social Democratic party split in all but name. The center-right of the party favored independence, but insisted that it be negotiated rather than unilateral. The attitude of the Social Democratic left remains clouded and a subject of contention even to this day.[7]

Finnish society was disintegrating when independence was declared, with both the left and the right assembling paramilitary forces. The presence in Finland of a large number to radicalized and undisciplined Russian soldiers led the right to fear that the Bolsheviks would attempt to spread their revolution to the Finnish part of the empire. The left wing of the Social Democrats, in turn, apparently feared the establishment of a right-wing authoritarian government. The left wing of the Social Democratic party attempted to seize power in Helsinki in January 1918. The Finnish Civil War was on. In the aftermath, right-wing historians would look upon the war as a war for national liberation; left-wing historians would view it as a class war; moderate Social Democrats, caught in the middle, would view it simply as national tragedy. The war ran through the spring months and was especially vicious, with battles fought not simply on urban streets, but on full-fledged military fronts. Some 7,000 men were killed in these battles. More than 1,500 were murdered during the "Red Terror" of the winter of 1917–18; over 8,000 were executed in postwar settlements of account. Another 9,000 died in prison camps, into which the victorious Whites herded as many as 80,000 men during the summer of 1918.[8]

The object of the Reds, who were subsequently to be represented in Finnish society by the Communist party, was at the least to destroy the bourgeois state and ally Finland with the new Soviet Union. More likely, although the matter remains murky, the Reds would have incorporated Finland into the Soviet Union.[9] The relationship with the Soviet Union has always remained the first cleavage of Finnish politics, and the line of cleavage has placed all bourgeois parties on one side and the Communist party on the other. The attitudes of the bourgeois parties were decided by the Russification campaigns and the Civil War. The Russophobia of these parties was simply reinforced by the Winter War (1939–40) and the Continuation War (1941–45). The behavioral meaning of the parties' attitudes has, of course, been radically conditioned by the European balance of power and has moved from open hostility in the interwar years to subdued and compliant neutrality since 1945.[10]

In December 1918, the moderate Social Democrats, who had opposed the Reds' attempt to seize power and had then largely sat out the Civil War, reconstituted the Social Democratic party. Having been caught in the middle between the Reds and the Whites, the Social Democrats always remained ambivalent toward the Soviet Union: they supported independence, but not unilateral independence; they opposed the attempted seizure of power, but stood aside during the Civil War. They later supported national resistance during the Winter War, but were divided over the Finnish attack that launched the Continuation War and were subsequently the principal proponents of an early negotiated peace with the Soviet Union.[11]

The surviving leaders of the defeated Reds regrouped in Moscow and established a Communist-party-in-exile. Those leaders who managed to remain free agents in Finland established a domestic Communist party in May 1920. The party was quickly suppressed, but reformed and managed to obtain twenty-seven seats and 14.8 percent of the vote in the 1922 elections.[12] In 1923, the Kallio government imprisoned the entire Communist parliamentary party, and the party's newspapers were suppressed. Large numbers of suspected Communists were arrested and imprisoned throughout the 1920s, and public activity by the Communists was suppressed completely in 1930. Nonetheless, the party was able to dominate the labor movement throughout the interwar years and retained extensive mass support in the impoverished and isolated North and East. It was not until October 1944—and then due to the changed relationship with the Soviet Union—that the party was again able to register as a legal association in Finland.[13]

In 1900, only about 12.5 percent of the Finnish population lived in urban areas. Such a Finnish working class as did exist prior to the end of the century consisted mainly of a rapidly growing rural proletariat. As world demand for timber rose in the second half of the nineteenth century, the Finnish forests became a kind of "green gold." Money from the sale of timber and the demands of the small but growing urban market enabled the peasant farmer to move from the traditional self-sufficiency of his ancestors toward modern farming methods. The increase in the world timber prices and the commercialization of agriculture produced a rapid rise in land values and laid the basis for the modern Finnish economy. But the newfound affluence of the freehold peasantry served to accentuate a growing gulf between the landowning minority and the impoverished majority of leaseholders and farm workers. The "green gold" brought wealth, but it also accelerated the disintegration of traditional rural society. In 1910, roughly 40 percent of those engaged in farming were freehold farmers; another 20 percent were leaseholders who were required to seek part-time and seasonal work to survive; an additional 40 percent were farm workers with little or no land.[14]

The main early beneficiary of the revolution in agricultural society was the socialist movement. The Social Democratic party was founded in 1899, and by 1906 had a peak pre–Civil War membership of nearly 100,000, drawn mostly from the rural proletariat and recently arrived immigrants from the countryside.[15] The party's rural character was dealt a severe blow, however, by its ambivalent position in the Civil War. When the war came, the party's former rural supporters either sided with the Whites, and subsequently supported the Agrarian party, or with the Reds, and thereafter remained loyal to the Communist party.[16]

The party's deruralization was carried further by gradual migration to the cities, the growth of the Agrarian party, and land reforms in the 1920s that allowed leaseholders to become independent farmers. By 1930, 90 percent of all rented farms and plots had been purchased by their tenants.[17] As these tenants became independent farmers, they shifted their political allegiance to the Agrarians. Leaseholders who could not buy land, and who continued to be heavily dependent on the seasonal labor market, gravitated toward the Communists, supported a series of smallholder protest parties that have been characteristic of Finnish politics since the 1920s or simply withdrew from political participation altogether.[18] As a result, the Social Democratic party was gradually transformed into a classic urban working-class movement.

Just as decisive for the party system as this transformation was the fact that the Agrarian party's supporters were not primarily well-to-do southern farmers, but the small, often economically marginal, independent farmers in the North and East. The upshot was in the 1920s an increasingly bitter conflict between the Social Democats and Agrarians over the distribution of national resources between agriculture and industry. The Social Democratic party's position of conflict with the Agrarian party on the consumer-producer dimension was accentuated by its opposition in the 1930s to the agricultural crisis support measures sponsored by the Agrarians and especially by its opposition to the postwar land settlement program, which it viewed as exactly contrary to the structural transformation the economy required. The 1945 Land Act was intended to resettle the large number of refugees from Karelia, most of whom were farmers. The act created some 142,000 new land holdings out of 2.8 million hectares of often low-quality land. In consequence, the average size of a farm in 1959 was a minuscule 8.9 hectares—even smaller than it had been before 1940.[19] Whereas the Agrarian party was committed to preserving the agricultural sector and its central place in the Finnish economy and society, the Social Democratic party was committed to the most rapid industrialization possible—and consequently a thoroughgoing rationalization of the agricultural sector.[20]

The Conservatives, too, came into constant conflict with the Agrarians and acquired a distinct consumer profile on the consumer-producer dimension. While the Agrarians wanted a massive state involvement to preserve the agricultural sector as it emerged from the postwar land settlement, and the Social Democrats wanted a state role to rationalize the sector, the Conservatives, who opposed the land settlement from the outset, wanted a drastic diminution of the state's role and the introduction of a free market in agricultural products. Since much of agriculture was dependent on the state for its existence, this was a position that guaranteed conflict with the Agrarians.[21] The Conservative party was overwhelmingly the representative of the interests of industry.[22] Withdrawal of the state from the agricultural sector would serve industrial interests in numerous ways: it would remove a program of income redistribution from industry to agriculture; it would accelerate migration from the countryside and contribute to an abundant supply of cheap labor for industry; it would reduce the price of raw materials.

We can speculate that the Conservatives in Finland, in contrast to their counterparts in Sweden, acquired a consumer profile just after World War II because Finland lacked a dominant Social Democratic party and united labor movement always ready and capable of defending consumer (and therefore industrial) interests. The Communist party, gaining half of the working-class vote, never assumed a distinct position on the cleavage, because much of its support was rural and agrarian. The Social Democrats could not become a dominant party because of the split in the labor movement. It was the Agrarian party that was dominant in Finland. Given its size and position on the left-right cleavage, it was virtually impossible to form a majority government without it, and it governed continuously from the 1930s to the 1970s. Given the dominance of the Agrarians and the weakness of the Social Democrats, the interests of industry probably compelled the Conservatives to acquire a profile in a way that was unnecessary in Sweden. The smaller bourgeois parties and the Communist party avoided a profile because, above all, their urban-rural heterogeneity discouraged them from seeking one.[23]

As the Agrarians became committed to the interests of farmers in the North and the Social Democrats and Conservatives to workers and industrialists in the South, the parties also came into conflict over the growing economic, social, and cultural disparities between the southern center and the northern periphery.[24] The cleavage has been apparent since the earliest days of industrialization, but did not become a primary feature of the party system until the late 1960s and 1970s. Before that time, the cleavage was important mainly in reinforcing the consumer-producer conflict, because of the predominance of agriculture, and especially marginal agriculture, in the North. Debates about agricultural support were, therefore, simultaneously debates about state assistance for the periphery. In the late 1960s, the cleavage assumed a more distinct life of its own as debates over the distribution of social services, investment, and the loci of decision making became more prominent. The Social Democrats, committed to a development strategy aiming at the most rapid and efficient possible industrialization, necessarily premised their economic policy preferences on national rather than local criteria. And national criteria necessarily led to preferences that favored the South at the expense of the North. The Conservatives' commitment to free market principles similarly resulted in preferences that necessarily favored the South, and they became *de facto* defenders of the center.[25]

The Communist party joined with the Agrarian party as the defender of the periphery. In many areas of the North and East, Finland has virtually a two-party system, with the Communists and Agrarians taking over 80 percent of the vote collectively. The origins of the Communists' disproportionate strength in the periphery are partly historical and partly economic. In the aftermath of the Civil War, it was much easier for Communists to operate in the remote and sparsely populated peripheral provinces, where the authority of the central government was much weaker. It was possible, in consequence, for the Communists to develop an organizational and cultural presence in the periphery that was much more difficult to establish in the Southwest. Moreover, the very remoteness of the area and the sparseness of its population discouraged other parties, in particular the Social Democrats, from seriously challenging the Communists.[26]

The high level of conflict in Finnish politics during the formative years of the party system resulted in a party system which contained a large number of cleavages. As we will see, the party system has, to a large degree, carried these conflicts forward to the contemporary era insofar as it has reinforced their sociological and psychological bases. To summarize, setting aside the socioeconomic dimension occupied by all parties: the Agrarians acquired profiles on the consumer-producer, ethnolinguistic, center-periphery, and foreign policy dimensions; the Social Democrats on the consumer-producer and center-periphery; the Liberals on the ethnolinguistic and foreign policy; the Conservatives on the center-periphery, ethnolinguistic, consumer-producer, and foreign policy; the Swedish People's party on the ethnolinguistic and foreign policy; and the Communist party on the foreign policy and center-periphery. Among these, only the foreign policy cleavage has been muted in the postwar era.

The Governments, 1955–1965

The 1956 Social Democratic–Agrarian–Liberal–Swedish Party Government

This majority coalition was formed under the formateurship of the Social Democratic party on March 3. The previous government, a coalition of the Agrarians and Social Democrats, resigned on January 27, because it had been defeated in the Eduskunta on a piece of vital economic legislation.[27] Each year since 1941 the Eduskunta had renewed emergency legislation granting the government very wide-ranging authority to regulate the economy. The constitution required that such exceptional grants of authority be enacted in one of two extraordinary ways. Under the more traditional procedure, such legislation would receive Eduskunta approval, followed by a general election, followed by a second Eduskunta approval by a majority of two-thirds. Alternatively, it could be declared urgent by a vote of five-sixths of the Eduskunta. If then approved by a majority of two-thirds, it could become effective immediately.[28]

Because the annual grant of authority was to expire on January 1, 1956, the previous coalition had to be successful in obtaining legislative approval by the second route, if stability of economic policy was to be maintained. Neither the time nor the desire for an early election existed. But in December 1955, the Conservatives, Swedish party, Liberals, and Communists joined together in the Eduskunta and prevented the existing government from obtaining the five-sixths vote necessary to process the legislation. This effectively killed the legislation, and on January 1, 1956, most economic regulations—including those controlling wages and prices—expired.[29] The immediate upshot was an explosion of prices in January and February. The Agrarian–Social Democratic coalition resigned because the two parties no longer felt they could carry out the economic policy to which they had committed themselves when they formed the government.[30]

In December 1955, the National Farmers Association announced a price rise of 5 to 6 percent on a range of basic commodities. The trade unions then demanded a twelve-mark-per-hour wage increase to offset the price rises and threatened a general strike from March 1 if the Employers' Association did not grant the increase. The farmers then threatened to withhold deliveries if their incomes were not maintained. On March 1, the general strike commenced. A few days later, agricultural deliveries were halted. The general strike lasted until March 20, and involved some violence, disruptions of critical supplies, and threats to shut off public heating. It was as the nation moved into this situation that the government was formed.[31]

Under the circumstances, the only issue of significance was whether the government's authority to regulate wages and prices would be restored. The Agrarians and Social Democrats had been committed to maintenance of the authority in the previous government and remained so. The Liberals and the Swedish party had opposed the renewal of the authority in the Eduskunta in December, but reversed their positions and endorsed the renewal in January when confronted with the consequences of abrupt deregulation. The Conservatives and the Communists remained opposed.[32] The government formed was a coalition of Social Democrats, Agrarians, Liberals, and the Swedish party. Social Democrats held the formateurship, and all members had a convergent relationship on the question of renewing economic regulation. The coalition had a majority of 133 out of 200 Eduskunta seats.[33]

The hypothesized limit of tolerance for conflictual

systems is the divergent-implicit relationship. In this case, we have no divergent-implicit relationships. We have only convergent and divergent-explicit relationships. So the case provides only a weak test of the hypothesis. Nonetheless, the formateurs, as we would expect, did include all parties with whom their party's relationships were below the limit of tolerance. This is significant because it produced an oversized government. The two liberal parties controlled thirteen seats apiece. The Agrarians controlled fifty-three. With fifty-four seats of their own, the Social Democrats could have created a minimum-winning government simply by recreating a coalition with the Agrarians.

The May 1957 Agrarian–Liberal– Swedish Party Government

The critical conflicts when this government was formed all involved economic and agricultural policy, for the Finnish economy was experiencing an annual inflation rate of 18 percent, unemployment had doubled in the past year, the balance-of-payments deficit was growing, and the state deficit was so large that the National Bank was threatening to cut off the government's credit.[34]

In February 1957, the parties in the then existing government had reached agreement on an economic stabilization plan. One of the key clauses in this agreement assured private sector workers of wage increases tied to the price index at a rate of .66 to 1. The unions had been demanding full compensation. But the Social Democratic Premier was able to persuade them to accept the .66 rate. He then sought a statement from the coalition parties reiterating the government's commitment to the .66 clause.[35] At this point, the Agrarian, Liberal, and Swedish parties reversed their positions on the clause. They refused to endorse it and decided that any wage index would be inflationary. After negotiations failed to bridge the impasse, the government resigned.[36]

President Kekkonen then asked the Agrarian parliamentary party leader, Sukselainen, to form a government. New negotiations between the Social Democrats and Agrarians were taken up immediately, but again came to naught on the wage indexation issue. The Social Democrats, Agrarians, Liberals, and Swedish party were in accord on the other elements of the outgoing government's economic stabilization program. The basic components of this program were a licensing scheme to reduce imports to 70 to 75 percent of the previous year's level; an export tax to raise new revenues and pay off a 1953 loan from the National Bank; new taxes on tobacco and other items; increased pension and residence taxes.[37]

Like the Agrarians and the other nonsocialist parties, the Conservatives rejected wage indexation. But they also opposed any licensing scheme to limit imports, the tax on exports, and the increased pension contributions and residence taxes. Rather than measures to increase revenues, they wanted a policy premised on drastic reductions in public expenditures. The main target of the Conservatives' reduction would be agricultural price supports. The party wanted to end the indexation of producer prices, and it wanted an end to the subsidies that the government paid to farmers. Since the country was experiencing an agricultural surplus, an end to indexation and supports would place the burden on producers rather than consumers. The Agrarians were most opposed to this.[38]

The question of agricultural subsidies was pressing when Suskelainen formed his first government in May, because the state's debt was nearing crisis proportions. While the parties were negotiating, the National Bank was threatening to end all further credit to the government unless the government introduced new measures to raise revenues or cut expenditures. The state's short-term debt had reached thirteen billion Finnish marks in May—equivalent to about 25 percent of the national money supply. The outgoing government had—possibly unconstitutionally—postponed payment of ten billion marks in past due debts.[39]

The members of the next government would thus be compelled to substantially increase revenues or reduce expenditures. The Agrarians, Social Democrats, Liberals, and

Swedish and Communist parties were all in agreement on the tax increases included in the outgoing government's stabilization program. The Social Democrats, however, wanted expenditure cuts in the form of reduced subsidies to farmers. These reductions would be obtained by reducing the support price. Thus, the reductions would not result in increased consumer prices. The Agrarians also wanted to reduce the state's deficit by reducing the subsidies paid to farmers. But they did not want to reduce the support prices: the reduced subsidies would be passed on to consumers in the form of higher prices. Farmers' incomes would be protected.[40]

Thus, the Agrarians had divergent relationships with the Social Democrats and Communists on wage indexation; with the Social Democrats and Conservatives on producer subsidies; and with the Conservatives on tax increases and import licensing. These must be classified as divergent-explicit relationships, because Social Democratic, Communist, and Conservative leaders all made their preferences the quid pro quo of their parties' participation in government with the Agrarians. The Communists, of course, had the burden of their dubious commitment to the parliamentary order, and that would have been sufficient by itself to guarantee their exclusion in 1957. With the Swedish party and the Liberals, the Agrarians had convergent preferences, for the former two shared the Agrarians' opposition to wage indexation, endorsed the economic stabilization program developed by the previous government, and lacked a profile on the consumer-producer cleavage.

The outcome, then, was a government based on convergent relationships—a coalition of the Agrarians, Liberals, and Swedish party. The government formed was a minority government. Because no divergent-implicit relationships were available to the formateurs, the case does not provide an ideal test of the proposition that the limit of tolerance will be divergent-implicit relationships in conflictual systems. Nonetheless, it does provide partial confirmation of the hypothesis: the formateurs were unwilling to go beyond a divergent-implicit relationship to build a government on divergent-explicit relationships—even when failure to do so meant the creation of a minority government. In the absence of a divergent-implicit relationship, the case does not fully confirm that the limit of tolerance is the divergent-implicit relationship; but it does indicate that the formateurs were unwilling to go beyond the divergent-implicit relationship.

The June 1957 Agrarian–Liberal Government

Within weeks of the new government's appearance it became apparent that the measures on which it was premised would not be sufficient to restrain the growth of the deficit and allow the government to meet its immediate obligations. The coalition was thus compelled to reduce expenditures or increase revenues still more. The parties in the coalition agreed that they would permanently defer payment of 25 percent of the trimonthly child support payments until the recipients were seventeen years of age. They also agreed to postpone all of the child support payments due at the end of the second quarter of 1957. This postponement would reduce immediate obligations by five billion marks. The parties also agreed to a five-billion-mark reduction in agricultural subsidies—to be passed on to consumers as higher prices.[41]

All of the opposition parties opposed postponement of the second-quarter support payments. The Social Democrats and Communists insisted that they be made within three months; the Conservatives insisted that they be made at least to families with low incomes. The opposition parties, with a majority in the Eduskunta, were able to reject the government's proposal of a postponement. The government was forced to make the second-quarter payments immediately and found itself lacking the five billion marks due in this payment. The National Bank rejected the Finance Minister's plea for a five-billion-mark loan to cover the payments. Confronted with this situation, the coalition parties debated where to find the five billion marks. The Swedish party insisted that the government now postpone payment of the *third*-quarter support payments. The Agrarians and Liberals opposed this because they recognized that the opposition in the Eduskunta would not permit it and because, in any event, it would not produce the immediately needed five billion marks. The Swedish party thereupon withdrew its ministers from the government.[42]

It is at this point—early June 1957—that the second Sukselainen government appears. The Agrarians continued in coalition with the Liberals. The Swedish party—having preferences convergent with the Agrarians on the other issues—had a divergent-explicit relationship because it made postponement of the third-quarter payment the quid pro quo of its return to the coalition. The Conservatives remained opposed to the tax increases in the economic stabilization package and to the import licensing scheme. They supported a reduction of agricultural subsidies, but opposed the increased consumer prices that were required to maintain farm incomes. They wanted incomes and prices determined by the market. The Social Democrats shared the Conservatives' opposition to the increased consumer prices and continued to insist that the subsidies be reduced by reductions in farm incomes. Both the Conservatives and Social Democrats made their taxation and producer-subsidy preferences respectively prerequisites of governmental cooperation. And so the Agrarians' relationships with these two parties were also divergent-explicit. Only the Liberals—with convergent preferences—remained available.[43]

The September 1957 Agrarian–Liberal–Social Democratic Opposition Government

In early July, the Eduskunta adjourned for the summer holiday, and the new government had a month to formulate further economic initiatives. It paid what it could, when it could, of the child support payments. It wrote new proposals excluding single-child families from the benefit. It also proposed to accelerate the collection of sales tax receipts; impose a surtax on incomes and wealth; reduce public works expenditures; and increase taxes on alcohol, tobacco, and other items. These proposals were presented to a special session of the Eduskunta that convened on August 6. Except for the income and wealth surtaxes, the proposals were acceptable to the opposition parties. The surtaxes became the latest focus of conflict. The opposition observed that the government's income tax proposal would raise taxes on moderate and higher incomes and thus affect virtually all urban residents. The wealth tax, however, would only take effect after a taxpayer's wealth had reached a very high level. Farmers, who had very low taxable incomes but substantial wealth (their land), would thus largely escape the impact on the new taxes. The Social Democrats, Conservatives, and Communists now demanded that the proposals be rewritten to spread the burden more evenly across all groups.[44]

In August, the Agrarians negotiated with the opposition parties in an attempt to enlarge the base of the still-minority government. These negotiations largely failed. None of the opposition parties was willing to budge on the surtax question or the issues that had divided the parties earlier. Indeed, the Agrarians and Social Democrats found themselves farther apart than ever on producer prices: the Social Democrats now demanded that the prices paid to agricultural producers be decoupled from the cost-of-living index. The Agrarians would not accept this.[45]

The negotiations were not, however, completely inconsequential. A group of dissident Social Democrats who had broken with the mother party over the summer and formed their own party—the Social Democratic Opposition—agreed to make a coalition with the Agrarians. In the spring of 1956, the left wing of the Social Democratic party had gained control of the central committee at a special national party congress. The shift of power within the party and intense personal antagonisms led to the departure of some center-right dissidents and the creation of the new party. Policy differences per se were probably less important than personal conflicts. The new party carried forward the profiles of the mother party: socioeconomic, center-periphery, and consumer-producer.[46]

In contrast to the Social Democrats, Conservatives, Swedish party, and Communists, the Social Democratic Opposition did not make its preferences prerequisites of cooperation with the Agrarians. It opposed the Agrarians' proposed surtax on incomes and wealth, but it was willing to disagree. So were the Agrarians; the two parties agreed to study the matter. The two parties likewise agreed to study the question of agricultural subsidies, on which they also disagreed. The Liberals continued to have preferences that converged with those of the Agrarians and participated in the third government of 1957.[47]

The outcome was a minority coalition of the Agrarians (still the formateurs), the Liberals, and the Social Democratic Opposition. Together, the three parties controlled 90 of the 200 Eduskunta seats.[48] On the first occasion, then, that the formateurs' party had the opportunity to make a coalition based on a divergent-implicit relationship, it exploited the opportunity. This is as the theory would have us expect; and it is especially significant, because making use of the divergent-implicit relationship did not give the Agrarians a majority government. Such a government would have required that the party make explicit concessions to one of the other opposition parties; it was not willing to do this for the sake of a majority government.

The coalition remained in office only until November 30, 1957, when it was replaced by a government of civil servants. This government was replaced by yet another government of civil servants on April 26, 1958. The second government remained in office until after the 1958 Eduskunta elections. Both of these governments were formed because policy conflicts among the parties were so intense that no party was both willing to govern and able to gain the tolerance of a majority of the Eduskunta. The conflicts that created this situation are discussed below.

The 1958 Social Democratic–Conservative–Agrarian–Liberal–Swedish Party Government

In the wake of the 1958 election, the formateurship passed from the Agrarians to the Social Democrats. The campaign and the subsequent negotiations were dominated by conflicts over producer price supports, unemployment insurance, and state support for home construction and agricultural colonization. The economic and fiscal crises that had overwhelmed government formation in 1957 now receded in importance as the condition of the economy improved.[49]

The most contentious issue in the period prior to this government's formation was agricultural income policy. The heart of the dispute was whether agricultural incomes should be tied to a general price index or to an index of costs of agricultural production. The Agrarians had long insisted that agricultural incomes must remain tied to the general price index; the Social Democrats demanded that the tie must be to an index of agricultural production costs. A tie to production costs would mean lower price increases for urban consumers; a tie to the general price index would mean higher incomes for farmers. The Conservatives, the third party with a producer-consumer profile, shared with the Social Democrats the demand that incomes be tied to producer cost indices. The other democratic parties were sympathetic to this view, but lacked a relevant profile.[50]

The second question at this time involved who should pay the costs of a new system of unemployment insurance, which all parties were committed to introducing. The Conservatives, the Swedish party, the Liberals, and the Agrarians argued that the employers' contribution should be limited to .25 of 1 percent of payroll and that the self-employed should pay only an employee's premium. The Social Democrats and the Social Democratic Opposition wanted the employers' contribution at .50 of 1 percent and wanted the self-employed to contribute as both employees and employers. It was the status of the self-employed rather than the amount of the employers' contribution that provided the conflict of policy principle.[51]

The third question involved the conditions attached to state loans for home construction and agricultural colonization. The Conservatives demanded that the rate of interest on the loans be indexed rather than fixed. The Social Democrats, the Agrarians, and the Social Democratic Opposition insisted that the rates remain fixed. Such loans were the state's primary and least expensive means of generating employment.[52]

In sum, the Social Democrats, the party of the formateurs, had divergent relationships with each party except the Social Democratic Opposition. With the Agrarians, they were in conflict over producer pricing; with the Conservatives, the Agrarians, the Swedish party, and the Liberals they were in conflict over the status of the self-employed in the new unemployment insurance scheme; with the Conservatives they were in conflict over the indexation of state loans for home construction and agricultural colonization. The Communist party's antidemocratic status insured that it was never seriously considered for inclusion in any government. There remained only the Social Democratic Opposition, with which the Social Democrats had only convergent preferences on the salient conflicts of policy principles.

Nonetheless, the Social Democrats formed a coalition with the Conservatives, Agrarians, Liberals, and Swedish party. On each of its points of disagreement with these parties, the parties agreed to disagree. They agreed to study alternative producer-pricing schemes; to study the possible formulas on which the unemployment insurance system could be based; and to defer the question of indexing state loans. In sum, the parties agreed across the board to make the divergent relationships implicit.[53] Once again, majority considerations do not provide an explanation for this behavior: the government formed was well oversized, controlling 137 of the 200 Eduskunta seats.[54] The Social Democrats could have had a majority without (a) the Swedish and Liberals parties, (b) the Conservatives, or (c) the Conservative and Swedish parties.

The broad willingness to accept implicit relationships as the basis for cooperation derived from the classical concern of democratic parties in conflictual democracies: the defense of the democratic order. The 1958 election had produced substantial gains for the Communist party, which rose from forty-three to an all-time high of fifty Eduskunta seats and became the largest party. The cooperation among the democratic parties was premised on their desire to isolate the Communists.[55]

The Communists aside, only the Social Democratic Opposition remained outside the government. The Opposition based its refusal to join on nonpolicy demands. It made the price of its participation a change in the membership of the central committee of the Social Democratic party. The Social Democratic leadership, not surprisingly, would not consider such a proposition.[56]

The new government served until December 3, 1958, when it resigned. It is impossible to know the full circumstances of its resignation, but several points are clear. Most important, the government resigned under the pressure of Soviet interference. Shortly after it was formed, Soviet-Finnish relations began to deteriorate sharply: the Soviet ambassador in Helsinki was recalled without replacement; negotiations on an international canal and a new trade treaty—essential to the Finnish economy—came to a halt; criticism of the government became conspicuous in the Soviet press. It was evident by the criticism that it was to the composition of the government rather than to its policies that the Soviets objected. In particular, the Soviets objected to Social Democratic participation as long as the party was under the leadership of Vainno Tanner and Vainno Leksinen, as it had been since the spring of 1957. Tanner and Leksinen, the former especially, had a history of bitter anticommunism and anti-Sovietism stretching back to the prewar years. Presumably, the Soviets found a government that was explicitly anticommunist and that included such figures to be intolerable.[57]

It is possible that the Soviets demanded either the inclusion of the Communists or the exclusion of the Tanner-Leksinen Social Democrats. Since no Finnish politicians at this time were willing to bring the Communists into a government, this would have meant the exclusion of the Social Democrats. What we do know is that after December 1958, President Kekkonen would not accept Social Democratic participation in a government until its leadership had been changed. That this was due to the Soviets' attitude was widely understood and accepted by Finnish politicians.[58] Indeed, in 1961 the matter was quite candidly debated in the Eduskunta.[59]

The short-term result of the Soviet intervention was that the coalition was replaced in January 1959 by a purely Agrarian government, which was apparently thought by Kekkonen and party leaders to be the most prudent outcome in the then very tense situation. Clearly this Agrarian government cannot be explained by any normal theory of government formation; for that reason I have omitted it.[60]

For the longer-term, the Social Democratic party was frozen out of government participation until it changed its leadership in the mid-1960s. In considering the intervening government formations, I will set aside the Social Democratic party, since its exclusion had nothing to do with the normal dynamics of government formation.[61]

The 1961 Agrarian Government

The minority Agrarian government formed in January 1959, remained in office until July 3, 1961, when it resigned because of a court ruling that implicated the Premier but had no consequences for the formation of the subsequent government. Except that the Social Democratic party remained barred from participation because of Soviet opposition, government formation now returned to the normal pattern of bargaining among the democratic parties. These negotiations proved fruitless, and on July 14 the Agrarians, with the formateurship, formed a single-party minority government.[62]

As was so often the case, the agricultural price law was a central issue. The existing law was scheduled to expire on September 1. The basic issues were unchanged. The Agrarians wanted the existing law, which tied producer prices to a general price index, renewed. The Conservatives wanted the link with the index broken and market forces to take over. The Social Democratic Opposition wanted immediate revisions that would make pricing decisions more favorable to consumers. The party's proposals would have taken authority to set prices away from the government and given it to a commission appointed by the Eduskunta. It also wanted pricing linked to an index of producer costs. Finally, it wanted producers to pay a tax on milk that would be used to increase support for smallholders and to finance milk exports.[63]

The second issue involved the state's authority to regulate housing prices in Helsinki and Tampere, which had expired on July 1. The Agrarians, Swedish party, and Social Democratic Opposition wanted the authority extended and strengthened. The Conservatives and the Liberals demanded an end to the regulation.[64]

The Agrarians were also in conflict with the Conservatives, the Liberals, and the Social Democratic Opposition over state support for Finnish industry. Specifically, the Agrarians wanted the state to purchase seventy new locomotives from France and Germany for the state railroad. The other three parties wanted these orders placed with Finnish industry. It was not a small matter, because the orders would have generated thousands of jobs in an economy suffering high unemployment. The Agrarians, however, more concerned to improve a decrepit railroad system as quickly as possible and to improve service in isolated areas, wanted the locomotives delivered at the earliest possible date. That meant ordering them abroad.[65]

The final point of conflict involved the status of the Swedish language, which had not been a point of bitter party division for twenty years. The 1922 Language Law had stipulated that a commune would be considered bilingual when the minority language group constituted 10 or more percent of the communal population. Communes that were designated as bilingual on this basis would remain bilingual unless the minority group fell below 8 percent of the population. By 1961, it was apparent that as a result of the immigration of Finnish-speakers and revised communal boundaries, the city of Turku would soon lose its bilingual status unless this percentage limit was revised. The Swedish party proposed that the bilingual status of Turku, Helsinki, and Vaasa be preserved so long as the Swedish-speaking population remained above 5,000. The advantage of such a proposal was that it would insure the bilingual status of the three cities without making towns that were currently only Swedish-speaking into bilingual towns. A general reduction in the 8 percent clause would have had this effect.[66]

When the issue was debated in the Eduskunta shortly before the outgoing government resigned, the four parties with profiles on the linguistic cleavage—the Conservatives, Liberals, Agrarians, and Swedes—were galvanized in defense of their language interests, and the debate was especially bitter. With the Social Democrats, the Social Democratic Opposition, and the Communists, none of which had relevant profiles, all ambivalent, neither side had a majority and the issue remained unresolved when the new government was formed.[67]

The Agrarians, then, had divergent relationships with every potential coalition partner. On none of the issues did any of the parties' leaders express an interest in converting the divergent relationships into implicit relationships. With no convergent or tangential relationships available, the Agrarians would thus have been compelled to make explicit concessions to one or more parties to gain partners in the government. The Agrarian leaders preferred governing alone as a minority government.

The 1962 Agrarian–Liberal–Conservative–Swedish Party Government

The minority Agrarian government remained in office until after the Eduskunta and presidential elections of February 1962. The Eduskunta balloting reduced the Social Democratic Opposition's presence in the legislature to three seats and deprived it of relevance.[68]

A prospective budget dificit of 76.6 billion marks in the 480-billion-mark state budget provided by far the most pressing issue at the time the new government was negotiated.

The next government would face the prospect of a severe cash shortage in the autumn. The basic division among the parties pitted the Communists, Social Democrats, and Social Democratic Opposition, all of which favored a tax increase, against the Agrarians, Liberals, Conservatives, and Swedish party, all of which wanted expenditure reductions as well as tax increases. In their campaigns, none of the parties indentified which taxes they would increase or which expenditures they would cut. This reticence was in part from electoral calculations. In part, it also derived from the difficulties the bureaucracy was having in estimating month-to-month revenue flows and the uncertain capacity of the capital markets to sustain the heavy level of public borrowing. Even so, the basic division among the parties was clear.[69]

The issue of a special language law for Turku, Helsinki, and Vaasa, already considered, remained very much alive. Final legislation had not yet passed the Eduskunta. The party positions remained unchanged.[70] The agricultural price law, too, was again a point of conflict. The outgoing Agrarian government had succeeded in having the legislation that was set to expire in September 1961 extended for an additional year, because the parties were so divided that no alternative could gain a majority. Little had changed in the interval. The Agrarians continued to demand that the extension be followed by a permanent law that tied prices to a general inflation index. The Conservatives continued to want an end to indexation. The Social Democrats and the Social Democratic Opposition wanted producer prices indexed to producer costs.[71]

A new issue between the parties involved the legislative introduction of a forty-hour workweek, which the trade unions and socialist parties were pressing for. The Agrarians were supportive; so was the Swedish party. The Liberals and especially the Conservatives were opposed to such legislation.[72] The course of the negotiations is telling in revealing the first tentative steps being taken by Finnish politicians to institutionalize corporatist patterns of policymaking. In the process, they were beginning Finland's transformation into an unconsolidated democracy. The forty-hour week became central to the negotiations because the Agrarians wanted the government to include representatives of the National Labor Confederation and the Employers' Association. The trade union leadership demanded the forty-hour week as the price of its cooperation. The Employers' Association insisted that it would not join any government that committed itself to such legislation. After extensive intervention by President Kekkonen, the Agrarian leaders did manage to bring both labor and management representatives into the government. The employers were represented by the Ministers of Industry and Commerce. Labor was represented by the Minister of Social Affairs and the Vice-Ministers of Finance and Communications.[73]

It was possible to reconcile the conflicts between the employers and labor and between the parties themselves by arranging an agreement to disagree. The Prime Minister designate, Karjalainen, was able to get everyone concerned to accept a statement that committed the government to support any policy which the two labor-market groups endorsed. Since the unions and employers were at loggerheads on the issue, this was a meaningless agreement. But it served its purpose. And it was supplemented by a government commitment to establish a commission to study the question.[74]

The parties reached the same sort of accommodation on the language dispute. The Agrarians, Conservatives, and Swedish party embraced a statement committing the next government to "respect the special needs of the Swedish-speaking minority." Each party could—and did—interpret this as it chose.[75] The Agrarians and Conservatives reached the same kind of agreement on the agricultural price law issue. They agreed to study it.[76]

Thus, the government was formed entirely on divergent-implicit relationships. The Agrarians had such a relationship with the Conservatives on the forty-hour week and the new agricultural price law; with the Liberals on the forty-hour week; and with the Swedish party on the status of Turku, Helsinki, and Vaasa.

The 1964 Agrarian–Conservative–Liberal–Swedish Party Government

The four-party coalition formed in 1962 came to an end on December 17, 1963. The ministers were unable to reach agreement among themselves and among their parliamentary parties on the 1964 budget and proposals for a one-year surtax on incomes, wealth, and property. In the wake of the coalition's resignation, none of the four parties in it was willing to form or serve in another government. With the Social Democrats still excluded by the Soviets, no party government was possible. After futile interventions by President Kekkonen, the result was a nonparty government of civil servants. This government, the Lehto ministry, took office on December 18 and served until September 1964.[77]

Much of significance occurred during the life of this administration. Not the least was that the four nonsocialist parties found themselves on several occasions during the spring Eduskunta compelled to support and preserve the Lehto ministry on some exceedingly unpopular measures, given their own unwillingness to form a government and the unwillingness of the Social Democrats to cooperate from their state of internal exile. This situation had the disadvantage of permitting the Communists and Social Democrats to blame the nonsocialist parties for the administration's unpopular measures during the summer communal elections. Such an infelicitous position gave the four parties reason to reconsider their attitudes toward participation in a government. With the sense that they were trapped, they renewed negotiations in the spring and again in the summer, but without success.[78]

When the Eduskunta reconvened in September, the Social Democrats and the Communists put forward an interpellation that, in the event, amounted to a motion of no-confidence against the Lehto administration. The administration had fifteen days in which to respond, and the nonsocialist parties had the same amount of time to decide whether to support the administration or replace it. They now had a double incentive to form a government, because the measures the administration had put forward were extremely unpopular. It had administratively enacted sharp increases in the prices of basic foodstuffs; administratively increased the rates of interest on state home construction and agricultural colonization loans; and proposed to the Eduskunta a continuation into the next year of the "one-year" surtax on incomes, wealth, and property. The administration proposed the tax extensions because the next budget would otherwise be 150 billion marks in deficit.[79]

These circumstances notwithstanding, the parties remained reluctant to govern, and threats from Kekkonen that he would dissolve the Eduskunta and call early elections were required. Under such pressures the Agrarians were given the formateurship on September 8 and succeeded in forming a new four-party majority coalition on September 13.[80]

The four parties were all committed to rejection of the proposed surtax extension and thus had convergent relations on that point. The question of how to address the then pending 150-million-mark deficit remained. Each of the parties was committed to major spending cuts, but not necessarily the same ones. The Liberals, Agrarians, and Swedish party were all agreed on one thing: they refused to declare in advance where these cuts would be made. The Conservatives were less reticent: they demanded that the cuts be made mainly in agricultural subsidies, agricultural colonization support, and public works. These proposals struck at the core interests of the Agrarians' constituents and were clearly unacceptable to the party—which refused to embrace them. As it happened, the Agrarians and Conservatives agreed to disagree. They simply proclaimed their intention to seek major cuts in public expenditures. They did not specify how, but did announce that the matter would be studied.[81]

The September food price increases that the Lehto ministry enacted were the last that would occur under the extended Agricultural Incomes Law. A permanent law was thus once again an issue. And the Agrarians continued to insist that the permanent law be based on the principle that producer prices would be tied to the general wage and price level. The Conservatives continued to insist that producer prices be de-indexed and that market forces be given greater play. The Social Democrats, also with a producer-consumer profile, but still not *salon fähig*, continued to demand a pricing formula that slowed consumer increases and government subsidies. Once again, the Agrarians and Conservatives agreed not to reach an agreement.[82]

That the Agrarians were committed to the formula in the old Agricultural Incomes Law did not mean that they supported the Lehto administration's consumer price increases. They, and all of the other parties from the Communists to the Conservatives, were committed to a rollback of the increases. The Agrarians were opposed because the increases reduced comsumption and aggravated an already serious oversupply, especially of butter. They wanted agricultural incomes to rise according to the law's formula; but they wanted the government to make good the increasing subsidies. How to deal with the consequences of a price rollback was an issue in itself and distinct from the broader question of how to deal with the deficit that would result from a cancellation of the surtax. Again, the Agrarians and Conservatives (and Social Democrats) were at loggerheads on the point. And, once again, they reached no policy agreement when they formed the new government.[83]

Because they did not have profiles on consumer-producer issues, the Liberals and Swedish party can be said to have had convergent preferences with the Agrarians. The question that had previously separated the Agrarians and the Swedish party—the linguistic status of Turku, Helsinki, and Vaasa—had been settled in the Swedish party's favor when the Communists and Social Democrats and Social Democratic Opposition decided to support the Swedish position. The issue was no longer on the agenda.[84]

The Agrarians and the Conservatives arranged implicit compromises on all of their differences. They were motivated to do so by the need to undo the measures taken by the Lehto administration and by Kekkonen's threats of an early election.[85]

Summary

Eight governments were formed in Finland between 1955 and 1965, if we discount the Soviet intervention in the formation of the January 1959 Agragarian Emergency government. We find that the theory correctly predicts the composition of seven of the eight governments. Among the eight governments, we have thirty-six relationships between formateurs' parties and the other democratic parties. In four of these relationships, nonpolicy considerations were decisive. Three of the four occurred when the Soviets vetoed Social Democratic participation between 1959 and 1965. The other instance occurred in 1958, when the Social Democratic Opposition demanded changes in the leadership of the Social Democratic party as the price of its cooperation. In the remaining thirty-two relationships, only policy preferences were important. In each case, the outcome conformed to the expectations of the theory.

It would be wrong to infer from the relative infrequency of nonpolicy demands that the party system was not intensely polarized. The polarization was, instead, manifested in other ways: above all, by the frequent inability of parties to form any kind of party government. Twice in 1957 and again in 1963, presidential governments of civil servants were appointed because there existed no party that was both willing to govern and could gain the toleration of a legislative majority. By toleration, I do not mean support for a governing program. I mean only the acceptance of the party's representatives as ministers. In such circumstances, the President was forced to appoint civil servants. As we saw, these governments were not caretakers in the generally understood sense that they limited their activity to day-to-day administration. They were appointed with the expectation that they would make major political decisions that the parties were unable to make. They routinely did so.

Between 1955 and 1965, such governments served for a total of eighteen months. They provided a relief valve of sorts for politicians by allowing them to escape coalition decisions that would have sorely tested the unity of their parties. These governments are the main reason that Finland has suffered less than Italy from party splits and debates about the "governing formula."

CHAPTER SEVEN

Finland as an Unconsolidated Democracy, 1966–1982

The unique feature of an unconsolidated democracy is that coalition outcomes are not systemically determined as they are in other democracies. Elsewhere, the systemic attributes of the democracy, in conjunction with the constant ambitions of party leaders and the variable constellation of bargaining relationships, determine the coalition outcome. The personalities and ideologies of leaders are inconsequential and are dominated by the ambitions inherent in their roles as party leaders. Moreover, there exist no leading politicians who are not party leaders and are therefore free of the constraints of the leadership role.

The Sources of the Transformation

The unconsolidated democracy is the exception to this. On the one hand, its very creation appears to require a powerful, autonomous politician—former President Kekkonen, in the Finnish case—capable of inducing and coercing a break in the practiced patterns of elite behavior. On the other hand, the unconsolidated democracy is the only one of the four democracies in which the systemic attributes are indeterminant: corporatism encourages party collaboration; polarization discourages it. These conflicting pressures have permitted the President—who is not subject to the role requirements of a party leader—to express decisively his personality in government formation in spite of opposition from party leaders. Precisely because the preferences of the President are so important, it is not possible to predict coalition outcomes.

Finland became an unconsolidated democracy in the late 1960s because of the corporatization of the Finnish economy. In this chapter I want to try to understand what caused this corporatization and the associated changes in the party system. I also want to try to understand the implications of unconsolidated democracy for government formation. Corporatization does not appear to have been brought about by economic change—in Finland's position in the international economy, in the level of development, in the mix of industries. None of these changes, so far as I can determine, explain why corporatization occurred when it did. Nor does corporatization seem to have been caused, at least directly, by changes in the party system. Theories of electoral change, embourgeoisement, postmaterialism, and so forth seem to have less resonance in Finland in the 1960s than in almost any European democracy.

Taking change in party-system fractionalization as an indicator of party-system change reveals that between 1955 and 1965 (the most critical period), only four of seventeen affluent democracies had more stable party systems. Between 1965 and 1975, only five of seventeen had more stable systems. Another indicator of party-system change, electoral volatility, also suggests that nothing exceptional was occurring in the Finnish party system and electoral society in the years before corporatization. Between 1948 and 1959, the volatility score for the Finnish electorate was half of the mean score for seventeen democracies. For the period 1960–69, the score was slightly below the mean. For the period 1970–77, the score was slightly above the mean.[1] Increased volatility, then, seems to have followed rather than caused the political and economic changes that interest us.

Finland changed to an unconsolidated democracy because of the latent potential for change that was inherent in its political institutions. The system changed because of the transformation first of the Finnish presidency, which made possible (but did not require) a transformation of the economy and some changes in party relationships. Finnish politicians in the 1960s inherited a constitution that already included a potentially powerful presidency. The presidency had not previously been a powerful office because Presidents until the 1960s were dependent on parties for their election. A President with an autonomous electoral base, however, could afford to make greater use of his latent authority to goad the economic interest groups and political parties into greater cooperation. He could encourage the greater cooperation in the economy that made possible greater cooperation in the party system and vice-versa. It was this heightened presidential intervention in both spheres that ultimately provoked corporatization and the transition to an unconsolidated democracy. In the pages that follow, I will first review the transformation of the Finnish presidency during the tenure of Uhro Kekkonen and the impact of the more powerful presidency on the parties and the interest groups. I will then consider the implications of this for coalition making. Finally, I will return to the contention that the transition to an unconsolidated democracy required a powerful, nonparty politician and that it is only in such a democracy that any politician is able to forcefully express his personality in coalition making.

Finnish presidents are selected indirectly by popular vote. Voters cast ballots for electors who are normally pledged to a candidate. Until Kekkonen established his political dominance in the 1960s, the multiparty format insured that no candidate received a popular majority. Negotiations within the electoral college thus decided who would be President. When Kekkonen was first elected in 1956, he received only 26.9 percent of the popular vote. He won on the thinnest possible majority in the electoral college after negotiations that stretched the balloting over an entire day.² Under the circumstances, Kekkonen, like his predecessors, could exercise little influence in domestic politics and was unable to intervene effectively in coalition negotiations. And, indeed, he was compelled in 1958 to accept the formation of the Fagerholm coalition, a government that took office in spite of his opposition to it.³

From the mid-1960s, Kekkonen was able to exercise a decisive influence in government negotiations. His greater authority derived from several sources: his ability to claim a popular mandate beyond the reach of any other Finnish politician; the personal esteem he commanded among Finnish voters; the divisions among the parties and their inability to form a united front; Finland's delicate foreign policy position and Kekkonen's masterful manipulation of it for his own domestic purposes; and, finally, Kekkonen's immense skill and determination.

Kekkonen was reelected in 1962. But his reelection was not assured until after the "Note Crisis" in Soviet-Finnish relations in December 1961 forced the withdrawal of Kekkonen's Social Democratic and Conservative challenger. Olavi Honka, sponsored by both the Social Democrats and Conservatives, withdrew from the campaign when the Soviets made known their dissatisfaction with him.⁴ Kekkonen went on to receive 44.3 percent of the popular vote in 1962 and won an easy victory in the electoral college.⁵ The election was a turning point. Kekkonen's share of the vote was extraordinary, but even more important, it was personal and cut across party lines. This exceptional support derived from Kekkonen's ability to portray himself as the guarantor of Finnish sovereignty and stability. The contrast with the always fractious parties could not have been sharper.⁶ After 1962, Kekkonen's position was never seriously challenged. He was reelected in 1968, receiving 61.6 percent of the popular vote.⁷ His third term was then extended by the Eduskunta from the normal six years to ten years. The extension was supported by all of the parties.⁸ In 1978, he was reelected yet again with only token opposition. When he finally left office in 1982, after twenty-six years as President, he did so because of failing health.⁹

Kekkonen was successful in using his augmented authority in part because the conflicts among the parties were frequently such that party leaders were unable to unite against his encroachments. Indeed, they sometimes did not want to resist these encroachments, because the viability of the parliamentary order depended on them and because they relieved party leaders of responsibility.[10] The President had, however, to observe certain rules of the game. The most important of these was that he did not involve himself in day-to-day governance.[11] The importance of the President's interventions was in making the process of governance more effective rather than in determining specific domestic policies to be pursued.

The President's more energetic role was a precondition of depolarization, but not a sufficient one. Greater cooperation among the parties required readmittance of the Social Democrats to the circle of ministerable parties and the equal participation of the Communist party in policymaking. It probably also required that the Communists not be automatically precluded from joining the government. Certainly, when the two parties, together representing the entire labor movement and about 50 percent of the voters, were in isolation, there was no possibility of depolarization. The Social Democrats were able to return to the government in 1966 because leadership changes within the party brought to the fore a new generation of leaders less antipathetic to the Soviet Union. The détente in party-Soviet relations made the Social Democrats once again acceptable to the other parties.[12]

The circumstances surrounding the Communist party's entrance into the circle of governing parties are less clear. The party joined the 1966 coalition of Social Democrats, Agrarians, and Liberals. It did not join because the other parties were suddenly persuaded of its commitment to the democratic order.[13] Kekkonen clearly wanted the party in government and argued that its strong position within the working class and the trade unions made its participation essential. The Agrarians and Social Democrats, each of which stressed that it would never govern alone with the Communists, could also find advantages in Communist participation in a broad coalition. The Agrarians could force responsibility on their main competitor for the votes of northern smallholders. The Social Democrats could do likewise to their competitor for the working-class vote. As well, the Social Democrats could always savor the prospect that participation would, as it eventually did, split and demoralize the Communist party.[14]

Calculations such as these may have been the only ones behind the decision to admit the party into the government. Or they may have been supplemented by Soviet pressure. Speculation has focused on the possibility that the Soviets told Kekkonen and the Social Democrats that Communist participation was the price Finland would have to pay for Soviet tolerance of the Social Democrats. Given the need to bring the Social Democrats back from isolation if the parliamentary order was to remain viable, Kekkonen and the democratic party leaders might have been willing to accept the Communists to get the Social Democrats.[15]

The unfreezing of the party system was paralleled by changes in the economy. Within a remarkably short time, the Finnish economy became among the most corporatized in the democratic world. This made union and employer involvement the *sine qua non* of effective policy and eased the centrifugal pressures in the party system. At the beginning of the 1960s, less than a third of the Finnish labor force was unionized and employers were only loosely organized. Workers were divided into competing socialist and communist unions, and party competition within the unions was bitter. In 1965, the Social Democratic–affiliated federation, the SAK, had only 248,000 members, while its Communist-affiliated competitor, the SAJ, had just 105,000. Once the two working-class parties emerged from their isolation, cooperation between the two unions grew steadily, as did their involvement in government policymaking.[16] In 1969, a unified Central Federation of Trade Unions was created by a merger of the old federations. The unified federation had 922,000 members by 1975, and two years later its membership had risen to 951,000. This made the Finnish labor force the best organized in the democratic world by 1977.[17] The turning point came in the first comprehensive incomes policy agreement reached among unions, employers, and the government in 1968. The agreement allowed for the withholding of union dues from wages and was followed by a rapid growth in union membership.[18] Employer organization has proceeded in tandem.[19]

The annual incomes policy agreements have dealt with wages and prices, but from the beginning have also included decisions on social benefits, the government's role in the marketplace, and, more recently, taxation. They have also embraced such social reforms as the introduction of the five-day workweek and codetermination in industry.[20] The parties and the Eduskunta have been left with the choice of embracing the agreements in their entirety and establishing the agencies necessary to implement them, or rejecting any part of the agreements and thus sabotaging the entire agreement. The parties and the parliament have thus found their roles reduced. In part, however, this has been because they have found it congenial to leave many major compromises to the labor-market groups.

Corporatism, the Party System, and Government Formation

The entrance of the working-class parties into government made the union's cooperation with each other, with the employer organizations, and with the government more likely. The greater cooperation in the economy in turn reduced the centrifugal pressure on the parties. The depolarization of the party system, however, should not be exaggerated. Throughout the 1970s, the party system continued to exhibit all the signs of an intensely polarized system. The Communist party, although divided internally between a reformist majority and Stalinist minority and electorally reduced, remained a critical force, receiving 17.9 percent of the vote in 1979.

The centrifugal pull of the system has been evident in the Communist party itself. When in government, the party's hard-line minority has in fact often acted as part of the opposition and voted against the government on critical issues.[21] The coalitions that included the Communists, Social Democrats, and Agrarians have placed great pressure on the Communists and Agrarians. This was evidenced in the Communists by the split between the reformist and hard-line wings, a split that has sometimes paralyzed the party. The Agrarians experienced the continued centrifugation of the system when a small protest group adjacent to it "began to claim that the party has 'betrayed the farmer' for the sake of the coalition." This splinter group, insignificant before 1966, eventually formed the Finnish Rural party and captured one-third of the Agrarians' parliamentary seats in the 1970 election.[22]

The upshot of the changes in the party system and economy has been a kind of mutual veto system in which no policy can succeed—or even be implemented—without broad support. It is a system in which corporatization has made it institutionally easier to develop this support than was the case twenty years ago. At the same time, it is a system in which centrifugal pressures—in the party system and the society at large—remain strong and continue to make cooperation among party leaders objectively difficult and dangerous.

It was in counteracting these centrifugal pressures that Kekkonen's interventions were decisive. In government formation, Kekkonen's main goal was to bridge the socialist-nonsocialist divide. Because of his strong position, his personal likes and dislikes had an impact on the choice of coalition partners and even individual cabinet ministers. "He has determined which parties are 'eligible' for entrance into a government, put pressure on parliamentary groups and hesitant ministerial candidates, and expressed a clear opinion concerning the government base and the individuals entering a cabinet—and concerning even the details of the government program."[23]

Kekkonen played a central role in the creation of every majority coalition formed after 1966. Reflecting Kekkonen's conviction that the country cannot be governed effectively otherwise, most of these were greatly oversized. They normally included the Communists, Social Democrats, Agrarians, and Swedish and Liberal parties. Six of the ten governments formed between 1966 and 1981 followed this popular front format. Collectively, they governed for almost eight of the fifteen years. Because Kekkonen was convinced that Communist participation was essential, he refused to sanction the participation of the Conservative party in any government formed after 1966.[24]

In 1968, Kekkonen was active in bringing about the first incomes policy agreement. This agreement was in turn essential to the formation of the 1968 coalition, because the Communists and Social Democrats had been unable to reach agreement with the Agrarians on several issues that the economic interest groups were able to resolve.[25] After the March 1970 election, in which the Agrarians lost about one-third of their Eduskunta seats, the Agrarians refused to join any government that did not include their arch-competitor, the Rural party. Kekkonen refused to sanction the latter's participation, because the Communists would then have refused to join. For their part, the Social Democrats were unwilling to govern with the Communists alone or with the Conservatives. Kekkonen would not accept a minority Conservative government because of the strain it would place on labor-market negotiations. The result was a sixty-three-day caretaker administration. It was only in late June that the Agrarians reversed their position and agreed to a government without the Rural party. They did so only because Kekkonen was on the verge of dissolving the Eduskunta for new elections. A popular front government followed the Agrarians' reversal.[26]

In 1971, the Communists withdrew from this government because of internal conflicts. Kekkonen made an effort to bring them back into the government, but was unsuccessful and had to accept a coalition of the Social Democrats, Agrarians, and Swedish and Liberal parties.[27] This government fell apart in October 1971 because of conflicts among the parties.

The result was a dissolution of the Eduskunta and a new election. Afterward, none of the parties was anxious to govern, and after six weeks of negotiations, Kekkonen appointed a minority Social Democratic government for lack of an alternative.[28]

Five months later, a government of the Social Democrats, Agrarians, and the two liberal parties was formed. It was possible to form this government only because the labor- and producer-market groups had been able to reach agreement on a comprehensive pension scheme that the Social Democrats and Agrarians had been unable to reach agreement on. Kekkonen first mediated the interest-group negotiations and then humiliated the Agrarian party leaders into accepting the compromise. He did so by forcing his way into an Agrarian party central committee meeting that was about to reject the compromise and, with media representatives in tow, berating the committee into acceptance.[29]

Following elections in 1975, all of the parties were again reluctant to govern. In order to force the Agrarians' hand, Kekkonen appointed a retired Agrarian leader as Prime Minister designate and insisted that no one else was acceptable. The Agrarians, who had hoped for the formation of a minority Social Democratic government, were compelled to govern or repudiate their former leader.[30] The Social Democrats and Communists were loath to participate in a government of any type because they did not want to be associated with the recession that Finland was then experiencing.[31] When a minority coalition of the Agrarians and the two liberal parties was about to be formed, Kekkonen made the most dramatic intervention of his career. Calling media representatives and all party leaders to his home for what was assumed to be a routine event, Kekkonen proceeded to shame the party leaders for half an hour on national television. In perhaps the most forceful speech ever given by a Finnish politician, he insisted that they form an oversized government within three days, that the only issue it should concern itself with was reducing unemployment, that they were not to bother with a detailed program, and that ministries should be distributed according to the size of each party's Eduskunta fraction. It was a remarkable performance. And it succeeded. Within three days a government of the Communists, Social Democrats, Agrarians, and the two liberal parties was in office.[32] Kekkonen again intervened, although less dramatically, in the formation of popular front governments in 1977 and 1979.[33]

The President's efforts were not always with effect. The Communists were sometimes too paralyzed by internal conflicts to participate in government. As well, Kekkonen was not always able to persuade the Social Democrats and Agrarians to serve together. In such instances, the outcome was a minority government led by one of the two parties. At other times, Kekkonen was unable to get any of the major parties to serve in any government. When this was the case, the outcome was a caretaker administration of civil servants. Finland had three of these governments between 1970 and 1979 (Aura I, Aura II, and Lininamaa I). They governed for a total of eleven months.

The Unconsolidated Democracy

The President's interventions entered the government-formation process as a kind of exogenous variable. Because he was not subject to the same pressures that party leaders were subject to, he was able to exert a powerful personal influence. He was instrumental in bringing the Communists into the 1966 coalition, which in turn eased the polarization in the labor market. He played a necessary role in the making of subsequent oversized governments and labor-market negotiations. It may be that an unconsolidated democracy can only develop where such a powerful nonparty actor exists. In any case, it is clear that it is only in an unconsolidated democracy that the personal preferences of a politician can be decisive with any regularity in government formation. In other democracies, there is no actor whose preferences are not dependent on the attributes of the system and the role requirements of party leadership.

The existence of such a politician in the unconsolidated democracy makes it impossible to predict government membership according to the model presented in part one. That model allowed us to deduce limits of tolerance elsewhere because system-level variables were compatible with each other. They did not place party leaders under contradictory pressures. In Finland, however, the system-level attributes—extreme corporatism and extreme party polarization—simultaneously urge politicians to cooperate and to avoid cooperation. The former urges them to defer cooperation from government formation to the alternative sites that corporatism provides. The latter urges them not to cooperate at all. These contradictory pressures provide ideal circumstances in which a determined President can intervene.

Party leaders tended to deal with their dilemma by striving to avoid coalition participation *and* cooperation outside of the cabinet during most of the 1970s. In place of the latter, they found it more congenial to leave much of the burden with the interest groups. The problem for party leaders has been that effective governance requires that the parties cooperate either inside or outside the cabinet. In the absence of the President's interventions, party leaders might, as they often did in the 1950s and early 1960s, have opted for ineffective governance as the less risky choice.

There is some evidence that in the late 1970s and early 1980s the system was becoming less dependent on presidential interventions. The first coalition formed under Kekkonen's successor, a coalition of the Social Democrats, Agrarians, and liberal parties, required no presidential intervention. As well, the corporatist practices now seem firmly institutionalized in the economy and are no longer dependent on Communist participation in the government. Indeed, the unions have grown increasingly independent of the Communist and Social Democratic parties. One clear sign of this has been the parties' call for proportional representation in union elections. Like conservative parties earlier in the century, they have wanted the rules changed to insure their own presence.[34] The Communist party has become less important as a source of party polarization. The Stalinist wing has declined in size and become a clear minority while reformists have become a dominant majority and, if not unambiguous members of the democratic circle yet, have moved closer to it. The democratic-antidemocratic cleavage itself has become less salient as years of Communist participation have passed. There are also some first, impressionistic signs of the emergence of a new elite political culture of the kind found in consensual democracies. Voitto Helander has written:

> Considerable evidence of the changed atmosphere was given by a congress convened by the government in the Korpilahti Hotel in autumn 1977.... The aim of the meeting was to influence the opinions of the politicians, administrators, and interest group leaders and thus to improve the atmosphere between these groups. The principal outcome was that the Finnish political terminology became enriched with a new term, "the spirit of Korpilampi," which means an improved atmosphere of cooperation between the elites of society. Altogether, the changes that have taken place in the Finnish political "elite culture" in recent years have smoothed over possible crises between the [parties and interest groups].[35]

It would be premature to suppose that Finnish democracy will continue to evolve in this way. But the transformation has been a remarkable one thus far and has been all the more so because it is a rare example of democratic stabilization by peaceful, internal change. In the concluding chapter, after summarizing the evidence in support of the hypotheses for the other systems, I will close by comparing the recent Finnish and Italian experiences.

CHAPTER EIGHT

Conclusions

Theory and Evidence

The path of causality developed in part one began with the transition from oligarchic to mass democratic rule. I argued that societies which experienced smooth transitions acquired unpolarized party systems. Those which had rough transitions developed enduring legitimacy problems reflected in the presence of antidemocratic parties and polarization. Where an unpolarized party system was combined with corporatist institutions, the result was a consensual democracy. Where it was not, the result was a competitive democracy. Where a political system lacked established legitimacy and corporatist institutions, the outcome was a conflictual democracy. Where corporatist institutions developed on top of a polarized party system, the result was what I called an unconsolidated democracy.

A second historical dimension involved the development of the individual parties. Parties which were instrumental in articulating a societal cleavage acquired an enduring profile on the cleavage. These profiles reflected the party's *raison d'être* and became a constant focus of policy concern. Within the profiles parties developed relatively coherent values.

I then took as axiomatic that party leaders are motivated above all by a desire to remain party leaders and that they will therefore attempt to minimize the extent to which questions of participation in governments become sources of conflict within their parties. They will therefore rest decisions to participate on the issues that generate the least dissension within their parties: those that engage within-profile principles of policy direction.

System attributes acquire importance by affecting the risks to their tenure that party leaders experience in making governments. Given that the system attributes are not readily manipulable and that the desire to remain a party leader is a constant one, the choices leaders make assume a predictable pattern.

The core of the argument as it applied to consensual democracies was that the consensus-building institutions and processes generated by corporatism provide a range of sites beyond the cabinet in which conflicts among parties can be resolved. Politicians find their interests best served by deferring policy compromises to these alternative sites, because their responsibility for concessions is then lessened. They, therefore, have a strong inducement not to compromise relevant preferences in government negotiations.

Corporatist interest structures make it difficult for any government to implement policies that are not widely embraced by the affected interests. Corporatism and an unpolarized party system together generate an elite political culture in which arbitrary policy decisions are widely viewed as illegitimate. For these reasons, the leaders of other parties have little defensive inducement to compromise their supporters' preferences for the sake of being in government. In view of the low incentive to compromise, the limit of tolerance should be the convergent relationship.

The theory was tested against ten Danish government formations in chapter 5. It could predict and explain the party composition of eight of these. It could not account for the 1957 Social Democratic–Radical–Justice coalition and the 1973 minority Liberal government. It failed in the first case because the three parties made explicit compromises. It failed in the

Conclusions 235

second case because convergent preferences were expected to lead to a coalition of the Liberals, Radicals, Conservatives, and Center Democrats. The single-party outcome that actually occurred is best explained by the centrifugation unleashed by the 1973 election and the Liberal formateurs' calculation that this could be more readily accommodated if a single centrist party formed the government. The test results for the Danish and other cases have been summarized in table 8.1, which appears at the end of this chapter. Readers may find reference to the table helpful in following the discussion below.

The theory has also been tested against fifteen governments formed in Sweden and Norway between 1955 and 1975.[1] These cases have been abstracted in appendix B. The theory could not account for the nonsocialist coalition that took office in Norway in 1965 and the Social Democratic–Agrarian coalition formed in Sweden in 1956. It failed in the Norwegian case because the four parties—the Conservatives, Liberals, Agrarians, and Christians—subordinated their policy differences to their mutual desire to end three decades of Labor party hegemony. These relationships could not be properly classified because it was the desire to form the government that led to the policy preferences rather than the obverse. Their appetites whetted by the experience of one month of coalition government in 1963, the four parties tailored their policies in 1964 and 1965 to their desire to form a government after the 1965 election, if that election produced a nonsocialist majority. Once they had won the election, they still did not hold the usual policy negotiations. Instead, negotiations were limited to who would gain the premiership and to the distribution of other portfolios.

The theory's other failure occurred in not predicting the Social Democratic and Agrarian coalition that was formed in Sweden in 1956. In this case, the formateurs decided that implicit concessions were not too great a price to pay for a majority government. The Agrarians agreed that the implicit compromises were outweighed by the benefits of participation.

There were 103 bargaining relationships between

formateurs' parties and the other democratic parties when these twenty-five governments were formed in the three consensual democracies. The theory could satisfactorily predict and explain the place of the second party in government or opposition in 91 of these 103 relationships. The 12 failures occurred when the governments discussed in the previous paragraph were formed. Of these 103 relationships, 81 were divergent. In only 4 of the 81 divergent relationships did one or both parties express a willingness to make the divergences implicit. On one occasion the formateurs rejected the offer (Denmark, 1955). On the other three occasions, the offer was accepted and led to the formation of two governments that could not otherwise have obtained majority status (Denmark, 1957; Sweden, 1956). In one other case (Norway, 1965), the relationships could not be classified, but it is certain that the four parties forming the government subordinated their policy differences for the sake of creating a nonsocialist majority.

The six other majority governments that appeared in consensual democracies between 1955 and 1975 were based on convergent relationships. The other sixteen governments that were formed during these years were minority governments. Seventy-seven divergent relationships existed when these minority governments were formed. In none of these relationships did either party express a detectable willingness to make the relationship divergent-implicit, even though the outcome would otherwise be a minority government.

In conflictual democracies the absence of alternative policymaking sites and the absence of a consensual culture make government formation a primary site for the resolution of party conflicts. The polarization induced by antidemocratic parties, creating a culture of hostility and suspicion, makes minority governments short-lived and places a premium on defensive participation. Polarization also places a premium on the creation of coalitions for the defense of the constitutional order. And when it is induced by an antidemocratic party, it creates a process of reciprocal delegitimization among parties and increases the policy distances between them. For party leaders, the meaning of these system attributes is found in reduced autonomy. Their freedom to create compromises is reduced because of the objective distances between parties, because of the difficulty of persuading their followers to accept compromises, and because of the tenuousness of their leadership positions. The acute polarization makes convergent preference relationships exceedingly rare. It also makes the risks of explicit compromises prohibitive for party leaders. The inference is that the limit of tolerance will be the divergent-implicit relationship.

Finland as a conflictual democracy provided us with eight governments. If we discount the effects of Soviet interventions on several bargaining relationships, the theory was able to predict and explain seven of the eight government formations. The single case of failure occurred in 1958, when one party declined to participate for nonpolicy reasons. Thirty-six bargaining relationships occurred during the formation of these eight governments. Three of them were decisively shaped by Soviet intervention. Another, mentioned above, was decided by nonpolicy calculations. The remaining thirty-two were based only on policies. All of the thirty-two led to outcomes anticipated by the theory.

The theory has also been tested against the seventeen governments formed in Italy between 1955 and 1975.[2] These cases have been abstracted in appendix B. The theory could satisfactorily predict and explain ten of these seventeen governments. For the seven other governments the theory failed because one or more parties based its decisions at least partly on nonpolicy calculations. Sixty-one bargaining relationships existed between the democratic parties and formateurs' parties when the seventeen governments were formed. Forty-seven led to outcomes that could be predicted and explained by the theory. The fourteen others were based on nonpolicy calculations.

Ninety-seven relationships have been examined across the twenty-five governments in Finland and Italy, and seventy-nine of the relationships produced outcomes that were consistent with the theory. There were no cases of failure when the participants defined the relationships entirely in policy terms. The eighteen relationships which led to outcomes we could not account for were all based decisively on nonpolicy calculations. We will return to these below when we consider the deviant cases in more detail.

Competitive democracies lack the variety of institutionalized alternative sites for conflict resolution that corporatism provides consensual democracies. They also lack the normative commitment to consensual politics that corporatism and an unpolarized party system together create.

The absence of corporatism and of a normative commitment to consensual politics make government formation a central site in the resolution of party conflicts, make minority governments short-lived, and encourage defensive participation. Lacking a polarized party system, leaders in these democracies do not suffer the reduction of autonomy that their counterparts in conflictual democracies experience. For the same reason, the elite culture is not one of intense hostility and suspicion. It might best be called a pragmatic culture. Leaders have substantial autonomy.

In undominated-competitive democracies, politicians making governments cannot expect the governments to last more than briefly unless they are majority governments. The scarcity of tangential and convergent preference relationships means that these will seldom provide a sufficient basis on which to make a majority government. But because of the majority premium, other parties will have little incentive to be satisfied with implicit compromises. In consequence, the government formed will be that combination of the formateurs' party and other parties which is both winning and based on minimal explicit compromises. This is the classical coalition situation.

In dominated-competitive democracies, the only opportunity a party has to influence policy is in government with the dominant party. But the dominant party can pick and choose among a range of potential partners and, given its size and ideological centrality, manipulate the conflicts among these potential partners. Oversized governments reduce the threat of policy blackmail and are therefore in the dominant party's interest if they can be arranged without excessive policy concessions. They normally can be because of the importance of defensive participation to flank parties. Since the dominant party is irreplaceable, its formateurs have little incentive to grant explicit concessions. Since oversized governments enhance their party's authority and since the divergent-implicit relationship will enhance the size of the government, they do have an incentive to accept such relationships. Other parties have an incentive to accept them because of the lack of alternative opportunities to participate and because of the premium the system attaches to defensive participation. The inference is that the limit of tolerance will be the divergent-implicit relationship.

Israel as a dominated-competitive democracy provided us with thirteen governments, eleven of which could be anticipated by the theory. The first failure occurred in 1952, when the formation of the government was made partly dependent on nonpolicy concessions as well as unanticipated policy concessions. The second occurred in 1961, when unanticipated policy concessions were again granted.

We looked at eighty-six relationships across these Israeli governments and found that seventy-six of them led to expected outcomes and did so for policy reasons that the theory could explain. Seven of the ten failures were attributable to the appearance of nonpolicy demands. The other three unpredicted outcomes occurred when unexpected policy concessions were made.

The theory has also been tested against the experience of the four Dutch governments that were formed between 1955 and 1967.[3] The studies of these governments are abstracted in appendix B. Two of the four governments were predicted correctly. A third government was also, save the nonparticipation of one party on nonpolicy grounds. In the fourth case, the dominant party, the Catholic party, made explicit concessions to several parties as the price of gaining their participation in a government. During the formation of these four governments, 16 bargaining relationships occurred; 15 of them were based only on policy questions, and 12 of the 15 led to outcomes that could be predicted and explained by the theory. For both Israel and the Netherlands together, then, thirteen of seventeen governments and 88 of 102 relationships were compatible with the theory.

Across all sixty-seven of the government formations in the seven countries, there occurred 302 bargaining relationships: 258 of the relationships led to outcomes predicted by the theory and explicable in terms of it; 27 of the 44 outcomes that could not be accounted for could not be because nonpolicy demands or motivations were decisive.

In 16 of these, the nonpolicy motivation was induced by centrifugation in the party system. In these cases, parties found themselves torn by whether to cooperate with a party on the left or right; or suffered major electoral losses because of such bilateral competition; or refused to join a government unless it included an electorally menacing flank party. Thirteen of these 16 relationships were found in Italy. As we saw in chapters 6 and 7, the frequent use of civil service governments in Finland conceals this manifestation of centrifugation to some extent. Were it not for the use of this rather unique pressure valve, the number of nonpolicy relationships would have been still greater in conflictual democracies. While these civil servant governments eased and concealed centrifugation, they were simultaneously caused by it. They invariably came into existence because parties were paralyzed by the pressures of bilateral competition. The three remaining instances in which bilateral competition was decisive occurred, appropriately enough, in Denmark in the wake of the 1973 "protest election." The concentration in conflictual democracies of outcomes affected by bilateral competition, although reducing the predictive power of the theory, certainly provides another form of confirmation of the model on which the theory is built. When the theory failed in these cases, it failed for reasons compatible with the model.

The other instances of failure are less easily classified. Six occurred in consensual democracies and were motivated by the desire to form majority governments (Norway, 1965; Sweden, 1956; and Denmark, 1957). The three formations suggest that, contrary to the stark terms in which the consensual model was cast, the majority consideration is occasionally important in these democracies. But only occasionally. For six of the nine majority governments were based only on convergent relationships. And sixteen minority governments were formed because larger governments would have required implicit or explicit concessions. None of these sixteen minority governments was based on a secure parliamentary majority. Preserving preferences thus dominated the majority motive on sixteen of the nineteen occasions on which formateurs had to choose between the two goals. Again, then, the theory seems to have been substantially confirmed.

One final empirical point needs to be made. I postulated that in dominated-competitive and in conflictual democracies, formateurs would not make explicit concessions to gain the support of a party. They would not do so in the former because their party's dominant position meant that they did not need to do so. They could not do so in the latter because of the threat to their leadership that such concessions would pose. The theory has been tested against forty-two government formations in the two kinds of democracies. In only three of these forty-two governments did the formateurs grant explicit concessions (Israel, 1952 and 1961; the Netherlands, 1963). The evidence, then, is that the theory is a credible one. It has received considerable empirical support.

Finland, Italy, Corporatism, and the Problem of Regime Stabilization

It has become commonplace to observe that the most corporatist democracies have been the democracies best equipped to cope with the economic crises of the 1970s and

1980s and the declining governability of Western societies.[4] Yet none of the democracies that lacked corporatist institutions in the 1960s, save Finland, was successful in creating them in the 1970s. If corporatism does make regimes more governable, and the evidence of the past chapter is that it does, its benefits are most needed in conflictual democracies. A comparison of Finland with Italy, where corporatism failed to take root in the 1970s, may shed some light on the preconditions of corporatism in conflictual democracies.

The two countries shared many characteristics in the early 1960s. Both were governed by center-right coalitions that sought the exclusion from power of Communist parties and trade unions. Both had party systems that were acutely polarized, with socialist parties pulled both ways by adjacent Communist and centrist parties. The outward pull of party competition meant that even the parties that governed found cooperation difficult. Governments were thus short-lived, and the agreements on which they were based were meaningless. The same issues reappeared regularly until they grew into crises that compelled the parties to act. Above all, the ruling coalitions in the two countries shared a common problem: declining electoral support compelled them to find a new governing formula.

They responded to their deteriorating positions in ways that produced divergent developmental paths. Finland entered an era of political depolarization and labor-market cooperation accompanied by a more stable political order and one of the better Western records of economic growth, price stability, and employment in the 1970s.[5] Italy experienced the convulsions of the Hot Autumn, economic stagnation cum rapid inflation, polarization, and even a sense for a time in the mid-1970s that the regime was on the brink of collapse.[6] From rather similar starting points in the early 1960s, then, one regime became more governable than it had been at any time in its history while the other became synonymous with crises and ungovernability.

Any account of these divergent paths must consider

Conclusions 243

the effects of corporatization in Finland and take as its starting point the different responses of the ruling coalitions to the crises of their governing formula. The Christian Democrat–led coalition in Italy responded by drawing the Socialist party (PSI) into the circle of governing parties. Mathematically, at least, this solved the problem of creating a ruling majority. But in practice the new coalition was no more effective than the old. The PSI, unable to deliver the social reforms it promised and under constant attack from the Communist party on its left, suffered a massive loss of credibility. The reforms could not be delivered because, with the party system so polarized, neither the Christian Democratic (DC) nor PSI leaders who supported the coalition could affort to make the hard compromises of their respective middle- and working-class interests that agreements required.[7] The PSI, being originally the party of change, was the bigger loser in this situation.

The opening to the left was superseded in the mid-1970s by the "Andreotti Solution": cooperation between the DC and PCI in making policy without actually bringing the PCI into government and concurrent attempts to arrange cooperation among the government, union, and employers. Both yielded only limited results. The PCI withdrew its support of the Andreotti government in 1978 when it concluded that, like the PSI before it, it was losing credibility in exchange for few tangible gains in power or policy. The incorporation of interests never proceeded far beyond participation of the unions in the administration of some social, especially pension, benefits. The unions were ever ready to give the government economic advice but refused to participate in a formal incomes policy. The largest union, the PCI-affiliated CGIL, demanded PCI participation in the government. It is not certain that the other unions would have been willing to join in an incomes policy if the CGIL had been persuaded to, but it is certain that they would not join without it.[8]

In contrast to the Italian experience, the Finnish ruling coalition responded to its weakened electoral position after the 1966 election by bringing both the Social Democratic and

Communist parties into the government. There was nothing exceptional about the return of the Social Democrats to government. Until the 1958 crisis in Soviet-Finnish relations, they had been a regular member of government since World War II. The inclusion of the Communist party was exceptional. We have already considered the circumstances surrounding this decision.[9]

The inclusion of the Communists critically affected the party system and labor market in ways that were preconditions of corporatization and are one-half of the explanation for the success of corporatization in Finland and its failure in Italy. In the first place, the inclusion of the Communists relieved the Social Democrats of the burden of constant harassment from their left whenever they compromised with the nonsocialist parties. In the second place, it profoundly shifted the center of gravity in the government. The center-right lost its dominance and was forced to accommodate the left in a way that the Italian Christian Democrats have never experienced. Had only the Social Democrats been included, the centrist Agrarian party would have remained at the center of the governing parties in much the same way that the cautious left of the DC did in Italy. In the third place, Communist participation provoked a split in the party between unreconstructed Stalinists and reformists that weakened the extreme left of the party system. It also provided reformers in the party with a rationale for a more cooperative attitude toward the Social Democrats. Thus, in relieving the Social Democrats of attacks from their left, in forcing the Agrarians to accommodate the left, in provoking the Communist party split, and in bolstering the position of the communist reformers, the participation of the Communists eased the polarization of the party system.

These changes in turn had important consequences for the labor market. Corporatism required centralization of authority within trade union confederations and greater cooperation among the confederations. With both working-class parties in government, trade union leaders were relieved of the burden of competition within the unions between supporters of a party in government and a party in opposition. Having both parties in government also legitimized cooperation with the government and the centralization that cooperation required. And it eased cooperation between the Social Democrat–and Communist–affiliated confederations. Above all, of course, union cooperation with the government was made easier because the union's political allies were now a part of the government and could be relied on to defend union interests in the cabinet. The situation would have been quite different had only the Social Democratic party been in government, for the trade union movement would then have been divided between support for and opposition to the government.

Improved relations among the unions and among the unions, government, and employers, in turn, made cooperation among the parties easier. We saw repeatedly in chapter 7 that broad coalitions were dependent for their formation on the prior resolution by labor-market groups of conflicts that also divided the parties. Thus the relationship between cooperation in the party system and in the labor market was a reciprocal one: cooperation in one domain contributed to cooperation in the other.

If Communist participation was a precondition of this, it was only an initial one. For we found that once the unions became engaged in the corporatist processes, they developed interests in them that were independent of the parties. Party influence in the unions declined, and the corporatist institutions continued to develop when the Communist party withdrew from government. The lesson is that the working class, however it is represented in a particular party system, must have united representation in the cabinet in the early years of corporatization.

The second distinction between Finland and Italy that helps account for the success of corporatization in Finland and its failure in Italy is to be found in the existence in Finland of a powerful political institution—the presidency as it was transformed by Uhro Kekkonen—independent of the parties and labor-market groups. Unlike his Italian counterparts, Kekkonen had the resources to pressure the labor-market groups and parties into cooperating when they were loath to do so. Kekkonen probably played a decisive role in the original decision to admit the Communists into the cabinet. Chapter 7 leaves no doubt that his personal interventions were critical to party and labor-market cooperation in the first decade after 1966. Finnish party leaders could not—as their Italian counterparts probably cannot—bring such changes about by themselves because of the extreme caution the precariousness of their positions forces on them.

One of the most striking features of the case studies, and especially of the studies of Finnish and Italian government formation, is the almost complete absence of evidence that the skills, ideologies, and aspirations of individual politicians made any difference in the final coalition outcome. That is, there is little evidence of politicians successfully creating coalitions other than those that would be created by party leaders concerned only to remain party leaders. Politicians in Finland and Italy especially did not use government negotiations as an occasion to change attitudes among their followers or to bridge conflicts with other parties. Indeed, the overwhelming thrust of their behavior was to avoid resolving conflicts, because to do so would put their own careers at risk. This ingrained conservatism reflects the peculiarly low level of autonomy of party leaders in conflictual democracies. It is because of this, too, that the changes that occurred in Finland are unlikely to occur in Italy and other conflictual democracies in the absence of a President or comparable figure with the authority to change the behavior of party leaders.

Table 8.1 Consolidated Results

Country	Governments			Bargaining Relationships				
	Number	Successfully predicted	Rate of success (in %)	Total number of relations	Successfully predicted	Rate of success* (in %)	Number of policy relations[†]	Rate of success[‡] (in %)
Denmark	10	8	80.00	45	37	82.22	42	88.09
Sweden	7	6	85.71	21	20	95.23	21	95.23
Norway	8	7	87.50	37	34	91.89	37	91.89
Consensual democracies	25	21	84.00	103	91	88.34	100	91.00
Finland	8	7	87.50	36	32	88.88	32	100.00
Italy	17	10	58.82	61	47	77.04	49	95.91
Conflictual democracies	25	17	68.00	97	79	81.44	81	97.93
Israel	13	11	84.61	86	76	88.37	79	96.20
Netherlands	4	2	50.00	16	12	75.00	15	80.00
Dominated-competitive democracies	17	13	76.47	102	88	86.27	94	93.61
Total	67	51	76.11	302	258	85.43	275	93.47

*This is the percentage of outcomes successfully predicted within the total universe of relationships.
[†]This is the number of bargaining relationships defined by participants solely in terms of immediate policy preferences.
[‡]This is the percentage of relationships successfully predicted strictly within the universe of policy relationships.

APPENDIX A

Methodological Notes

The Limits of the Theory and the Selection of Test Cases

One of the theory's central propositions is that decisive policy preferences can be known by studying the historical crises and challenges that shaped party profiles. This limits the theory to multiparty democracies with proportional representation. It was only in such democracies that a party, once established, could be relatively confident of a place—of whatever size—in the party system by mobilizing those voters motivated by profile issues. In majority and plurality electoral systems, parties are compelled, except where their constituency is geographically concentrated, to make general appeals across cleavages and to attempt to aggregate as many interests as possible. This has the effect of substantially "washing-out" the original profiles and, when they can be identified at all, making them poor predictors of coalition behavior. Thus the theory should fit only democracies with proportional representation: Norway, Sweden, Denmark, Finland, Belgium, the Netherlands, West Germany, Italy, Austria, Ireland, Iceland, Israel, Spain, Portugal, Weimar Germany.

Appendix A

A further limit to the theory, following from the requirement that profiles be formed and preserved, is that the theory does not apply where parties arose as a recent response to a rapid transition from authoritarianism to democracy. Parties formed in such circumstances will often lack well-formed profiles. If the democratic order was established suddenly as a result of a collapse of an authoritarian regime, and most of the parties played no role in bringing about the change, they will have only a weak sense of identity and organization in the early years of the democratic order. This means that we cannot account for coalition behavior in such regimes as Republican Spain, and in the new democracies of Greece, Portugal, and Spain. Roy Macridis' characterization of the Greek parties is much to the point. They exhibit

> lack of membership; lack of internal organization; lack of institutionalized forms of selecting leaders and for establishing leader and rank-and-file relationships; internal party decentralization, with emphasis on local and regional party bosses; and the lack of a coherent program. Party members vote in different ways in the parliament even if belonging to the same party, and powerful magnates and their followers frequently desert one party to join another. In Greece, parties have been personal creations holding together as long as the leader remained present.[1]

This characterization also applies to many of the parties that have existed in the brief periods of Portuguese and Spanish democracy.

An authoritarian interlude as such does not preclude the application of the theory. We can test it against cases of Italian government formation. The Italian parties have roots that precede the Fascist period. And by their role in the resistance, the liberation, and the immediate postwar years, the parties played a decisive role in the birth of the democratic order. In doing so, they established themselves in Italian society and gained a certain stability of profiles.

The Weimar Republic, like the modern Greek regime, was a regime that came about by default. But the Weimar parties did have origins that preceded the establishment of the regime, and on this count the theory should apply. Yet, among all of the Weimar coalitions, only three were parliamentary-based, noncrisis governments. The others were formed either in periods of acute emergency or were personality-based governments with no definite support in the Reichstag. Indeed, among these latter, most could survive only so long as they could rule by presidential decree or so long as the Reichstag was prorogued.[2] Normal parliamentary politics, then, was only exceptionally a feature of the republic. Crisis governments—governments formed when the survival of the regime is immediately threatened—require a different kind of explanation.

When these limits are entered, we are still left with almost all of the European parliamentary democracies. The theory should be applicable to Norway, Sweden, Denmark, Belgium, the Netherlands, Ireland, Germany, Iceland, Finland, Austria, and Italy. It should also account for the Israeli experience.

The hypothesis for consensual democracies has been tested against all government formations in Denmark, Sweden, and Norway between 1955 and 1975. The hypothesis for conflictual democracies has been tested against all of the governments formed in Italy between 1955 and 1975 and in Finland between 1955 and 1966. The hypothesis for dominated-competitive democracies has been tested against the governments formed in Israel between 1950 and 1975 and against those formed in the Netherlands between 1955 and 1967. The hypothesis for the undominated-competitive democracies does not require testing. So cases from Ireland, Belgium, Iceland, and the Federal Republic of Germany have not been used. These countries have been undominated and competitive for most or all of the postwar period. The time frame—generally, 1955–1975—was chosen arbitrarily. The governments formed in Israel between 1950 and 1955 were included to increase the number of cases in the undominated-competitive type. The study of the Finnish governments stopped in 1966 because it was at this point that the transition to the unconsolidated type began. That change is considered separately in chapter 7. The study of the Dutch governments stopped in 1967 because it was at that point that the party system became undominated. The post-1967 experience is reviewed in chapter 3.

The Dependent Variables

There are two dependent variables: the government formed and the bargaining relationships on which the government was based. In the first instance, using the predicted limit of tolerance, we predict the party composition of the government. All parties that meet the limit are expected to be in the government. The predicted government can then be compared with the actual government. In this, the government is the unit of analysis.

A second approach, which provides us with a much larger number of cases, is to use the relationship between the formateurs' party and each of the other democratic parties in the legislature as a dependent variable. We compare the predicted limit with the relationship that exists between the formateurs' party and each party in government and outside of it. Of course, when the predicted government conforms perfectly with the actual government, the predicted limit of tolerance will be the same as the observed limit. But when the predicted government does not match the observed government, the mismatch could occur because a single relationship or every relationship was unanticipated. Using the individual relationship as the dependent variable permits a more sensitive test of the theory.

Identifying Parties and Governments

The first requirement of a party is that it have at least one profile. Parties that are formed on the basis of personalities are not defined as parties. In the countries against which the theory is tested, such parties are rare and short-lived.

Methodological Notes

Even if it has a profile, a party is not always relevant to the outcome. A criterion of relevance defined in terms of a percentage of legislative seats is unsatisfactory, because it can lead us to ignore small parties whose existence is decisive. Alternatively, it can lead us to count larger parties whose existence is of no consequence. A party is relevant when its presence in the legislature can affect (assuming party discipline) whether a government is formed.

The most basic consideration in the formation of a government is whether it has any prospect of legislative success. Stated otherwise, the question is: When is a party so small that its existence can make no difference positively or negatively to a prospective government's legislative success? The general rule is that a party is of such size whenever it is numerically incapable of making a necessary contribution to any legislative majority (assuming a 50-percent-plus-one-vote requirement) the prospective government might construct while in office.

Take the hypothetical example of a legislature with 150 seats, a majority requirement of 76, a distribution of seats as follows, and E as the formateurs' party.

PARTY	A	B	C	D	E	F	G
SEATS	45	13	4	9	50	26	3

With E the party of the formateur, there exist three possible legislative majorities: EF (76), EA (95), and EBCD (76). There is no possible winning combination in which G is relevant. If A had been the party of the formateur, a potential winning combination would have existed in which G was a necessary member: ACFG (78). Thus, in the first instance, G would be defined as irrelevant; in the second, it would be relevant. In the first, with or without G, the formateur and later the Prime Minister must recruit the same amount of support from other parties, whether as members of the government or independent parties in the legislature, to obtain legislative success. This element of the definition of a relevant party eliminates only a few legislative groups, and they are usually those already excluded by the profile requirement. They are noted on a case-by-case basis in part two.

There is a final question: When is a party a single party, and when is it actually two parties allied with each other? A party is defined here as a group that places candidates for office on a single list. In the event of an interelection merger, the two parties become one when they adopt a common parliamentary caucus. Likewise, one party becomes two if separate caucuses are established.

To sum up, a legislative group will be classified as a party when it has at least one profile, has numerical relevance to some legislative majority the formateur might construct, and places candidates for office on a single list or holds a common parliamentary caucus.

A party is classified as a member of government when at least one of its representatives holds a cabinet position and its pertinent decision-making body (the parliamentary party, central committee, leadership bureau, as the case may be) endorses participation in the government. The only exception to this is in the event of a party of such small size that it does not receive a cabinet position because of its smallness, but nonetheless binds itself to the government through formal endorsement.

A new government is considered to have been formed (a) in the wake of a parliamentary election, (b) whenever the party composition of the government is altered by the entrance or withdrawal of one or more parties, and (c) whenever the previous government is brought down by a parliamentary vote or the Prime Minister's submission of its resignation, except when the resignation was purely technical. These criteria were selected because they constitute the principal occasions on which parties are required to overtly negotiate with each other and state explicitly their attitudes toward a hypothetical government and its program.

Caretaker governments are excluded from the study. By caretaker, I mean those governments formed to hold office only until an impending election and those formed only to remain until a political agreement can be reached among parties; or until it is agreed that negotiations have broken down and only a minority, but politically competent, government can be formed. A politically competent government is one with the clear and committed support of at least one parliamentary party.

The Empirical Procedures

Each chapter in part two begins with an analysis of the origins of a party system. These are intended not to be comprehensive histories, but to identify the cleavages on which parties that survived into the test period acquired profiles. The studies of individual governments are likewise highly selective. They ignore the process of negotiations, various bargaining ploys, personality clashes, and so forth, except where they are decisive for the final outcome. I am only concerned to predict and explain the final outcome.

The heart of the task is to identify for each party the dominant policy preferences within its profiles. These preferences are then compared with the preferences of the formateurs' party to determine whether the bargaining relationships are tangential, convergent, or divergent. The comparisons are made on the basis of positions held prior to the negotiations. In the event of divergent preferences, it is necessary to determine whether in negotiations one or both parties agreed to an implicit or explicit compromise or refused to alter its position.

The classification assigned to each relationship is not an attempt to average the policy components of the relationship. The classification reflects the highest relationship type that exists in the entire relationship of the two parties. If, for example, three policy questions exist, on one of which the parties have tangential positions, on another of which they have convergent preferences, and on the third of which they have divergent-implicit preferences, the relationship is divergent-implicit.

If the parties are concerned with the same issue, but initially have divergent preferences, the conflict can be handled in several ways, and determining the relationship type requires that we compare prenegotiation positions with postnegotiation positions. The decisive point is that in an implicit compromise the parties do not, by joining a government, obligate themselves to support a definite policy at variance with their initial preference. In an explicit compromise, they do so obligate themselves.

There will always be a compromise of one type or the other. When conflicting preferences exist before negotiations, it is not possible for parties to conclude negotiations and form a government without announcing publicly how the conflict was dealt with. On the issues that I have defined as government-formation relevant, it is virtually impossible for the parties to make a secret pact, because the policy basis of the new government must be approved by party bodies. Since negotiations capture the almost undivided attention of the media and party dissidents, it is virtually impossible to win secret approval of major policy concessions. The consequence is that we can always gain an accurate understanding of the outcome from publicly available sources.

APPENDIX B

Case Summaries for Sweden, Norway, the Netherlands, and Italy

The summaries that follow are abstracted from case studies similar to the studies that appear in the main body of the book. The abstracts identify the issues that were critical in each coalition negotiation and the bargaining relationships that the issues created. The abstracts allow readers with specialized knowledge of the individual countries to compare their understanding of the key issues with ours. For brevity's sake, the abstracts are limited to policy questions that arose among parties that were both relevant (see appendix A) and proregime. They do not provide explanations of the issues, their origins, and resolution. Nor do they provide background information on party politics. Thus, the nuances and subtleties are omitted. In the Italian abstracts, for instance, Christian Democratic positions were normally classified as those of the party's dominant center-left, even though the DC right frequently exerted a decisive influence on coalition negotiations through its ability to obstruct the implementation of agreements. Readers interested in more complete analyses may obtain copies of the full-length studies from me. The definitions and rules of classification and case selection that are discussed in the main text and in appendix A were employed in these studies also.

For each country I have provided an introductory table that identifies the cleavages on which each party was assigned a profile. This table is followed by a brief textual discussion of the policy questions relevant to each government formation and a table that summarizes the bargaining relationships on each issue between the party of the formateur and the relevant, proregime parties. I also note the expected outcome and the actual outcome and explain briefly any discrepancies between them. The findings for each country are summarized and reviewed in chapter 8.

Sweden: 1955–1975

The 1956 Social Democratic–Agrarian Government

The Social Democratic party had the formateurship. The first issue involved the universal, obligatory national pension scheme on which the Social Democrats had recently campaigned. Only the Communists endorsed the idea. Following extensive negotiations, however, the Agrarians and the Social Democrats agreed to disagree, with the former claiming that they would not be taking a final position until the appearance of a party committee report scheduled for the next year.

The second issue turned on family assistance payments (*barn-bidragen*): whether parents should be eligible to receive the payments after the birth of the first child or only after the birth of a second child. The Conservatives and the Liberals demanded the elimination of the payments after the first child, whereas the Social Democrats wanted them increased. More generally, the Conservatives and Liberals wanted across-the-board cuts in social spending. They also called for a general reduction in income tax rates. By contrast, the Social

Table B.1 Policy Profiles of Swedish Parties

	Cleavages			
Party	Socioeconomic	Consumer-producer	Center-periphery	Regime
Conservatives	+			
Liberals	+			
Agrarians	+	+	+	
Social Democrats	+	+	+	
Communists*	+			+

*The Swedish Communist party is not a "relevant" party. See the definition of relevant party in appendix A.

Democrats were committed to increases in social expenditures and were at this time examining various tax increases.

Contending economic strategies provided the third issue. The Social Democrats' primary concern was full employment, and their preferred policy was one that kept interest rates low and stable. By contrast, the Conservatives and Liberals were concerned about inflation and were committed to using a deflationary monetary policy.

The fourth issue involved forest lands. The Agrarians demanded that the government provide smallholders with subsidized credit that would enable them to purchase state-owned and absentee-owned forest lands. The Social Democrats were opposed to the proposal. Fifth, the Agrarians wanted the government to provide the smallholders with easier credit for general investment. The Social Democrats rejected this request, yet both parties agreed to provide a credit subsidy through a budgetary proposition. The subsidy would also be available to small industry, a constituency of greater interest to the Social Democrats. In effect, the parties were able to turn a divergent preference into a tangential one. Sixth, the Agrarians demanded the removal of the urban-rural pay differentials for public employees. The Social Democrats opposed this. The two parties agreed to study the question once in government.

Despite three implicit differences with the Agrarians, the Social Democrats were willing to include them in a

Appendix B

Table B.2 Parties' Relationships with the Social Democrats (1956)

Party	Issues					
	Obligatory pensions	*Social spending*	*Economic management*	*Forest lands*	*Agricultural investment assistance*	*Pay differentials*
Conservatives	divergent	divergent	divergent	no profile	no profile	no profile
Liberals	divergent	divergent	divergent	no profile	no profile	no profile
Agrarians	divergent-implicit	convergent	convergent	divergent-implicit	tangential	divergent-implicit

government. None of the issues on which the two parties disagreed were of the sort that required immediate policy action. Even the pension question would not face a definitive Riksdag decision for at least a year. The outcome is contrary to the expectations of the theory.

Expected outcome: a Social Democratic minority government.
Actual outcome: a Social Democratic–Agrarian coalition.

The 1957 Social Democratic Government

The Social Democratic party received the formateurship. After an inconclusive referendum, the pension issue came to dominate the agenda. As previously, the Social Democrats favored an obligatory scheme. The other parties wanted to keep the voluntary formula. Yet this time the Social Democratic and Agrarian leaders were no longer willing to disagree; in February 1957, the Agrarian party had made public its negative report on the question.

Expected outcome: a minority Social Democratic government.
Actual outcome: same.

The 1958 Social Democratic Government

Faced with the rejection of their pension proposal in the second chamber, the Social Democratic government dissolved the chamber and scheduled new elections. The campaign focused entirely on the pension issue and resolved nothing. Again, no party expressed an interest in making the conflict implicit; the government outcome was a minority Social Democratic government.

Expected outcome: a minority Social Democratic government.
Actual outcome: same.

The 1960 Social Democratic Government

The Social Democrats retained the formateurship. The pension issue was still the dominant issue, although it no longer overshadowed all other issues. The Social Democrats'

Table B.3 Parties' Relationships with the Social Democrats (1960)

Party	Issues	
	Pension fund	State deficit
Conservatives	divergent	divergent
Liberals	convergent	divergent
Agrarians	divergent	divergent

obligatory scheme was now established, but not yet accepted by the Conservatives and the Agrarians (also known since 1958 as the Center Party).

A second issue sprang from the budget deficit. The Social Democrats had previously been able to obtain the passage of a legislation establishing a 4 percent sales tax. The Conservatives wanted the tax repealed. Instead, they wanted the deficit made good by the cancellation of first-child family assistance payments, cuts in housing subsidies, cuts in school expenditures for meals and textbooks, and reduced communal support. The Liberals and Agrarians, too, wanted the tax repealed, but wanted the deficit to be financed by state borrowing. No party expressed an interest in making the conflicts implicit.

Expected outcome: a minority Social Democratic government. Actual outcome: same.

The 1964 Social Democratic Government

The Social Democrats again had the formateurship. Four issues were on the table. The Conservatives were still trying to limit the size of the national pension fund. They proposed that the resources of the existing system be drawn on to pay pensions to individuals outside the fund's scope: invalids and individuals born before 1896. The Conservatives' proposal was resisted by all the other parties. The state budget deficit still provided the second source of conflict. The Social Democrats proposed to remove the tax-exempt status of pension contributions, mostly paid by the middle class. All the bourgeois parties rejected the proposal. The Conservatives wanted expenditure cuts rather than tax increases. The Liberals argued for an increase in the pension-fund-contributions rate from 4 to 5 percent and increased indirect taxes on cigarettes, alcohol, and so forth. The Agrarians wanted no changes in the pension fund contributions but supported the increases in indirect taxes that the Liberals proposed.

A third issue involved the corporate purchase of agricultural and forest lands. Seeking some rationalization, the Social Democrats wanted to give companies that used agricultural and forest products as raw materials access to the land market. The Agrarians opposed the proposal on the grounds that the increased land prices it would set in train would make it more difficult for small farmers to enlarge their holdings. The two parties also disagreed on the issue of regional development, with the Social Democrats wanting to base state aid on criteria of national efficiency and the Agrarians arguing that it be made available to all municipalities in development regions—mainly in the North and West. By the same token, the Agrarians opposed the Social Democrats' plan to reduce public works employment for the seasonally unemployed in Norrland province. Whereas the Social Democrats preferred programs to transfer surplus labor from such regions to the South and East, the Agrarians wanted expanded employment programs in the depressed regions. No party leaders expressed an interest in making the relationships divergent-implicit and forming a government on that basis. This government remained in office until it was replaced by a majority Social Democratic government after the 1968 elections. That government then remained in power until the elections of 1970.

Expected outcome: a Social Democratic minority government.
Actual outcome: same.

The 1970 Social Democratic Government

The Social Democrats retained the formateurship. Three issues divided the parties. First, the Social Democrats had proposed a tax reform, of which the net effect would be to shift

Table B.4 Parties' Relationships with the Social Democrats (1964)

Party	Pension fund	Budget deficit	Land market	Regional development
		Issues		
Conservatives	divergent	divergent	no profile	no profile
Liberals	convergent	divergent	no profile	no profile
Agrarians	convergent	divergent	divergent	divergent

the tax burden more toward higher incomes. The Agrarians and the Liberals endorsed the reform. The main opposition came from the Conservatives, who, instead, made proposals that would reduce taxes on individuals in upper brackets.

Second, the bourgeois parties objected to two Social Democratic government economic measures: a credit freeze and an investment tax on a selected range of enterprises. The bourgeois parties proposed instead a negotiated incomes policy, presumably accompanied by agreements on prices, investment, and taxes. The Agrarians and Liberals, in addition, wanted the V.A.T. raised immediately to reduce domestic demand. The Social Democrats refused to employ indirect taxes as instruments of demand management (as opposed to social goals).

The third issue was again regional development. To stem the depopulation of the less developed regions, the Agrarians wanted growth controls placed on major population centers—controls on further building, investment, and job creation. Committed to policies that encouraged the migration of the unemployed to the South, where labor was in short supply, the Social Democrats could not agree. No party leaders expressed an interest in making the policy conflict implicit and establishing a coalition on that basis.

Expected outcome: a minority Social Democratic government. Actual outcome: same.

The 1973 Social Democratic Government

The Social Democrats had the formateurship. First, in response to growing unemployment and sluggish growth, all

Case Summaries

Table B.5 Parties' Relationships with the Social Democrats (1970)

	Issues		
Party	Tax reform	Economic management	Regional development
Conservatives	divergent	divergent	no profile
Liberals	convergent	divergent	no profile
Agrarians	convergent	divergent	divergent

of the bourgeois parties demanded tax reductions. The Social Democrats rejected any tax reductions that were not offset by other tax increases or agreements among labor-market organizations. The second issue involved the Social Democrats' proposal to raise the minimum capital requirements for stock companies, which were widely used as a tax shelter. It was strongly opposed by the bourgeois parties.

The National Pension Insurance Fund offered the third point of conflict. The Social Democrats had passed legislation vesting the fund with the authority to buy unlimited shares of stock in private enterprises. The legislation was viewed by bourgeois parties as an unprecedented expansion of state power.

The fourth and fifth issues pitted the Social Democrats against the Agrarians. The former wanted to establish a system of taxation on forest lands and subsidies for reforestation that would accelerate the harvesting of old timber stocks. The Agrarians opposed the program, because it would discriminate against small farmers and reduce the individual farmer's control over the disposition of his product. Moreover, the Agrarians wanted primary responsibility for local planning vested in county assemblies (*landstingen*), whereas the Social Democrats wanted it to remain the responsibility of country administrations (*lansstyrelserna*). The former solution would produce a distribution of resources across the county, while the latter emphasized efficiency and thus concentration.

No party leaders expressed an interest in making the conflicts implicit. That the Social Democrats were unwilling to

Table B.6 Parties' Relationships with the Social Democrats (1973)

| | Issues | | | | |
Party	Tax reductions	Capital requirements	Pension fund	Forest program	Local planning
Conservatives	divergent	divergent	divergent	no profile	no profile
Liberals	divergent	divergent	divergent	no profile	no profile
Agrarians	divergent	divergent	divergent	divergent	divergent

make the differences implicit in this instance is particularly important because the government would have a minority status even if it could assume the support of the Communist party.

Expected outcome: a minority Social Democratic government. Actual outcome: same.

Norway: 1954–1975

The 1961 Labor Party Government

From 1955 to 1961, Norway was governed by Labor party majority governments. At the 1961 elections, Labor lost its majority. It retained the formateurship. Five issues divided the parties. NATO membership was the first. All the parties with a foreign policy profile supported membership, except for the Socialist People's party. EEC membership was the second issue. The Socialist People's party rejected membership. The Agrarians and the Christians did not want more than a treaty of association. (For these two parties the relevant profiles were consumer-producer, and cultural and moral. This is discussed in more detail in the study of the 1971 government.)

The Socialist People's party demanded that the next government nationalize private banks and insurance companies. Labor proposed instead that greater public control of bank activity be gained by requiring that one-quarter of each private bank's directors be appointed by communal governments. This was opposed by all of the nonsocialist parties and by the Socialist People's party.

Case Summaries

Table B.7 Policy Profiles of Norwegian Parties

Party	Socio-economic	Center-periphery	Consumer-producer	Cultural-linguistic	Moral-religious	Foreign policy
Conservatives	+	+		+	+	+
Liberals (1954–1973)*	+			+		
Christians	+	+		+	+	
Agrarians	+	+	+	+		
Labor	+	+	+		+	+
Socialists†	+					+

*In 1973, the Liberal party split into two parties—the Liberals and the New People's party. Neither had relevance.

†The Socialist People's party was unrepresented from 1969 until 1973, when it formed the Socialist Alliance with the Norwegian Communist party.

Income and indirect taxes provided the fourth point of conflict. The nonsocialist parties wanted across-the-board rate reductions; they opposed an increase in indirect taxes. By contrast, Labor would not support income tax reductions and wanted increases in taxes on tobacco, alcohol, and gasoline to finance enlarged spending on social programs.

Assistance for less developed regions provided the final point of conflict. Labor proposed the targeting of public and private investment in a few regional centers. It also proposed that the development fund be financed by a special tax. The Agrarians and Christians responded by saying that such concentration would compound the problems of outlying areas and argued for a more equal distribution. Further, except for the Liberals, all nonsocialist parties preferred to have the fund sustained by regular budgetary appropriations.

With all parties in the Storting, then, Labor had divergent relationships. None of the parties expressed a willingness to make these conflicts implicit.

Expected outcome: a minority Labor government.
Actual outcome: same.

Table B.8 Parties' Relationships with Labor (1961)

Party	Issues				
	NATO Membership	EEC Membership	Control of Banks	Taxation	Regional Assistance
Conservatives	convergent	convergent	divergent	divergent	divergent
Liberals	no profile	convergent	divergent	divergent	no profile
Christians	no profile	divergent	divergent	divergent	divergent
Agrarians	no profile	divergent	divergent	divergent	divergent
Socialists	divergent	divergent	divergent	convergent	no profile

The 1963 Conservative–Liberal–Agrarian–Christian People's Party Government

Following the scandal of the "King's Bay Affair," the King offered the formateurship to the second largest party, the Conservatives. At issue were NATO membership (see above), the subsidization of basic foodstuffs, and taxation. The Conservatives opposed the previous Labor government's commitment to stabilize food prices through increased subsidies for producers. Conservatives wanted the price increases passed on to consumers. The other bourgeois parties sided with the Conservatives. By contrast, the Socialist People's party shared Labor's preference. The third issue was taxation. Labor and the Socialist People's party demanded an increase in the automobile registration tax and a gasoline tax increase. The other parties opposed this.

No party leader expressed an interest in making the differences implicit.

Expected outcome: a minority Conservative-Liberal-Agrarian-Christian government.
Actual outcome: same.

The 1963 Labor Party Government

The Labor party received the formateurship. The issues and bargaining relationships were the same as they had been a month earlier, when the Conservatives formed the previous government. From table B.9 we can see that Labor had

Table B.9 Parties' Relationships with the Conservatives (1963)

Party	NATO membership	Food prices subsidies	Tax increases
Liberals	no profile	convergent	convergent
Christians	no profile	convergent	convergent
Agrarians	no profile	convergent	convergent
Labor	convergent	divergent	divergent
Socialists	divergent	convergent	divergent

no convergent relationship with any other party. Again, no party leader expressed the interest in making the conflicts implicit. As the theory would predict, the formateur formed a minority government on its own.

The 1965 Agrarian–Conservative–Liberal–Christian People's Party Government

The formateurship passed from the Labor party to the four bourgeois parties. In addition to NATO membership, five issues were on the table. The Liberals wanted to reverse Labor's policy of restricting investment in housing. They proposed a program that would encourage lenders to increase such investments and encourage market activity. The other nonsocialist parties endorsed the Liberals' proposal. Second, Labor's measures to increase state control on bank loans were opposed by all bourgeois parties. More generally, whereas Labor emphasized public saving, the other parties emphasized private saving. A similar cleavage divided the parties on a third issue: whether the government should intervene to tie the annual wage and producer price settlements and limit the former to productivity increases. While the nonsocialists supported the measure, the two socialist parties opposed it.

A fourth issue was regional development. Whereas Labor wanted to pursue a development scheme that maximized the efficient use of investments from a national perspective, the Agrarians and the Christian People's party were concerned with insuring that investments were made in the periphery.

The final point of conflict was between the Christian People's party and Labor. The former wanted the state to increase support for Christian private schools, wanted communities to have the right to extend the number of hours weekly of religious instruction given in public schools, and wanted the establishment of a Christian teachers' college. Labor opposed all of this.

In the absence of a clear formateurs' party, we cannot draw the kind of table we used in previous cases to summarize the bargaining relationships. Although all the nonsocialist parties had divergent relationships with the two socialist parties on one or more issues, they all had convergent relationships among themselves. However, convergence is not the appropriate concept in this case. During the six months preceding the elections, the parties intentionally overlooked their differences so that, if they received a Storting majority, they would be able to form a government together. Once the majority was obtained, the parties avoided policy discussions and, instead, concentrated the negotiations entirely on the distribution of ministries. The desire to form a particular government determined the bargaining relationships, rather than the bargaining relationships determining the government formation. Therefore, the theory succeeds neither in predicting nor explaining the outcome.

The 1969 Agrarian–Conservative–Liberal–Christian People's Party Government

The Agrarian party nominally had the formateurship, although, in fact, the role was again acted out in a collegial fashion. Two issues dominated the negotiations. The first was tax reform. The nonsocialists wanted a reduction in the progressiveness of the income tax rates, especially on upper incomes. In addition to a smaller V.A.T., Labor wanted the opposite: higher wealth and property taxes, and the elimination of the tax exemption the nonsocialists had introduced for savings accountants. Abortion provided the second issue. Labor wanted a liberalization of the abortion law; the Christian People's party defended the prevailing restrictive law. The other

Table B.10 Parties' Relationships with the Agrarians (1969)

	Issues	
Party*	Taxation	Abortion
Conservatives	convergent	no profile
Liberals	convergent	no profile
Christians	convergent	tangential
Labor	divergent	divergent

*The Socialist People's party had no representatives in this Storting.

bourgeois parties expressed sympathy for the Christian party position.

Expected outcome: an Agrarian-Conservative-Liberal-Christian government.
Actual outcome: same.

The 1971 Labor Party Government

Labor had the formateurship. Two issues dominated Norwegian politics at this time. First, EEC membership. Only Labor and the Conservatives favored membership. The Agrarians feared the devastation of the uncompetitive Norwegian agricultural sector. They also argued that membership would further diminish local control over investments and regional developments. The Christians shared the Agrarians' concern about the further peripheralization of the Norwegian periphery. They added a moral concern, contending that membership would accelerate the secularization of Norwegian society and threaten traditional values. The Liberals were divided, with the rural wing opposing membership and the urban wing supporting it.

Second, the Conservatives and Labor were in conflict over public spending and taxation. Labor wanted an increase in state spending matched by an increase in revenues. The revenues would be gained through increased railroad fares, increased charges for electric power, telephones, telegrams, and telexes. The party also wanted to increase the National Insur-

Table B.11 Parties' Relationships with Labor (1971)

Party	Issues	
	EEC membership	Public spending and taxation
Conservatives	convergent	divergent
Liberals	no coherent policy	divergent
Christians	divergent	divergent
Agrarians	divergent	divergent

ance Fund premiums for employers. The Conservatives opposed all of this. So did the other nonsocialist parties.

No party leaders expressed an interest in making the conflicts implicit as a basis for government.

Expected outcome: a minority Labor government.
Actual outcome: same.

The 1972 Christian People's–Agrarian–Antimarket Liberal Party Government

After the negative results of the referendum on EEC membership, the resigning Labor government could only be replaced by an antimarket government. The Christian People's party received the formateurship. EEC membership was the sole issue. Only the Agrarians and the rural wing of the Liberal party (now established as the Antimarket Liberal party) opposed membership. The Conservatives, Labor, and the urban wing of the Liberals had campaigned in its favor.

Expected outcome: a Christian–Agrarian–Antimarket Liberal government.
Actual outcome: same.

The 1973 Labor Party Government

Labor received the formateurship. Five issues stirred Norwegian politics. The question of EEC membership was kept alive by the Conservatives, who pledged to work for it in the

Case Summaries

Table B.12 Parties' Relationships with Labor (1973)

Party	EEC membership	NATO membership	Inflation	Religious education	Abortion
Conservatives	divergent	convergent	divergent	no profile	no profile
Christians	convergent	no profile	divergent	divergent	divergent
Agrarians	convergent	no profile	divergent	no profile	no profile
Socialists	convergent	divergent	convergent	no profile	no profile

next Storting. For Labor, however, the fight was over; it adopted the associate relationship negotiated with the EEC by the previous government.

NATO membership came back on the political agenda with the reentry in the Storting of the Socialist People's party through an electoral alliance—called the Socialist Alliance—with the Norwegian Communist party. The Socialist Alliance wanted Norway to withdraw from NATO; all the other parties with a foreign policy profile opposed the withdrawal.

A third issue was the management of price increases. Labor wanted the income tax reduced on the lower half of the scale. It also proposed a substantial reduction in private investment. The Conservatives, and with them the Agrarians and Christians, wanted an incomes policy based on coordinated wage and price settlements and the establishment of a council to administer the settlement. Labor refused, contending that it was unworkable.

The fourth issue involved the Christian party's proposals to make religion a mandatory component of the high school curriculum. It also wanted to revise the existing law on public support of private Christian schools. Labor opposed all of this. The liberalization of abortion provided the last issue (see 1969 government). No party leaders expressed an interest in making the conflicts implicit as a basis for government.

Expected outcome: a minority Labor government.
Actual outcome: same.

Table B.13 Policy Profiles of Dutch Parties

Party	Cleavages	
	Socioeconomic	Religious
Liberals (VVD)	+	+
Antirevolutionary Party (ARP)	+	+
Christian Historical Union (CHU)	+	+
Catholic People's Party (KVP)	+	+
Social Democrats (PvdA)	+	+

The Netherlands: 1956–1966

The 1956 PvdA–ARP–CHU–KVP Government

PvdA nominally received the formateurship, but KVP was the dominant party and *de facto* holder of the formateurship. Eight issues played a central role in the negotiations. The first issue involved rent control. The Socialists agreed on the need for an increase in regulated rents, but insisted on regulations or a tax that would prevent owners of rental units from receiving excessive profits. All nonsocialist parties opposed this.

The second issue involved private investment in housing. The Socialists favored increased public investment. The nonsocialists wanted tax changes that would help future home owners to save the necessary down payments. The third issue turned on income tax reduction. The nonsocialist parties wanted the reduction; the socialists preferred to expand social services and public investment. The elimination of the investment tax deduction provided the fourth point of conflict. Only the Socialists supported the elimination; all the others opposed it. The fifth issue involved the continuation of wage and price controls. The Socialists supported the continuation, whereas the nonsocialist parties opposed it.

The sixth issue turned on whether individuals should be entitled to substitute private health insurance for the mandatory public insurance. All parties, except the Socialists, agreed that individuals should be provided with this alternative. The seventh issue was whether to drop the legal prohibition against civil service employment for married women. Only the KVP wanted it retained. Last, the debate focused on the issue of higher education spending, with KVP requesting an increase for Catholic institutions. All other parties opposed the increase.

The outcome of the negotiations was an agreement to disagree across all issues. Although the parties agreed to join the government, none of them agreed to endorse the program. The program was only an agreement among ministers, and all of the parties in government reserved the right not to support it. Eventually, VVD rejected participation because it was dissatisfied with the distribution of portfolios among its party leaders and wanted to avoid an internal confrontation.

Expected outcome: a PvdA-ARP-CHU-KVP-VVD government.
Actual outcome: a PvdA-ARP-CHU-KVP government.

The 1959 KVP–ARP–CHU–VVD Government

KVP received the formateurship. The old issues were still active, pitting the Socialists against the nonsocialists. In addition, the Socialists demanded that wage settlements be advanced and made contingent on rent increases. They also insisted on the establishment of price controls on agricultural land. Two other issues were on the agenda. First, the tax financing the general family allowance. KVP supported the allowance and tax, whereas VVD, ARP, and CHU did not. This conflict was reinforced by a second one over changes in funding for various denominational and secular universities.

On all these disputes, the parliamentary groups agreed to disagree. The parties per se agreed to join the government, but none agreed to endorse the program. One exception to this pattern was the PvdA; the party insisted on explicit

Table B.14 Parties' Relationships with the KVP (1956)

Party	Issues							
	Rent control	Housing investment	Income tax reductions	Investment tax deduction	Wages and prices controls	Private health insurance	Married women employment	Higher education spending
VVD	convergent	convergent	convergent	convergent	convergent	convergent	convergent	divergent-implicit
ARP	convergent	convergent	convergent	convergent	convergent	convergent	convergent	divergent-implicit
CHU	convergent	convergent	convergent	convergent	convergent	convergent	convergent	divergent-implicit
PvdA	convergent divergent-implicit	convergent divergent-implicit	convergent divergent-implicit	convergent divergent-implicit	convergent divergent-implicit	convergent divergent-implicit	convergent divergent-implicit	divergent implicit

*For explanation of abbreviations, see table B.13.

Table B.15 Parties' Relationships with the KVP (1959)

		Issues			
Party*	Wages and prices controls	Investment tax incentives	Rents	Family allowance	University Funding
VVD	convergent	convergent	convergent	divergent-implicit	divergent-implicit
ARP	convergent	convergent	convergent	divergent-implicit	divergent-implicit
CHU	convergent	convergent	convergent	divergent-implicit	divergent-implicit
PvdA	divergent-explicit	divergent-explicit	divergent-explicit	convergent	divergent-explicit

*For explanation of abbreviations, see table B.13.

compromises and demanded that the program be binding on the parliamentary groups. As a result, its differences with the KVP remained explicit.

Expected outcome: a KVP-ARP-CHU-VVD government.
Actual outcome: same.

The 1963 KVP–ARP–CHU–VVD Government

KVP had the formateurship again. The debate on the family allowance continued. KVP wanted an increase in the allowance. CHU and ARP wanted pension increases instead. The Socialists supported both measures, whereas the Liberals opposed both and urged legislation that would allow individuals to opt out of the compulsory health insurance program.

Tax reduction was the second issue. VVD wanted reductions, the other nonsocialist parties were ambivalent, supporting rather a reduction in the progressiveness of the income tax. The Socialists opposed both a tax reduction and a reduction in the progressiveness. The third issue involved price controls on agricultural land. The Socialists wanted such controls; the KVP and VVD firmly opposed them. Housing policy provided the fourth point of conflict. Although KVP and the Social-

Table B.16 Parties' Relationships with the KVP (1963)

	Issues				
Party*	Family allowance and pension increases	Tax reduction	Price controls on land	Home construction	Commercial television
VVD	divergent-explicit	convergent	convergent	divergent-explicit	divergent-implicit
ARP	divergent-explicit	convergent	no policy	divergent-explicit	convergent
CHU	divergent-explicit	convergent	no policy	divergent-explicit	divergent-implicit
PvdA	divergent-explicit	divergent-explicit	divergent-explicit	convergent	convergent

*For explanation of abbreviations, see table B.13.

ists favored working-class and public housing, the liberals and ARP favored middle-class and private sector housing.

The fifth issue involved the establishment of commercial television, the amount of broadcast time the different pillars of the Dutch consociational society would receive, and the criteria that would be used to allocate this access. KVP, ARP, and PvdA, the parties most satisfied with existing arrangements, wanted the most restrictions on new broadcast facilities. By contrast, CHU and VVD, the least satisfied, wanted the most liberal access.

KVP, ARP, CHU, and VVD agreed to form a coalition based on divergent relations and explicit compromises. The theory entirely fails to explain this outcome; instead, it predicts that KVP would not need to make such concessions.

Expected outcome: a minority KVP government.
Actual outcome: a KVP-ARP-CHU-VVD government.

The 1965 KVP–ARP–PvdA Government

KVP had the formateurship. The television broadcasting issue remained unresolved. CHU now insisted that KVP make explicit concessions on the access criteria, and VVD re-

Case Summaries

Table B.17 Parties' Relationships with the KVP (1965)

	Issues		
Party	Television Broadcasting	Price Controls on Real Estate	Oil and Gas Development
VVD	divergent-explicit	convergent	convergent
ARP	convergent	convergent	convergent
CHU	divergent-explicit	convergent	convergent
PvdA	convergent	divergent-implicit	divergent-implicit

*For explanation of abbreviations, see table B.13.

quested similar concessions on the legalization of Radio Veronica, the access criteria, and the issue of commercialization. KVP refused. Once this issue was disposed of, the negotiations concentrated on the differences between the Catholics and the Socialists: whether price controls should be imposed on real estate and whether the government should participate in oil and gas development. The two parties decided to refer the former difference to the Social-Economic Council; they agreed to the "possibility" of such participation as regards the latter.

Expected outcome: a KVP-ARP-PvdA government.
Actual outcome: same.

Italy: 1955–1975

The 1955 DC–PSDI–PLI Government

In all of the governments studied below, the DC formed the government. Except as noted, it was actually the DC center-left which formed the governments. As a result, DC policies are usually defined as those of the center-left. One of the constant features of these governments was the gulf that separated the DC from the PCI, MSI, Monarchists, and, for a time, the PSI. That gulf was created above all by the latter parties' hostility, or what the DC perceived to be hostility, to the constitutional order. This basic division was reinforced by

Appendix B

Table B.18 Policy Profiles of Italian Parties

Party	Cleavages			
	Socio-economic	Foreign policy	Clerical-anticlerical	Regime
Monarchists (Mon)	+			+
Neo-Fascists (MSI)	+			+
Liberals (PLI)	+	+	+	
Christian Democrats (DC)	+	+	+	
Republicans (PRI)	+	+	+	
Social Democrats (PSDI)	+	+	+	
Socialists (PSI)	+	+	+	until 1963
Communists (PCI)	+	+	+	+

many policy conflicts. The studies below (and the test of the theory) are limited to the relationships among the proregime parties. We shall pay closer attention to the PSI's policy preferences as we approach its break with the PCI and its entrance into the circle of democratic parties.

Among the democratic parties, four issues were on the table in 1955. The first involved the conditions under which a landowner could remove a tenant farmer. The DC position was to require that landowners demonstrate "just cause" for evictions during the first nine years of a contract. The second issue involved the so-called Vanoni Plan, or more generally the question of whether any comprehensive, coordinated program of state intervention in the economy should be adopted. The DC supported such a program. The third issue turned on whether the *Enti Nazionale Idrocarburi* (E.N.I.) should have the exclusive right to develop recently discovered Po Valley oil and gas deposits. The DC (or its dominant center-left) thought so.

On the first issue, the PSDI and the PRI insisted that the owner had no right to evict during the life of the contract. The PLI insisted on an unconditional right of eviction. Only the PSDI and the PLI were willing to defer the issue to a study group. On the second and third issues, only the PLI was in disagreement. Yet the PLI agreed to diagree, confident in both

Case Summaries

Table B.19 Parties' Relationships with the DC (1955)

	Issues		
Party*	Sharecropper tenancies	Vanoni plan	E.N.I.
PLI	divergent-implicit	divergent-implicit	divergent-implicit
PRI	divergent-explicit	convergent	convergent
PSDI	divergent-implicit	convergent	convergent

*For an explanation of abbreviations, see table B.18.

cases that the DC right would join in with it in sabotaging unsatisfactory measures if they appeared in parliament.

Expected outcome: a DC-PSDI-PLI government.
Actual outcome: same.

The 1957 DC Government

The old conflicts over landlord-tenant relationships, the Vanoni Plan, and Po Valley oil and gas remained. On the first, DC's position had changed somewhat; it now stipulated six conditions under which a landowner could evict a tenant. To these issues was added a new one: whether the state should nationalize the telephone service. The DC advocated nationalization.

On the first issue, the positions of the PRI, PSDI, and PLI had not changed, except that the PRI and the PLI were no longer willing to defer the issue. On the next two issues, planning and the Po Valley oil and gas, positions were unchanged. On the telephone issue, only the PLI opposed nationalization. Unlike the DC, the PLI, PSDI, and PRI were now unwilling to defer these issues. The PRI and PLI felt the need to distance themselves from the DC in view of the upcoming elections. The PSDI was torn apart by internal conflicts and wanted to avoid a coalition agreement that would only aggravate these conflicts.

Expected outcome: a DC minority government.
Actual outcome: same.

Table B.20 Parties' Relationships with the DC (1957)

	Issues			
Party*	Sharecropper tenancies	Planning	E.N.I.	Telephone
PLI	divergent-explicit	divergent-explicit	divergent-explicit	divergent-explicit
PRI	divergent-explicit	convergent	convergent	convergent
PSDI	divergent-explicit	convergent	convergent	convergent

*For an explanation of abbreviations, see table B.18.

The 1958 DC–PSDI Government

The first issue was a law that would guarantee the validity of collective labor agreements. The DC endorsed the proposal. The PLI opposed it. The second issue turned on the renewal of the Fund for the South. The DC supported the renewal. The Vanoni Plan was still at issue. Positions were unchanged. A fourth issue involved the legislation that would nationalize the production and distribution of electrical power and guarantee workers in this industry the right to participate in plant management. The DC had no clear position on this demand and was only willing to commit the next government to a study of the matter. The PSDI was the only party to have a clear position (in favor); but it accepted the DC's offer to study the matter. Finally, the DC was committed to a ten-year plan of school construction and a raising of the school-leaving age to fourteen. The PSDI and PRI shared the DC's commitment. The PLI would not commit itself to these programs, but neither would it reject them.

The PLI insisted on explicit concessions as the quid pro quo for its cooperation. The DC refused to go along. The PRI removed itself from the negotiations for reasons the theory does not anticipate: it insisted that the DC negotiate with the PSI. In effect, the PRI understood that unless the left wing of the governing circle was reinforced, the DC would not be able to win legislative approval of the governmental program because of the DC-right opposition.

Expected outcome: a DC-PRI-PSDI government.
Actual outcome: a DC-PSDI government.

Case Summaries

Table B.21 Parties' Relationships with the DC (1958)

	Issues				
Party*	Labor contracts	Fund for South	Planning	Electric power	School
PLI	divergent-explicit	divergent-explicit	divergent-explicit	divergent-explicit	no policy
PRI	convergent	convergent	convergent	no policy	convergent
PSDI	convergent	convergent	convergent	divergent-implicit	convergent

*For an explanation of abbreviations, see table B.18.

The 1959 DC Government

The issues were the same as in the previous case. Yet this time two parties were unwilling to consider joining a DC-led government. The PRI continued to insist that the DC negotiate with the PSI. The PSDI was unwilling to join a coalition because of internal conflicts that followed from the secession of its left wing (which formed the Moviménto Unita Italiano Socialista). Only the PLI remained available in principle, but it continued to demand explicit concessions, and DC negotiators were unwilling to grant these.

Expected outcome: a DC-PRI-PSDI government.
Actual outcome: a DC minority government.

The 1960 DC Government

The PRI and the PSDI continued to refuse to participate in a DC-led government that did not engage the PSI in direct negotiations. However, the regime commitment of the PSI remained ambiguous in the eyes of the DC leaders. In addition, the PSI continued to reject Italian membership in NATO and in the EEC and the stationing of U.S. Jupiter missiles on Italian soil. These foreign policy conflicts were supplemented by the PSI's insistence that the DC government would have explicitly to commit itself to nationalization of the electric power industry. The DC would not commit itself to do more than study this.

The PLI, the only democratic party available, had divergent-explicit relationships with the DC on three new issues. It was opposed to DC proposals that would provide the state with authority to regulate monopolies. It also opposed a DC-sponsored "Green Plan" for agriculture, a program premised on state provision of subsidized credits for smallholders. And it rejected a DC plan to structure electric power rates in a way that subsidized agriculture and the South. In addition to these new disagreements, the PLI remained opposed to legislation that made collective bargaining agreements binding on employers. On the entire range of issues, the PLI expressed no inclination to make these disagreements implicit.

Expected outcome: a DC-PRI-PSDI government.
Actual outcome: a DC minority government.

The 1962 DC–PRI–PSDI Government

Although they included for the first time the PSI, negotiations were limited to a program on which collaboration in the legislature could be based. The DC continued to define the democratic circle as including only itself, the PRI, PLI, and PSDI.

Many issues were at stake, most of which we have already encountered: economic planning, the nationalization of the electric industry, the "Green Plan" for agriculture, and various subsidies for the South. Two new issues involved educational reforms. First, provided that church-run schools were granted financial parity, the DC supported the establishment of a system of secular, state-supported kindergartens and nursery schools. Second, the DC supported legislation establishing a unified national middle-school system. At stake was the substance of the curriculum; specifically, whether it would include mandatory Latin instruction. The DC wanted Latin included.

The PSI, PSDI, and PRI were all campaigning to reduce the role of the church in education and opposed the principle of financial parity. They also opposed obligatory Latin instruction, on the grounds that it reinforced class discrimination

Case Summaries

Table B.22 Parties' Relationships with the DC (1962)

Party*	Issues				
	Economic planning	Electric industry	Agriculture and South	Financial parity	Latin courses
PLI	divergent-explicit	divergent-explicit	divergent-explicit	divergent-explicit	convergent
PRI	convergent	divergent-implicit	convergent	divergent-implicit	divergent-implicit
PSDI	convergent	divergent-implicit	convergent	divergent-implicit	divergent-implicit

*For an explanation of abbreviations, see table B.18.

in Italian education in favor of children of middle- and upper-class backgrounds and that the humanistic, spiritual orientation such instruction implied was exactly contrary to the historical, material, and empirical worldview they wanted conveyed. Yet in both cases of disagreement, the issues were left unresolved when the government was formed. The PLI wanted mandatory Latin courses, but opposed the creation of a state system of kindergartens and nursery schools as well as state support for the church-sponsored schools. It refused to make these conflicts implicit.

Expected outcome: a DC-PRI-PSDI government.
Actual outcome: same.

The 1963 DC–PSDI–PRI–PSI Government

After the secession of its left wing (which formed the Partito Socialista Italiano de Unita Proletaria), the PSI and the DC were, for the first time, willing to discuss PSI participation in a DC-led government. The issues of Latin instruction and financial parity for church schools were and remained unresolved. The parties likewise remained divided on the meaning of economic planning; while the PLI opposed any planning, the DC, PSDI, and PRI wanted limited, indicative planning, and the PSI proposed the imposition of obligatory investment programs on private industry. The parties agreed to disagree.

Three new issues were on the agenda. First, the DC

Table B.23 Parties' Relationships with the DC (1963)

Party*	Lay education	Economic planning	Property speculation	Tenants legislation	Regional governments
PLI	divergent-explicit	divergent-explicit	divergent-explicit	divergent-explicit	convergent
PRI	divergent-implicit	convergent	divergent-implicit	convergent	divergent-implicit
PSDI	divergent-implicit	convergent	divergent-implicit	convergent	divergent-implicit
PSI	divergent-implicit	divergent-implicit	divergent-implicit	convergent	divergent-implicit

*For an explanation of abbreviations, see table B.18.

opposed legislation that would empower municipalities to expropriate real estate at below-market prices to curb speculation. The PSDI, PRI, and PSI wanted this legislation. The parties agreed that the new government would study the problem and pass legislation to curb speculation. The crucial issue of how this would be done was ignored. Second, the DC supported legislation that would force landowners to sell their land to the sharecroppers who worked it as tenancy contracts expired; the DC also supported legislation providing tenants with subsidized credits to make this possible. This was supported by all parties save the PLI. Third, the DC opposed the establishment of the regional governments originally mandated by the 1948 constitution. This was supported by the PSI, PRI, and PSDI and opposed by the PLI. The coalition parties agreed only to "study" the question.

The PLI required explicit concessions as the price of its cooperation. Such concessions would have precluded DC cooperation with the PSI, PSDI, and PRI.

Expected outcome: a DC-PSDI-PRI-PSI government.
Actual outcome: same.

The 1964 DC–PRI–PSDI–PSI Government

Six issues divided the parties. Three of them have already been explained in previous cases: state subsidies to church schools, legislation that would eliminate sharecropping, and the establishment of regional governments. On all these issues, party positions remained unchanged. The fourth, economic planning, was becoming a greater source of division, with the PLI opposed to it, the DC wanting targets, the PRI and PSDI advocating indicative planning, and the PSI wanting obligatory planning. The fifth concerned escalating urban real estate prices. The DC now took the position that below-market expropriation was permissible, but only when it was part of a detailed and approved program of urban planning. The DC was opposed to the legislation that would require municipalities to formulate such plans and that would provide the financial support that expropriation required. Last, the DC and its previous partners supported a package of tax increases. The PLI opposed the tax increases.

On all points of disagreement, the DC and its coalition partners avoided concessions by agreeing only to very general goals.

Expected outcome: a DC-PRI-PSDI-PSI government.
Actual outcome: same.

The 1966 DC–PSU(PSI+PSDI)–PRI Government

The 1964 government fell when DC integralists broke ranks with the government and voted down a proposal to establish a system of state-supported nursery schools and kindergartens. The DC reformed the four-party coalition. The issues and parties' positions were unchanged from the previous governments. So were the expected and actual outcomes.

Expected outcome: a DC-PSU(PSI+PSDI)-PRI government.
Actual outcome: same.

The 1968 DC–PSU(PSI+PSDI)–PRI Government

Four issues were debated. First, the devolution of limited authority to regional governments. A devolution bill passed in 1967 did not provide for election procedures or finances. The DC was divided: most of all it sided with the PRI

Table B.24 Parties' Relationships with the DC (1964)

Party*	Issues					
	Church schools	Share-cropping	Regional government	Economic planning	Urban planning	Tax increases
PLI	divergent-explicit	divergent-explicit	convergent	divergent-explicit	convergent	divergent-explicit
PRI	divergent-implicit	convergent	divergent-implicit	divergent-implicit	divergent-implicit	convergent
PSDI	divergent-implicit	convergent	divergent-implicit	divergent-implicit	divergent-implicit	convergent
PSI	divergent-implicit	convergent	divergent-implicit	divergent-implicit	divergent-implicit	convergent

*For an explanation of abbreviations, see table B.18.

and PSU (the outcome of the 1966 merger between the PSI and the PSDI) in support of the enactment of the election and finance legislation. By contrast, the DC right and the PLI were opposed. The second issue was social security reform. The debate focused on the creation of a guaranteed-minimum old-age pension, indexation of pensions, and an increase in the percentage of previous income that pensions provided. The DC, PSU, and PRI favored the reforms; the DC right and PLI opposed them all. The third issue was university reform. The parties debated whether admission should be open or selective, whether universities should be autonomous, self-governing bodies, and whether students should be granted rights of participation in university governance. Again, the dividing line ran between the DC, PSU, and PRI on the one hand, and the DC right and the PLI on the other. The fourth issue was the liberalization of divorce. All of the lay parties rallied around it; the DC opposed it.

The DC, PSU, and PRI agreed to disagree on the divorce issue: the coalition would not have a policy. By contrast, the PLI was not willing to make its differences with the DC implicit.

Expected outcome: a DC-PSU-PRI government.
Actual outcome: same.

Case Summaries

Table B.25 Parties' Relationships with the DC (1968)

	Issues			
Party*	Regional government	Social security reform	University reform	Divorce
PLI	divergent-explicit	divergent-explicit	divergent-explicit	divergent-explicit
PRI	convergent	convergent	convergent	divergent-implicit
PSU	convergent	convergent	convergent	divergent-implicit

*For an explanation of abbreviations, see table B.18.

The 1969 DC Government

The issues and relationships were the same as they had been in 1968, and the outcome would have been the same had not the three lay parties on the left of the DC decided to stay out for tactical reasons. The PSU split over cooperation with the PCI. Its left pressed for an end to cooperation with the DC and a return to cooperation with the PCI. The PSU right (the old PSDI and centrists from the old PSI) opposed such a strategy. Now the PSDI insisted that it would not participate in another coalition unless the parties pledged that they would not cooperate with the PCI at the local level. The PSI refused. Further, none of the parties of the lay left was willing to govern with the DC unless all of the lay left participated. The outcome was, therefore, a purely DC minority government.

Expected outcome: a DC-PRI-PSU government.
Actual outcome: a DC minority government.

The March 1970 DC–PSI–PSDI–PRI Government

Four issues were on the table. Three were not new: liberalization of divorce, pension indexation, and university reform. The fourth issue was labor law reform: the Workers' Charter. The charter limited a variety of employers' rights, including the right to dismiss and lay off workers. Most important, it guaranteed the position of trade unions in the workplace. The PLI and DC right opposed the charter.

The DC and lay left parties found a way to set aside the divorce issue: senators would be free to vote as they

Table B.26 Parties' Relationships with the DC (March 1970)

		Issues		
Party*	Divorce	Pension indexation	University reform	Workers' charter
PLI	divergent-explicit	divergent-explicit	divergent-explicit	divergent-explicit
PRI	divergent-implicit	convergent	convergent	convergent
PSDI	divergent-implicit	convergent	convergent	convergent
PSI	divergent-implicit	convergent	convergent	convergent

*For an explanation of abbreviations, see table B.18.

wished, and once the constitutional provision for national referenda was enacted, the issue would be put to a national vote. By contrast, the differences with the PLI remained explicit.

Expected outcome: a DC-PSI-PSDI-PRI coalition.
Actual outcome: same.

The August 1970 DC–PSI–PSDI–PRI Government

Three issues were still unresolved: divorce legislation, indexation of pensions, and university reform. Positions remained unchanged on these issues. The fourth issue was the response to spiraling inflation. The PLI wanted to cut expenditures for several basic social programs. DC and PSDI wanted to reduce the rate at which public spending was growing and to raise indirect taxes. PRI wanted to reduce the rate of increase in public spending, but opposed increased indirect taxes. The PSI wanted tax increases, but no slowing of public spending.

The DC and PLI expressed no interest in understating their differences. As usual, cooperation with the PLI would have precluded a center-left coalition, produced a minority government, and been even more incompatible with DC preferences than a center-left government. By contrast, the DC and the three lay left parties agreed to form a government that would have no common economic policy. Instead, they merely committed themselves to measures (unspecified) that would improve the national economy.

Expected outcome: a DC-PSI-PSDI-PRI government.
Actual outcome: same.

Case Summaries

Table B.27 Parties' Relationships with the DC (August 1970)

		Issues		
Party*	Divorce	Pension indexation	University reform	Economic management
PLI	divergent-explicit	divergent-explicit	divergent-explicit	divergent-explicit
PRI	divergent-implicit	convergent	convergent	divergent-implicit
PSDI	divergent-implicit	convergent	convergent	divergent-implicit
PSI	divergent-implicit	convergent	convergent	divergent-implicit

*For an explantion of abbreviations, see table B.18.

The 1972 DC–PSDI–PLI Government

The unwillingness of the PSI to participate in negotiations left the DC left with no place to turn for a potential majority. As a result, it, too, decided to remain on the sidelines. The formateurship thus went to Giulio Andreotti, then a leader of the DC right. Three issues were debated. Management of the economy was the first. The DC right's preferred response to the economic crisis was orthodox: deflationary fiscal and monetary policies. Whereas the PLI supported such a policy, the other parties, including the DC left, wanted the reverse: expansionary policies combined with the maintenance of price controls on a range of basic items. This conflict was reinforced by further conflicts over a range of social investments. The DC right and the PLI opposed the DC left and the lay left parties in their demands for expanded state investments in hospital, housing, and school construction and the South. Finally, the divorce question still isolated the DC, both left and right, from the other parties.

The DC right and PLI agreed to understate their differences on all three issues. Hence, notwithstanding their unambiguous opposition to them, both the DC right and PLI endorsed continued efforts to implement the enlarged programs of social investments. On the left, however, only the PSDI went along. The DC left and the PRI refused to participate. The DC right, the PLI, and the PSDI were willing to agree to disagree on the issue of divorce. In short, the DC right formed a government with the PLI on the basis of a program that was largely the property of the DC left. This outcome came about because, although the DC left could not form a government without the PSI, it could prevent the DC right from forming a government based on the DC right preferences. Under these circumstances, the DC right and PLI jettisoned their policy ambitions for the rare opportunity to gain unshared ministerial power. Causality, then, was the reverse of that proposed by the theory: it ran from the desire to form a government to policy preferences rather than vice versa. Therefore, the theory predicts the right outcome, but for the wrong reasons.

The 1973 DC–PSI–PSDI–PRI Government

The divorce issue was not resolved. The economic issues were the same as those which existed when the outgoing government was formed. The PLI, PRI, and PSDI wanted a contractionary program and cuts in social projects. By contrast, the PSI wanted an expansionary monetary and fiscal policy and increased state investment in social programs. The DC had no coherent policy: it was now committed to a contractionary monetary policy and an expansionary fiscal policy and to major increases in state investment in hospitals, housing, and universities.

The lay left parties were willing to ignore their differences with the DC provided that the PLI was not included in the government. Once again, the coalition parties merely committed themselves to the common good rather than concrete policies.

Expected outcome: a DC-PSI-PSDI-PRI government.
Actual outcome: same.

The March 1974 DC–PSI–PSDI Government

Following the rise in world oil prices, the economic crisis dominated the agenda. The conflicts among the parties were compounded by attempts to negotiate an emergency loan from the International Monetary Fund. The fund demanded restrictive monetary policies and reductions in the budget deficit. These conditions were in line with the preferences of the PLI, PRI, and PSDI. But the PSI continued to insist on expan-

Table B.28 Parties' Relationships with the DC (1973)

	Issues	
Party*	Divorce	Economic management
PLI	divergent-explicit	divergent-explicit
PRI	divergent-implicit	divergent-implicit
PSDI	divergent-implicit	divergent-implicit
PSI	divergent-implicit	divergent-implicit

*For an explanation of abbreviations, see table B.18.

sionary policies. And the DC remained incapable of reconciling its commitments to monetary contraction and fiscal expansion.

The DC, PSDI, and PSI agreed to disagree and support a policy of monetary contraction and fiscal expansion. In effect, the coalition adopted inconsistent policies to avoid reconciling its differences. The PRI and PLI would not go along with this.

Expected outcome: a DC-PSI-PSDI government.
Actual outcome: same.

The November 1974 DC–PRI Government

Again, a single issue dominated Italian politics. Having accepted the I.M.F. conditions, the DC now had preferences compatible with those of the PRI, PSDI, and PLI. Only the PSI remained committed to an expansionary policy. The PSDI refused to negotiate. In its view, the positions of the PSI made an effective majority impossible, and it thus called for a new election. The PLI's participation was precluded by the DC's movement toward cooperation outside the cabinet with the PCI. What Moro called a "strategy of attention" to the PCI was unacceptable to the PLI.

Expected outcome: a DC-PLI-PRI-PSDI government.
Actual outcome: a DC-PRI government.

Notes

Introduction: Governing Coalitions and Democratic Politics

1. Among the most important works in recent years are Browne and Dreijmanis, eds., *Government Coalitions;* Dodd, *Coalitions;* and De Swaan, *Coalition Theories.* As well, a special issue of *Comparative Political Studies* (vol. 17, no. 2), published in summer 1984, has been devoted to theories of coalitions. It contains several important articles and extensive bibliographies.
2. Luebbert, "Coalition Theory," pp. 235–49.
3. *Ibid.,* pp. 236–41.

1. Varieties of Multiparty Democracies

1. See, among others, Crozier, Huntington, and Watanuki, *The Crisis;* O'Connor, *Fiscal Crisis;* and Schmitter, "Interest Intermediation."
2. Leonardi, "Polarizzazione," pp. 299–319; Pridham, *Italian Party System.*
3. See, among others, Anton, "Policy Making," pp. 88–102, and *Administered Politics;* Groenings, "Cooperation"; McDaniels, "Unicameral Parliament"; Rustow, *Politics of Compromise;* Rokkan, "Numerical Democracy"; Stjernquist, "Sweden: Stability or Deadlock?"; Torgersen, "The Trend" and "Chapter Six: Political Institutions."
4. Sartori, *Parties and Party Systems,* pp. 122–23.
5. See Leonardi, "Polarizzazione"; Pridham, *Italian Party System;* and Sartori, "Il pluralismo polarizzato," pp. 3–44.
6. Election returns can be compared in von Beyme, *Parteien in westlichen Demokratien,* pp. 467–92.

1. Multiparty Democracies

7. See note 3, and Kaarsted, *Dansk politik i 1960'erne;* Hadenius et al., *Sverige;* Nordic Council, *Nordisk kontakt,* vols. 6–26.
8. See notes 3 and 7.
9. Torgersen, "The Trend," p. 103.
10. Safran, *Israel;* Irving, *Christian Democratic Parties,* pp. 164–92; Wahlbäck, *Från Mannerheim.*
11. Lijphart, *Politics of Accommodation,* p. 135.
12. Cited in Daalder, *Parlement en politieke besluitvorming,* p. 28.
13. Lijphart, *Politics of Accommodation,* p. 78.
14. Ibid., pp. 115–20.
15. The data on attitudes are from Anton, *Administered Politics,* pp. 129–59.
16. Ibid., pp. 137–40.
17. Ibid., p. 140.
18. Ibid.
19. Ibid., p. 142.
20. Ibid.
21. Ibid., pp. 142–43.
22. Ibid., p. 143.
23. Ibid.
24. See, among others, Grew, ed., *Crises of Political Development.*
25. The literature is reviewed by Gerhard Lehmbruch in "Introduction," pp. 1–29.
26. Johansen and Kristensen, "Corporatist Traits," p. 192.
27. Headey, "Trade Unions," pp. 407–31.
28. Schmitter, "Interest Intermediation," p. 293.
29. See Galenson, *Labor in Norway* and *The Danish System;* Galenson and Adams, *Comparative Labor Movements* and "Current Problems"; Myers, *Industrial Relations in Sweden;* Wheeler, *White-Collar Power.*
30. Galenson and Adams, "Current Problems," p. 284.
31. Among the recent studies of interest group integration in Scandinavia are Ruin, "Participatory Democracy"; Rokkan, "Votes Count"; Peterson, "Interest Group Incorporation"; Meijer, "Bureaucracy and Policy"; Kvavik, *Interest Groups;* Jarlov, Johansen, and Kristensen, "Danish Committee System"; Hallenstvedt and Vraa, "Det organiserte samfunn"; Elvander, ed., *Interessorganisationerna;* Christensen, "Normerne for samspiellet"; Buksti and Johansen, "Organisationssystemet" and "Variations in Organizational Participation"; Christensen and Egeberg, "Organized Group-Government Relations"; Olsen, ed., *Politisk organisering;* Gaasemyr, *Organisasjonsbyrakrati.*
32. Olsen, Roness, and Saetren, "Norway: Still Peaceful Coexistence," p. 61.
33. Ibid., pp. 61–62.
34. Ibid., p. 62.
35. Johansen and Kristensen, "Corporatist Traits," pp. 204–5.
36. Heckscher, "Interest Groups in Sweden."
37. Ibid., p. 166.
38. Ibid., p. 170.
39. Rokkan, "Numerical Democracy," pp. 106–7.
40. On Finland, see Wahlbäck, *Från Mannerheim;* and Alapuro and Allardt, "The Lapua Movement." On Austria, see Simon, "Democracy in the Shadow."

3. Party Leaders and Coalitions

41. See, among others, the essays by John R. Gillis on Germany, David Bien and Raymond Grew on France, Aristide Zolberg on Belgium, and Grew on Italy in Grew, ed., *Crises of Political Development*. On Ireland, see O'Hegarty, *A History*. For the Netherlands and Belgium, Geyl, *History*. For Italy, Farneti, "Social Conflict."

42. Torgersen, "The Trend," p. 103.

43. Dovring, "Scandinavia"; Rustow, *Politics of Compromise*.

44. Torgersen, "The Trend," p. 103.

45. The transition to parliamentary democracy and the development of the party system in Denmark are discussed in chapter 5. Comparable studies of Norway and Sweden are available from me.

46. Postwar Austrian politics to the end of the Grand Coalition is reviewed in Bluhm, *Building an Austrian Nation*.

2. Policy Preferences and the Imperatives of Party Leadership

1. Dorpalen, *Hindenburg*, pp. 119–20.

2. Sirkin, "Coalition, Conflict, Compromise," pp. 166–67.

3. Lipset and Rokkan, "Cleavages, Structures, Party Systems," pp. 1–64.

4. This was first suggested by Lipset and Rokkan, "Cleavages, Structures, Party Systems," pp. 1–64.

5. The literature on cleavages and party systems is now extensive. In addition to the classic Lipset and Rokkan piece above, my discussion has been aided by Allardt and Littunen, eds., *Cleavages*; Bendix, ed., *Nation Building*; Rose and Urwin, "Persistence and Change"; and Rokkan, ed., *Approaches*.

6. On the rural-urban relationship in the Middle Ages, see the works of Henri Pirenne, especially his *Medieval Cities*. On the eighteenth and nineteenth centuries, see Milward and Saul, *The Economic Development*, pp. 40–110.

7. Lijphart, "Political Parties," pp. 27–42.

8. Inglehart, *Silent Revolution*; Dalton, Beck, Flanagan, eds., *Electoral Change*.

9. Numerous works have contributed to my understanding of bargaining relationships. Among the most important have been Walton and McKersie, *A Behavioral Theory*; Ikle, *How Nations Negotiate*; Cross, *Economics of Bargaining*; Snyder and Diesing, *Conflict Among Nations*; Zartman, ed., *Fifty Percent Solution* and *The Negotiating Process*.

3. Party Leaders and Governing Coalitions

1. See "Consensus Building" and "The Institutional and Historical Bases of Consensual Politics" in chapter 1.

2. It is important to keep in mind that the party was able to form the government in the first place because it was for some substantial part of the legislature

3. Party Leaders and Coalitions

the least undesirable party available. For this part of the legislature, bringing the government down is a sound strategy only when another party becomes less undesirable.

3. Di Palma, *Political Syncretism*.

4. For examples of this in the Italian context, see Tamburrano, *Storia e cronaco*.

5. A party has majority-relevance when it is capable of making a necessary contribution to any mathematically feasible majority that includes the formateurs' party. This is discussed in appendix A. See "Identifying Parties and Governments" therein.

6. Grosser, *Geschichte Deutschlands*, p. 200.

7. Irving, *Christian Democratic Parties*, pp. 164–92.

8. *Financial Times*, April 24, 25, 1974, p. 1, June 14, 15, 1974, p. 1; *Neue Zürcher Zeitung*, April 22–25, June 14, 1974, p. 1; *The Times*, June 14, 1974, p. 1.

9. These governments were Leburton (1973); Tindemanns (1974); Tindemanns (1977); Martens (1979); Martens (April 1980); Martens (October 1980). For their party composition, see Irving, *Christian Democratic Parties*, p. 190, and *Keesing's Contemporary Archives*, pp. 25817, 26534, 28460, 29679, 30420, and 31129.

10. See Irving, *Christian Democratic Parties*, pp. 164–92; Mabille and Lorwin, "The Belgian Socialist Party"; and Mabille and Lorwin, "Belgium."

11. *Economist*, December 26, 1981, pp. 15–16.

12. For the composition of the governments, see Tomasson, *Iceland*, pp. 40–41.

4. Israel

1. The only exception to this was the small, ultra-orthodox Agudah party's initial opposition to female voting rights. See Isaac, *Party and Politics*, p. 40.

2. See Laqueur, *A History*, chs. 6–8; Sachar, *A History*, pp. 65–82, 138–63; Horowitz and Lissak, *Origins*, pp. 37–105.

3. For my understanding of the three basic ideologies that motivated Zionist pioneers, I have relied heavily on Isaac, *Party and Politics*, chs. 1 and 2.

4. *Ibid.*, p. 17, and table 2.1 on p. 50.

5. Sachar, *A History*, ch. 15.

6. Zohar, *Political Parties*, introduction.

7. Isaac, *Party and Politics*, chs. 1 and 2.

8. Kalischer, "Seeking Zion," p. 112 and passim.

9. Isaac, *Party and Politics*, p. 19.

10. *Ibid.*, p. 3.

11. *Ibid.*, ch. 4.

12. *Ibid.*, ch. 5.

13. *Ibid.*, p. 23.

14. During the First Aliyah (1882–1903), about 25,000 Jews emigrated to Palestine. Some of them were Zionists. But the majority were passive, religious Jews who came for study and meditation. See Sachar, *A History*, pp. 26–30.

15. On the relative electoral strength of the parties in the WZO elections,

4. Israel

see Horowitz and Lissak, *Origins*, pp. 102–3. For a discussion of the development of Yishuv institutions, see Horowitz and Lissak, *Origins*, pp. 68–105, and Shapiro, *Formative Years*, entire, but especially chs. 2, 3, and 8.

16. Isaac, *Party and Politics*, pp. 16–49.
17. *Ibid.*, p. 29.
18. *Ibid.*; Laqueur, *A History*, pp. 410–14.
19. Isaac, *Party and Politics*, pp. 27–31; Laqueur, *A History*, pp. 410–14.
20. Shapiro, *Formative Years*, pp. 9–16; Isaac, *Party and Politics*, p. 24.
21. Isaac, *Party and Politics*, p. 25.
22. Shapiro, *Formative Years*, chs. 2–4.
23. *Ibid.*, ch. 8.
24. Isaac, *Party and Politics*, p. 26.
25. *Ibid.*, p. 27; Shapiro, *Formative Years*, ch. 5.
26. Isaac, *Party and Politics*, p. 27; Shapiro, *Formative Years*, ch. 5; Sachar, *A History*, ch. 7.
27. See note 26.
28. Isaac, *Party and Politics*, pp. 26–27.
29. *Ibid.*
30. Shapiro, *Formative Years*, ch. 5; Sachar, *A History*, pp. 160–63.
31. Isaac, *Party and Politics*, pp. 27–28.
32. *Ibid.*, p. 28.
33. Shapiro, *Formative Years*, ch. 8; Sachar, *A History*, pp. 154–60; Laqueur, *A History*, pp. 332–33.
34. Isaac, *Party and Politics*, p. 30.
35. Laqueur, *A History*, pp. 297–301, 323, 333, 487–88.
36. Paltiel, "The Progressive Party," p. 3.
37. Sachar, *A History*, pp. 171–95; Laqueur, *A History*, pp. 338–84; Schechtman and Benair, *History of the Revisionist Movement*.
38. See note 37.
39. Isaac, *Party and Politics*, pp. 37, 41–44.
40. *Ibid.*, p. 42.
41. *Ibid.*
42. *Ibid.*, pp. 43, 46.
43. *Ibid.*, pp. 44–45.
44. Zohar, *Political Parties*, p. 62.
45. Isaac, *Party and Politics*, p. 45.
46. Zohar, *Political Parties*, pp. 50–54.
47. Sirkin, "Coalition, Conflict, Compromise," pp. 152–86.
48. *DV*, October, 14, 1950, p. 1; *JP*, October 13, 1950, p. 1.
49. See note 48.
50. *DV*, October 20, 1950, p. 1; *DHK*, 1st Knesset, 179th Session 7 (October 16, 1950), p. 9; *JP*, October 17, 19, 1950, p. 1.
51. See note 50.
52. *JP*, October 24, 1950, p. 1.
53. *JP*, October 24, 25, 1950, p. 1.
54. *Ibid.*; Sirkin, "Coalition, Conflict, Compromise," pp. 172–77.
55. See note 54.

4. Israel

56. JP, October 25, 26, 1950, p. 1.
57. JP, October 27, 29, 1950, p. 1; Sirkin, "Coalition, Conflict, Compromise," p. 177.
58. DHK, 1st Knesset, 179th Session 7 (October 16, 1950), p. 18.
59. JP, October, 25, 27, 29, 1950, p. 1; HA, October 25–27, 1950, p. 1.
60. Sirkin, "Coalition, Conflict, Compromise," p. 240; Kraines, "Israel," p. 522.
61. Palestine Post, March 15, 1950, p. 1; Norman, "Israel After Two Years," p. 42.
62. JP, January 5, 8, 24, 1951, p. 1; HA, January 5, 8, 9, 1951, p. 1.
63. HA, February 5, 14, 15, 1951, p. 1.
64. DHK, 2d Knesset, 13th Session 10 (October 8, 1951), pp. 241, 296; DV, August 12, September 19, 1951, p. 1; Birnbaum, The Politics, p. 151; Bentwich, "Israel, the Sixth Year," p. 403.
65. Isaac, Party and Politics, p. 139; Herut Movement, Working Platform, p. 3.
66. Birnbaum, The Politics, pp. 141–42; DV, September 28, October 4, 1951, p. 1; HB, September 28, 1951, p. 1; DHK, 2d Knesset, 13th Session 10 (October 8, 1951), p. 224.
67. See note 66.
68. Sirkin, "Coalition, Conflict, Compromise," p. 323; Birnbaum, The Politics, pp. 147–49.
69. Birnbaum, The Politics, pp. 154–58; Bentwich, "Fourth Year of Israel," p. 252; DHK, 2d Knesset, 13th Session 10 (October 8, 1951), pp. 223, 248; HZ, August 6, 1951, p. 1, and September 18, 1951, pp. 1–2, editorial; DV, September 10, 1951, p. 1; JP, September 30, October 4, 1951, p. 1.
70. See note 69.
71. Sefer Ha-Huquim, September 15, 1949, p. 271.
72. Birnbaum, The Politics, p. 161.
73. Ibid., p. 162.
74. Ibid., pp. 165–66; JP, October 14, 1952, p. 1, and December 25, 1952, pp. 1–2.
75. The quote is from HZ, December 18, 1952, p. 1; see also JP, December 16, 18, 23, 25, 1952, p. 1.
76. HZ, December 25, 1952, p. 1.
77. JP, January 13, 1953, p. 1.
78. Safran, Israel, p. 163.
79. Ibid.; JP, December 14–17, 1952, p. 1.
80. JP, December 14–17, 1952, p. 1; Birnbaum, The Politics, p. 164; HB, December 12, 17–18, 1952, p. 1.
81. DHK, 2d Knesset, 156th Session 13 (December 22, 1952), p. 287.
82. Safran, Israel, p. 163.
83. Ibid.; Isaac, Party and Politics, pp. 138–43, 149.
84. See the coverage in JP, December 1952.
85. See notes 75–78.
86. The most insightful discussion of this aspect of government formation in Israel is to be found in Sirkin, "Coalition, Conflict, Compromise," pp. 266–303.
87. Ibid.

4. Israel

88. This inference is supported by the analyses of contemporary observers. See the citations of the Israeli press in notes 75, 76, and 79.
89. *HB*, May 3, 1953, p. 1.
90. *HB*, May 13, 1953, p. 1.
91. *HB*, May 26, 1953, p. 1.
92. *DV*, May 29, 31, 1953, p. 1.
93. *HZ*, May 29, 1953, p. 11.
94. *Ibid.*
95. *JP*, May 31, June 1–3, 1953, p. 1.
96. *Ibid.*
97. *Ibid.*
98. *JP*, January 26, 1954, p. 1.
99. For background on the "Kastner Case," see Sachar, *A History*, pp. 371–76.
100. *JP*, November 22, 1955, p. 1.
101. *Ibid.;* and above, chapter 4, "The 1952 Government."
102. *JP*, August 30, November 22, 1955, p. 1; *HA*, November 3, 1955, p. 1.
103. Sirkin, "Coalition, Conflict, Compromise," p. 328.
104. *JP*, September 30, 1955, p. 1; *HA*, September 30, 1955, p. 1.
105. Sirkin, "Coalition, Conflict, Compromise," pp. 158–61, 347; *JP*, August 30, 1955, p. 1.
106. *JP*, August 4, September 9, 1955, p. 1; *DV*, August 30, 1955, p. 1; *HA*, November 2, 3, 1955, p. 1.
107. Sirkin, "Coalition, Conflict, Compromise," pp. 102–22, especially pp. 102–14.
108. *Ibid.*, pp. 115–18.
109. For a discussion of the economic difficulties Israel faced in its first decade, see Sachar, *A History*, pp. 395–429.
110. Sirkin, "Coalition, Conflict, Compromise," p. 331.
111. *Economist*, November 12, 1955, "Israel's New Government," p. 57; *JP*, September 20, 1955, p. 1; *HA*, September 26, 1955, p. 1.
112. Sirkin, "Coalition, Conflict, Compromise," p. 331.
113. Isaac, *Party and Politics*, pp. 135–53; Sirkin, "Coalition, Conflict, Compromise," pp. 214–17.
114. Isaac, *Party and Politics*, pp. 104–6.
115. *Ibid.*, p. 148.
116. *HA*, July 21, 1955, p. 3.
117. Sachar, *A History*, pp. 464–70, 559–67; Isaac, *Party and Politics*, pp. 148–49, 154.
118. *HA*, December 21, 1954, p. 1; *DV*, July 23, 1955, p. 3.
119. For the 1955 case, see the coverage of the negotiations in *DV*, *HA*, and *MA*, August–October 1955; see also, Sirkin, "Coalition, Conflict, Compromise," pp. 339–43.
120. *JP*, December 18, 1957, p. 1; *DV* December 20, 1957, p. 1; *HA*, December 20, 1957, p. 1.
121. *JP*, December 17, 1957, p. 3.
122. *HZ*, January 6, 1958, p. 1; *HA*, January 6, 1958, p. 1.

123. *HA*, January 6, 1958, p. 1.
124. *Ibid.; DHK*, 3d Knesset, 387th Session 23 (January 7, 1958), p. 575.
125. Goldman, *Religious Issues*, p. 67.
126. For a general discussion of the issue, see Sachar, *A History*, pp. 602–8; Sirkin, "Coalition, Conflict, Compromise," pp. 186–93; Isaac, *Party and Politics*, pp. 73–77.
127. Sirkin, "Coalition, Conflict, Compromise," pp. 186–93.
128. *Ibid.*
129. *JP*, June 24, 1958, p. 3, and June 25, July 4, 1958, p. 1.
130. *Ibid.*
131. *HA*, July 7, 1959, p. 1.
132. *HZ*, November 17, 1959, p. 1; *HA*, November 17, 1959, p. 1; Birnbaum, *The Politics*, p. 242.
133. Sirkin, "Coalition, Conflict, Compromise," p. 315; *JP*, December 14, 1959, p. 1.
134. *JP*, November 29, December 1, 6, 11, 1959, p. 1.
135. Sirkin, "Coalition, Conflict, Compromise," p. 329.
136. *JP*, November 11, 1959, p. 3, and November 25, 26, 1959, p. 1.
137. *JP*, November 15, December 1, 9, 16, 1959, p. 1.
138. *Ibid.*
139. *JP*, November 24, December 2, 1959, p. 1.
140. *Ibid.*
141. For background on the Lavon affair, see Sachar, *A History*, pp. 543–47; Sirkin, "Coalition, Conflict, Compromise," pp. 53–69.
142. *JP*, September 17, 21, October 17, November 2, 1961, pp. 1, 3; see also *HA* and *MA* for August and September 1961.
143. See the Histadrut's paper, *Davar*, August–September 1961.
144. *JP*, November 2, 1961, p. 1; *HZ*, November 2, 1961, p. 1.
145. See note 144.
146. *JP*, September 21, 1961, p. 1.
147. *Ibid.*
148. *JP*, August 22, October 13, 17, 1961, p. 1.
149. *JP*, October 26, 1961, p. 1.
150. *JP*, August 22, October 13, 1961, p. 1.
151. Sirkin, "Coalition, Conflict, Compromise," pp. 61–63; *JP*, August 25, 1961, p. 1.
152. *JP*, October 19, 22, 1961, p. 1.
153. *Ibid.*
154. Sachar, *A History*, pp. 548–49.
155. *HA* and *MA*, June 25–28, 1961, p. 1.
156. *HA*, December 15–25, 1963; Sirkin, "Coalition, Conflict, Compromise," pp. 69–76.
157. For background on the establishment first of Rafi and later of the Alignment, see Isaac, *Party and Politics*, pp. 116–35; Sirkin, "Coalition, Conflict, Compromise," pp. 76–87.
158. See note 157.
159. Sirkin, "Coalition, Conflict, Compromise," pp. 127–52.

160. See *HA* and *MA*, November 1965.
161. Sirkin, "Coalition, Conflict, Compromise," pp. 127–52.
162. *JP*, November, 8, 10, 18–19, 30, 1965, p. 1.
163. *Ibid.*
164. Sirkin, "Coalition, Conflict, Compromise," pp. 203–30.
165. *Ibid.*, p. 330.
166. *HA*, November 2, 1965, p. 3.
167. *Economist*, July 31, 1965, "Israel: Escape from the Sabbath," p. 43; *JP*, December 31, 1965, p. 1.
168. See note 167.
169. See note 167.
170. See the reporting in *JP* and *HA*, June 3–6, 1967, March 1969, December 1969, July 28–August 2, 1970.
171. Inspector General of Elections, *Results*, pp. 4–5.
172. See the reporting in *JP* through spring and summer 1974.
173. Akzin, "The Likud," pp. 104–10; Isaac, *Party and Politics*, pp. 155–58.
174. See note 173; and Reich, "Israel's Foreign Policy," pp. 255–83.
175. Reich, "Israel's Foreign Policy," pp. 255–83.
176. *JP* and *HA*, December 1, 1973–April 11, 1974, and October 15–-November 1, 1974.
177. *JP*, March 2, 1974, June 1974, October 3, 1974, p. 1.
178. Isaac, *Party and Politics*, pp. 78–79.
179. *JP*, February 12, 1974, p. 1; Sachar, *A History*, pp. 801–7.
180. *JP*, December 1975.
181. Rubinstein, "The Lesser Parties," pp. 188–89; *JP*, December 13, 1973, p. 1, and June 2, 1974, p. 1.
182. Inspector General of Elections, *Results*, pp. 4–5.
183. Sachar, *A History*, pp. 803–5; *JP*, March 8–11, 1974, p. 1.
184. See note 183.
185. See note 183.
186. Sachar, *A History*, pp. 802–3.
187. *Ibid.*, p. 805; *JP*, June 3–4, 1974, p. 1.
188. *JP*, June 3–4, 1974, p. 1.
189. *JP*, October 30, 1974, p. 1.

5. Denmark

1. Engelstoft and Wendt, *Haandbog*.
2. Jones, *Denmark*, pp. 44–72.
3. *Ibid.*, pp. 73–79 and passim.
4. Hvidt, *Venstre og forsvarssagen*, chs. 2 and 3.
5. *Ibid.*
6. *Ibid.*
7. Haue et al., *Det ny Danmark*, pp. 42–81.
8. Hansen, *Landbrugs historie*, vol. 2, ch. 3; Østerud, "Agrarian Structure."

5. Denmark

9. Jones, *Denmark*, p. 96.
10. *Ibid.*
11. Haue et al., *Det ny Danmark*, pp. 57–58.
12. *Ibid.*, pp. 57–69.
13. Bertolt, ed., *En bygning vi rejser:* Svensson, "Support for the Danish Social Democratic Party"; Thomas, "Social Democracy in Denmark."
14. Haue et al., *Det ny Danmark*, pp. 73–88.
15. Berglund and Lindstrom, *Scandinavian Party Systems*, p. 108.
16. Kuhnle, *Patterns*, pp. 106–16; Rasmussen and Skovmand, *Det radikale Venstre*.
17. Milward and Saul, *Economic Development*, p. 510.
18. *Ibid.*, pp. 470–534; Skrubbeltrang, *Agricultural Development;* Jensen, *Danish Agriculture;* Jorberg, "Industrial Revolution"; Østerud, "Agrarian Structure," ch. 3.
19. Haue et al., *Det ny Danmark*, ch. 23.
20. Rhode, "The Communist Party."
21. Kolding, *Retsforbund.*
22. Kaarsted, *Regeringskrisen*, p. 8.
23. Krag and Andersen, *Kamp og fornyelse*, p. 20.
24. *Ibid.*, p. 23.
25. Kaarsted, *Regeringskrisen*, pp. 22–24; Einhorn, *National Security*, pp. 43–44.
26. Einhorn, *National Security*, pp. 42–43.
27. Kaarsted, *Dansk politik*, p. 21.
28. Einhorn, *National Security*, p. 63.
29. *Ibid.*
30. *Ibid.*, p. 64.
31. *Ibid.*
32. Kaarsted, *Regeringskrisen*, ch. 20.
33. Kaarsted has written an entire book on the formation of this government. For a detailed and well-documented discussion of the Social Democrats' economic policies, see his *Regeringskrisen* generally and, in particular, pp. 26–35, 81–84, 121–28, 145–51, 157–64.
34. *Ibid. PTK*, April 29, 1957, pp. 1–2.
35. Kaarsted, *Regeringskrisen; BLT,* April 28, 1957, pp. 1, 3.
36. Kaarsted, *Regeringskrisen*, p. 30 and passim.
37. *Ibid.*, chs. 18 and 20.
38. *Ibid.*, ch. 2.
39. *Ibid.*, ch. 14.
40. For a sample of the attacks directed against Starcke when he led his party into the government, see *Berlingske Tidende, Aftenbladet,* and the reporting in the (Swedish) *Dagens Nyheter* on the days of July 7–13, 1957. For discussions of subsequent divisions within Starcke's party, see Kaarsted, *Dansk politik*, ch. 2, and Pedersen, *Erindringer.*
41. Kaarsted, *Dansk politik*, p. 21.
42. *Nk* 5(1): 6–7; 5(6):281–84. *Nordisk kontakt* is a serial that follows day-to-day party and parliamentary politics in the five Nordic Council countries. It is published by the council and is by far the most reliable and detailed source of information.

5. Denmark

43. Haue et al., *Det ny Danmark*, pp. 265–68.
44. *Nk* 5(12):637–41; 5(3):120–21; 5(5):229–31.
45. *Nk* 5(5):229.
46. *Nk* 5(6):285–87; 5(10):505–6; 5(9):446–49; 5(11):578–81.
47. Kaarsted, *Dansk politik*, ch. 2; Pedersen, *Erindringer*.
48. Larsen, *Den levende vej*, "Beretning om den XX Kongress i Sovjet Unionens Kommunistike Parti," p. 345.
49. Norlund, "Fornyelsen," pp. 205–9 and passim; Petersen, "Socialistik folkeparti."
50. *Nk* 5(13):703.
51. Rimstad, "De Uafhaengige," pp. 90–93.
52. *Ibid.*
53. *Nk* 7(10):566–69; 7(11):628–33.
54. Kaarsted, *Dansk politik*, ch. 2. See also the *Nk* citations in notes 42 and 44.
55. *Nk* 7(9):439–40.
56. *Nk* 7(10):566–69; 7(11):628–33.
57. See note 56.
58. *Nk* 7(11):637; 7(13):761. See also notes 33, 34, and 37.
59. Sorensen, "Politics Since 1964"; Bille, *S-SF: Kilder*. See also the coverage of the campaign and the coalition negotiations in *Dagens Nyheter, Politiken*, and *Information*, September and October 1964.
60. *Nk* 9(19):579 and passim; 9(6):330–35.
61. *Nk* 9(10):580–81; *PTK*, September 3, 1964, p. 2.
62. *Nk* 9(1):77–78.
63. Kaarsted, *Dansk politik*, ch. 4; Ninn-Hansen, *Svy år*, pp. 19–20 and passim; Pedersen, "The First Socialist Majority," pp. 144–57.
64. For an overview of the campaign, see Pederson, "The First Socialist Majority," pp. 144–57, and Glans, "Election of 1966."
65. Kaarsted, *Dansk politik*, pp. 54–57.
66. *Ibid.*; Pedersen, "First Socialist Majority"; Glans, "Election of 1966"; Nielsen, *Danmarks forste arbejderflertal*, chs. 1 and 2.
67. Kaarsted, *Dansk politik*, pp. 54–57.
68. *Ibid.*, pp. 52–62.
69. *Ibid.*, p. 55.
70. Ninn-Hansen, *Syv år*, pp. 20–21.
71. *Ibid.*, p. 20.
72. Kaarsted, *Dansk politik*, pp. 44–48.
73. *Nk* 12(1):70–75.
74. Ninn-Hansen, *Syv år*, p. 40 and passim.
75. *Nk* 13(1):1–7; Ninn-Hansen, *Syv år*, pp. 13–69.
76. *Nk* 13(1):6–8, 11.
77. *Ibid.*, pp. 7–8.
78. *Ibid.*
79. *Nk* 13(2):70–78; Ninn-Hansen, *Syv år*, pp. 43–69.
80. Ninn-Hansen, *Syv år*, pp. 61–77.
81. *Nk* 13(2):76.

5. Denmark

82. Ninn-Hansen, *Syv år*, pp. 69–75.
83. Kaarsted, *Dansk politik*, pp. 63–68.
84. Eklit and Pedersen, "Denmark Enters the EEC"; Fitzmaurice, "Scandinavian Referenda."
85. *Nk* 16(6):338–40.
86. Ninn-Hansen, *Syv år*, pp. 181–95.
87. *Nk* 16(2):103–4.
88. *Nk* 16(11):674; 16(15):977–78; 16(12):751–52; 16(9):549–51; 16(3):130.
89. *Nk* 16(9):549–50; 16(12):751–52.
90. *Nk* 16(9):549–50; 16(12):751–52.
91. For a discussion of the developments leading up to the 1973 election, see Nilson, "Norway and Denmark," pp. 205–35.
92. *Ibid.*, p. 225.
93. *Nk* 18(4):224–27; 18(14):909–11.
94. See note 93; and Ninn-Hansen, *Syv år*, pp. 241–51.
95. *Nk* 18(14):909–11.
96. *Nk* 18(12):764–67; 18(13):839–41.
97. *Nk* 18(9):559–61; 18(12):769–70.
98. Moller, ed., *De politiske partier:* Maddeley, "Scandinavian Christian Democracy," pp. 276–86. On the party's unwillingness to participate in a government of any sort, see Ninn-Hansen, *Syv år*, p. 245, and the coverage in *Politiken* and *Information* throughout November and December 1973.
99. See note 98.
100. *Nk* 18(12):770 and passim.
101. *Nk* 18(15):979 and passim.
102. Ninn-Hansen, *Syv år*, pp. 241–51. See also the coverage in *Politiken, Information*, and *Berlingske Tidende* in December 1973.
103. See note 102.
104. See note 102.
105. See note 102.

6. Finland

1. Hamalainen, *In Time of Storm*, p. 7.
2. Pogorelskin, "The Politics of Frustration," pp. 231–46.
3. *Ibid.*; Upton, *Finnish Revolution*, ch. 1; Kirby, *Finland*, chs. 1 and 3.
4. Kirby, *Finland*, ch. 2.
5. Colliander, *Svenska folkepartiet;* Lindman, *Den svenska partibildningen.*
6. Arter, *Bumpkin Against Bigwig.*
7. Hamalainen, *In Time of Storm*, ch. 6; Upton, *Finnish Revolution*, chs. 2–11; Kirby, *Finland*, ch. 3; Wahlbäck, *Från Mannerheim*, pp. 11–62.
8. Kirby, *Finland*, p. 64.
9. Hamalainen, *In Time of Storm*, ch. 6; Upton, *Finnish Revolution*, chs. 2 and 3.
10. Kirby, *Finland*, chs. 6 and 8; Wahlbäck, *Från Mannerheim*, pp. 116–55.

6. Finland

11. Upton, *Finnish Revolution*, chs. 2, 8 and 11; Krosby, *The Petsamo Dispute*.
12. Kirby, *Finland*, p. 72.
13. Hodgson, *Communism*; Kalela, "Right-Wing Radicalism"; Billington, "Finland," pp. 117–44.
14. Kirby, *Finland*, p. 10.
15. *Ibid.*, p. 19.
16. Rasila, "Finnish Civil War," pp. 110–42; Allardt, "Social Sources," pp. 49–72; Allardt and Pesonen, "Citizen Participation," pp. 27–39.
17. Kirby, *Finland*, p. 75.
18. Rasila, "Finnish Civil War"; Allardt and Pesonen, "Citizen Participation"; Nousiainen, *Finnish Political System*, pp. 28–55.
19. Kirby, *Finland*, p. 170.
20. *Ibid.*, pp. 169–75 and passim.
21. Nousiainen, *Finnish Political System*, pp. 96–100.
22. *Ibid.*
23. *Ibid.*, pp. 39–55.
24. For the historical development of the center-periphery cleavage, see Kirby, *Finland*, pp. 162–78; 201–9; Rantala, "The Political Regions," pp. 116–40; Wahlbäck, *Från Mannerheim*, pp. 205–13; Sankiaho, "A Model."
25. See note 24.
26. Hodgson, *Communism*, ch. 5.
27. *Nk* 2(2):24–27.
28. Nousiainen, *Finnish Political System*, ch. 6.
29. *Nk* 2(1):17; 2(2):24–27; 1(14):20; 1(15):18.
30. *Nk* 2(2):24–28; 2(3):19.
31. See note 30.
32. *Nk* 2(3):17–19; 2(4):12–13; 2(5):14–24; 2(6):15–17.
33. See note 32.
34. *Nk*, 3(1):21.
35. *Nk* 3(6):22–23.
36. *Nk* 3(6):22–23; 3(5):15–20; 3(7):21–22; 3(9):13.
37. See note 36.
38. See note 36. Also: *NK* 3(10):14–16; 3(11):31–37.
39. See note 38.
40. See note 38.
41. *Nk* 3(11):31–37.
42. *Ibid.*
43. *Ibid.*
44. *Nk* 3(12):23–26.
45. *Ibid.*, p. 20.
46. Nousiainen, *Finnish Political System*, p. 27; Knoellinger, *Labor in Finland*, pp. 221–22.
47. *Nk* 3(12):19–23, 30.
48. *Ibid.*
49. *Nk* 4(7): 348 and passim; 4(9):459 and passim; 4(12):624–26.
50. See note 49.
51. See note 49.

52. See note 49.
53. See note 49.
54. See note 49.
55. See note 49; also *Nk* 4(12):615–17.
56. *Nk* 4(12):616.
57. Wahlbäck, *Från Mannerheim*, pp. 166–94.
58. *Ibid.*
59. *Nk* 7(11):605–8.
60. Wahlbäck, *Från Mannerheim*, pp. 166–94.
61. *Nk* 7(11):605–8.
62. *Ibid.*, pp. 599–604.
63. *Nk* 7(3):137; 7(9):481.
64. *Nk* 7(10):532–33; 7(15):815.
65. *Nk* 7(10):533–34.
66. *Ibid.*, pp. 537–40.
67. *Ibid.*
68. Wahlbäck, *Från Mannerheim*, pp. 187–94.
69. *Nk* 8(1):19–22; 8(7):389–93; 8(8):445–46, 449–50.
70. *Nk* 8(1):26; 8(5):266; 8(6):328–30.
71. *Nk* 8(6):328–30.
72. *Nk* 8(7):383–87.
73. *Ibid.*
74. *Ibid.*
75. *Nk* 8(6):328–30.
76. *Ibid.*
77. *Nk* 9(1):17–21.
78. *Nk* 9(8):458–61; 9(10):590–92.
79. *Nk* 9(11):662–65.
80. *Ibid.*, pp. 654–68.
81. *Ibid.*
82. *Ibid.*
83. *Ibid.*
84. *Ibid.*
85. *Ibid.*

7. Finland as an Unconsolidated Democracy, 1966–1982

1. Dalton, Beck, Flanagan, "Electoral Change," tables 1.1 and 1.2, and pp. 8–11.
2. Nousiainen, *Finnish Political System*, p. 215.
3. *Ibid.*, p. 275.
4. For background on the "Note Crisis" and its role in the 1962 election, see Wahlbäck, *Från Mannerheim*, pp. 161–204.
5. Nousiainen, *Finnish Political System*, p. 224.

7. Finland, 1966–1982

6. Wahlbäck, *Från Mannerheim*, pp. 161–204; Pesonen and Rantala, "Change and Stability," pp. 36–40.
7. Nousiainen, *Finnish Political System*, p. 224.
8. Pesonen and Rantala, "Change and Stability," p. 7.
9. *Economist*, August 28, 1982, "Survey Finland," p. 5.
10. Nousiainen, *Finnish Political System*, pp. 239–40.
11. *Ibid.*, p. 275.
12. Pesonen and Rantala, "Change and Stability," p. 6.
13. *Nk* vol. 12, "Finland" sections in nos. 7–10, especially pp. 580–90.
14. *Nk* 12(10):580–90.
15. *Dagens Nyheter*, April 28–May 5, May 24–28, 1966, pp. 1, 3.
16. Nousiainen, *Finnish Political System*, p. 115; Pesonen and Rantala, "Change and Stability," pp. 13–14; Helander, "A Liberal Corporatist Sub-system," pp. 163–87.
17. Pesonen and Rantala, "Change and Stability," pp. 39–40.
18. Helander, "A Liberal Corporatist Sub-system," p. 171.
19. Pesonen and Rantala, "Change and Stability," pp. 39–40.
20. See note 16.
21. Pesonen and Rantala, "Change and Stability," p. 12.
22. Nyholm, "Finland," pp. 86–87.
23. Nousiainen, *Finnish Political System*, p. 239.
24. See the "Finland" sections of *Nk*, vol. 18, nos. 10–12, and vol. 21, nos. 13–15; 21(16):1066–68; Suhonen, "Finnish Recession," pp. 185–87; Nyholm, "Finland," p. 87; Pesonen and Rantala, "Change and Stability," pp. 39–40; Helander, "A Liberal Corporatist Sub-system," p. 186; and reporting in *HSB*, August 3–27, 1972, p. 1 and passim, November 10–30, 1975, p. 1 and passim, May 1–16, 1977, p. 1 and passim, May 10–27, 1979, p. 1 and passim.
25. Husu, "Economic Stabilization Programs," pp. 254–65. For an account of the 1968 coalition negotiations, see the "Finland" sections in *Nk*, vol. 14, nos. 15–17, and the coverage in *HSB*, February 20–March 4, 1968, p. 1 and passim.
26. For an account of the 1970 coalition negotiations, see the "Finland" sections in *Nk*, vol. 16, nos. 8–12; *HSB*, May 22–June 15, 1970, p. 1 and passim.
27. See the "Finland" sections in *Nk*, vol. 17, nos. 4–6; *HSB*, March 21–26, October 25–30, 1971, p. 1 and passim.
28. For an account of the first 1972 government, see the "Finland" sections in *Nk*, vol. 18, nos. 1–5; *HSB*, January 20–February 3, 1972, p. 1 and passim.
29. For an account of the second 1972 government, see *Nk*, vol. 18, nos. 10–12; *HSB*, August 3–27, 1972, p. 1 and passim.
30. *Nk* 21(13):868.
31. Suhonen, "Finnish Recession," pp. 185–87; Pesonen and Rantala, "Change and Stability," p. 39.
32. For the text of Kekkonen's speech and an account of the events surrounding it, see *Nk* 21(16):1066–68. For the details of the earlier negotiations, see the "Finland" sections of *Nk*, vol. 21, nos. 13–15; *HSB*, November 10–30, 1975, p. 1 and passim.
33. Nyholm, "Finland," p. 87; *HSB*, May 1–16, 1977, and May 10–27, 1979, p. 1 and passim.

34. Pesonen and Rantala, "Change and Stability," pp. 39–40.
35. Helander, "A Liberal Corporatist Sub-system," p. 186.

8. Conclusions

1. The Norwegian governments are: 1961, Labor (minority); 1963, Conservative-Christian-Agrarian-Liberal (majority); 1963, Labor (minority); 1965, Conservative-Agrarian-Liberal-Christian (majority); 1969, Conservative-Agrarian-Christian-Liberal (majority); 1971, Labor (minority); 1972, Christian-Agrarian-Antimarket Liberal (minority); 1973, Labor (minority). Between 1955 and 1961, Norway was governed by Labor party majority governments. The Swedish governments are: 1956, Social Democrat–Agrarian (majority); 1957, Social Democrat (minority); 1958, Social Democrat (minority); 1960, Social Democrat (minority); 1964, Social Democrat (minority); 1970, Social Democrat (minority); 1973, Social Democrat (minority). Between 1968 and 1970, the Social Democrats formed a majority government.

2. The seventeen Italian governments are: 1955, Christian Democrat–Social Democrat–Liberal (majority); 1957, Christian Democrat (minority); 1958 Christian Democrat–Social Democrat (minority); 1959, Christian Democrat (minority); 1960 Christian Democrat (minority); 1962, Christian Democrat–Republican–Social Democrat (minority); 1963, Christian Democrat–Republican–Social Democrat–Socialist (majority); 1964, Christian Democrat–Republican-Socialist–Social Democrat (majority); 1966, Christian Democrat–Social Democrat–Republican-Socialist (majority); 1968, Christian Democrat–Social Democrat–Republican-Socialist (majority); 1969, Christian Democrat (minority); March 1970, Christian Democrat–Socialist–Social Democrat–Republican (majority); August 1970, Christian Democrat–Socialist–Social Democrat–Republican (majority); 1972, Christian Democrat–Social Democrat–Liberal (minority); 1973, Christian Democrat–Socialist–Social Democrat–Republican (majority); March 1974, Christian Democrat–Socialist–Social Democrat (majority); November 1974, Christian Democrat–Republican (minority).

3. The four Dutch governments are: 1956, Catholic-Socialist-Antirevolutionary–Christian Historical (majority); 1959, Catholic–Antirevolutionary–Christian Historical–Liberal (majority); 1963, Catholic-Antirevolutionary–Christian Historical–Liberal (majority); 1965, Catholic-Socialist-Antirevolutionary (majority).

4. See the essays in Lehmbruch and Schmitter, eds., *Trends*, and in Berger, ed., *Organizing Interests*.

5. Average annual rate of unemployment, 1979–1983, was 5.7% for Finland and 8.3% for Italy. Average annual private consumption deflator, 1971–1981, was 11.8% for Finland and 16.0% for Italy. Average annual real GDP growth, 1971–1981, was 3.5% for Finland, 3.0% for Italy. Sources: *OECD Observer* (January 1984), no. 126, pp. 224–27; *OECD Economic Survey, Italy* (December 1982), table D; and *OECD Economic Survey, Finland* (December 1982), table F.

6. See the essays in Penniman, ed., *Italy at the Polls, 1976* and *Italy at the Polls, 1979*.

7. Tarrow, "Three Years," pp. 14–18; Lange, "Sindicati," pp. 943–72; Salvati, "Two Ruling Classes," pp. 331–66; Regini, "Changing Relationships," pp. 109–32.

8. See note 7.
9. See chapter 7, "The Sources of the Transformation."

Appendix A. Methodological Notes

1. Macridis, Allen, and Anselem, "The Mediterranean," p. 511.
2. Bracher, *Die Auflösung*.

Bibliography

Primary Sources

Aftenbladet (Stockholm).
Ha-Aretz (Tel Aviv).
Berlingske Tidende (Copenhagen).
Ha-Boquer (Tel Aviv).
Dagens Nyheter (Stockholm).
Davar (Tel Aviv).
Divrei Ha-Knesset (Israel Parliamentary Proceedings). Jerusalem: Government Printer.
The Economist (London).
Financial Times (London).
The Herut Movement. *Working Platform for the Second Knesset.* Jerusalem: Herut Office, 1951.
Huvudstadbladet (Helsinki).
Information (Copenhagen).
Inspector General of Elections. *Results of Elections to the Eighth Knesset and the Local Authorities, 31 XII 1973.* Jerusalem: Central Bureau of Statistics, 1974.
Jerusalem Post (Jerusalem).
Keesing's Contemporary Archives. London: Longman.
Ma'Ariv (Tel Aviv).
Al Ha-Mishmar (Tel Aviv).
Neue Zürcher Zeitung (Zurich).
Nordic Council. *Nordisk kontakt. Parlamentarisk orientering/Pohjolan Parlamenttien Tiedonantoja.* Stockholm: Nordic Council Offices.

OECD Economic Survey, Finland (Paris).
OECD Economic Survey, Italy (Paris).
OECD Observer (Paris).
Palestine Post (Jerusalem).
Politiken (Copenhagen).
Sefer Ha-Huquim (Tel Aviv).
Svenska Dagbladet (Stockholm).
The Times (London).
Ha-Zofeh (Tel Aviv).

Books and Articles

Akzin, Benjamin. "The Likud." Penniman, ed., *Israel at the Polls,* pp. 104–10.
Alapuro, Risto and Erik Allardt. "The Lapua Movement: The Threat of Rightist Takeover in Finland, 1930–32." Linz and Stepan, eds., *The Breakdown of Democratic Regimes: Europe,* pp. 122–44.
Allardt, Erik. "Social Sources of Finnish Communism: Traditional and Emerging Radicalism." *International Journal of Comparative Sociology* (1964), 5(1):49–72.
Allardt, Erik and Pertti Pesonen. "Citizen Participation in Political Life in Finland." *International Social Science Journal* (1960), 12(1):27–39.
Allardt, Erik and Y. Littunen, eds. *Cleavages, Ideologies, and Party Systems.* Helsinki: Westermarck Society, 1964.
Anton, Thomas. "Policy Making and Political Culture in Sweden." *Scandinavian Political Studies,* (1969), O.S. 4:88–102.
—— *Administered Politics: Elite Political Culture in Sweden.* Boston: Martinus Nijhoff, 1980.
Arter, David. *Bumpkin Against Bigwig: The Emergence of a Green Movement in Finnish Politics.* Tampere: Institute of Political Science Research, 1978.
Axelrod, Robert. *Conflict of Interest: A Theory of Divergent Goals with Application to Politics.* Chicago: Markham, 1970.
Bayne, Edward A. *Transition in Zion: Aspects of Social and Political Change.* American Universities Field Staff Report (EAB-6-62). S. W. Asia Series, vol. 2, no. 1.
Bendix, Reinhard, ed., *Nation Building and Citizenship.* New York: Wiley, 1964.
Bentwich, Norman. "The Fourth Year of Israel." *Fortnightly* (April 1952), n.s. 171:249–54.
—— "Israel, the Sixth Year." *Fortnightly.* (June 1954), n.s. 175:401–7.
Berger, Suzanne, ed. *Organizing Interests in Western Europe: Pluralism, Corporatism, and the Transformation of Politics.* Cambridge: Cambridge University Press, 1981.

Berglund, Sten and Ulf Lindstrom. *The Scandinavian Party Systems*. Lund: Studentlitteratur, 1978.
Bertolt, O., ed. *En bygning vi rejser, Den politiske arbejderbevaegelses historie: Danmark*. Vols. 1–3. Copenhagen: Fremed, 1954.
Beyme, Klaus von. *Parteien in westlichen Demokratien*. Munich: Piper, 1982.
Bile, Lars. *S-SF: Kilder til belysning af forholdet mellom Socialdemokratiet og Socialistisk Folkeparti, 1959–1973*. Copenhagen: Gyldendal, 1974.
Billington, James. "Finland." Cyril Black and Thomas Thornton, eds., *Communism and Revolution: The Strategic Uses of Political Violence*. Princeton: Princeton University Press, 1964.
Birnbaum, Ervin. *The Politics of Compromise*. Madison, N.J.: Fairleigh Dickinson University Press, 1970.
Bluhm, William T. *Building an Austrian Nation: The Political Integration of a Western State*. New Haven: Yale University Press, 1973.
Böltken, Ferdinand and Wolfgang Jagodzinski. "In an Environment of Insecurity: Postmaterialism in the European Community, 1970–1980." *Comparative Political Studies* (1984) 17(4):453–85.
Bracher, Karl Dietrich. *Die Auflösung der Weimarer Republik: Eine Studie zum Problem des Machterfalls in der Demokratie*. Stuttgart: Institut für Politische Wissenschaft, 1955.
Bretton, Henry L. *Stresemann and the Revision of Versailles*. Stanford: Stanford University Press, 1953.
Browne, Eric. *Coalition Theories: A Logical and Empirical Critique*. Beverly Hills: Sage Publications, 1973.
Browne, Eric and John Dreijmanis, eds. *Government Coalitions in Western Democracies*. New York: Longman, 1982.
Buksti, J. and L. N. Johansen. "Organisationssystemet i Danmark." *Økonomi og politik* (1977), pp. 386–415.
——— "Variations in Organizational Participation in Government: The Case of Denmark." *Scandinavian Political Studies*, (1979) n.s. 2:197–220.
Castles, Francis. "Scandinavia: The Politics of Stability." Macridis, ed., *Modern Political Systems*.
Christensen, J. "Normerne for sampspillet mellem den danske centraladministration og interessorganisationerne i centraladministrativt perspektiv." Paper delivered to the 1978 Conference of the Nordic Political Science Association, Bergen, Norway.
Christensen, T. and M. Egeberg. "Organized Group-Government Relations in Norway: On the Structured Selection of Participants, Problems, Solutions, and Choice Opportunities." *Scandinavian Political Studies*, (1979) n.s. 2:239–60.
Colliander, Rafael. *Svenska folkpartiet i Finland, 1906–1926*. Helsinki: Tidningsaktiebolaget-Nylands Tryckeri, 1926.
Craig, Gordon. *Germany, 1866–1945*. London: Oxford University Press, 1980.

Cross, John G. *The Economics of Bargaining.* New York: Basic Books, 1969.
Crozier, Michel, Samuel Huntington, and Joji Watanuki. *The Crisis of Democracy.* New York: New York University Press, 1975.
Daalder, Hans. "Cabinets and Party Systems in Ten Smaller European Democracies." *Acta Politica.* (1971) 6(3):282–303.
—— "In Search of the Center of European Party Systems." *American Political Science Review* (1984) 78(1):92–109.
——, ed. *Parlement en politieke besluitvorming in Nederland.* Alphen aan den Rijn: Samson Uitgeverij, 1975.
Dahl, Robert, ed. *Political Oppositions in Western Democracies.* New Haven: Yale University Press, 1966.
Dalton, Russell, Paul Beck, and Scott Flanagan. "Electoral Change in Advanced Industrial Democracies." Dalton, Beck, and Flanagan, eds., *Electoral Change in Advanced Industrial Democracies,* pp. 3–25.
—— "Partisan Forces and Political Change." Dalton, Beck, and Flanagan, eds., *Electoral Change in Advanced Industrial Democracies,* pp. 451–77.
——, eds., *Electoral Change in Advanced Industrial Democracies: Realignment or Dealignment?* Princeton: Princeton University Press, 1984.
Danstrup, J. *A History of Denmark.* Copenhagen: Gyldendal, 1949.
De Swaan, Abram. *Coalition Theories and Cabinet Formation: A Study of Formal Theories of Coalition Formation Applied to Nine European Parliaments After 1919.* Amsterdam: Elsevier, 1973.
Di Palma, Giuseppe. *Political Syncretism in Italy: Historical Coalition Strategies and the Present Crisis.* Policy Papers in International Affairs, no. 7. Berkeley: Institute of International Studies, 1978.
Dodd, Lawrence. *Coalitions in Parliamentary Government.* Princeton: Princeton University Press, 1976.
Dorpalen, Andreas. *Hindenburg and the Weimar Republic.* Princeton: Princeton University Press, 1964.
Dovring, Folke. "Scandinavia." Grew, ed., *Crises of Political Development,* pp. 139–63.
Einhorn, Eric. *National Security and Domestic Politics in Post-War Denmark: Some Principal Issues, 1945–1961.* Odense University Studies in History and Social Science, vol. 27. Odense: Odense University Press, 1975.
Elklit, J. and J. N. Petersen. "Denmark Enters the EEC." *Scandinavian Political Studies,* (1973) o.s. 8:200–205.
Elvander, Nils, ed. *Interessorganisationerna i dagens Sverige. Andra reviderade upplaga.* Lund: Gleerup, 1969.
Engelstoft, Povl and Frantz Wendt. *Haandbog i Danmarks politiske historie fra Freden i Kiel til vore dage.* Copenhagen, 1934.
Farneti, Paolo. "Social Conflict, Parliamentary Fragmentation, Institutional Shift, and the Rise of Fascism: Italy." Linz and Stepan, eds., *The Breakdown of Democractic Regimes: Europe.*

Fitzmaurice, J. "Scandinavian Referenda and EEC Entry." *European Review* (Spring 1973), pp. 12–19.
Gaasemyr, J. *Organisasjonsbyrakrati og korporativisme.* Oslo: NKS-Forlaget, 1979.
Galenson, Walter. *Labor in Norway.* Cambridge: Harvard University Press, 1949.
—— *The Danish System of Labor Relations: A Study in Industrial Peace.* Cambridge: Harvard University Press, 1952.
Galenson, Walter and John Clarke Adams. *Comparative Labor Movements.* New York: Prentice-Hall, 1952.
—— "Current Problems of Scandinavian Trade Unionism." Karl H. Cerny, ed., *Scandinavia at the Polls,* pp. 267–96. Washington, D.C.: American Enterprise Institute, 1977.
Gamson, William A. "A Theory of Coalition Formation." *American Sociological Review* (1961) 26(2):373–82.
Gerlich, Peter. "Consociationalism to Competition: The Austrian Party System Since 1945." Paper delivered to the Colloquium on Recent Changes in European Party Systems, European University Institute, Florence, December 1978.
Geyl, Pieter. *History of the Low Countries: Episodes and Problems.* London: Macmillan, 1964.
Glans, Ingemar. "The Danish Parliamentary Election of 1966." *Scandinavian Political Studies,* (1967) o.s. 2:23–38.
Goldman, Eliezer. *Religious Issues in Israel's Political Life.* Jerusalem: Religious Party Press, n.d.
Grew, Raymond, ed. *Crises of Political Development in Europe and the United States.* Princeton: Princeton University Press, 1978.
Griffiths, John C. *Modern Iceland.* New York: Praeger, 1969.
Groenings, Sven. "Cooperation Among Norway's Non-Socialist Political Parties." Ph.D. diss., Stanford University, 1962.
Grosser, Alfred. *Geschichte Deutschlands seit 1945: Eine Bilanz.* Munich: Deutschen Taschenbuch, 1980.
Hadenius, Stig, Björn Molin, and Hans Wieslander. *Sverige efter 1900.* Stockholm: Bonniers, 1978.
Hallenstvedt, A. and M. Vraa. "Det organiserte samfunn." N. Ramsoy and M. Vraa, eds., *Det norske samfunn.* Oslo: Gyldendal Norskforlaget, 1975.
Hamalainen, Pekka Kaleui. *In Time of Storm: Revolution, Civil War, and the Ethnolinguistic Issue in Finland.* Albany: State University of New York, 1979.
Hansen, K. ed. *Det danske landbrugs historie.* Vol. 2. Copenhagen: Gads Forlag, 1945.
Haue, Harry, Jorgen Olsen, and Jorn Aarup-Kristensen. *Det ny Danmark, 1890–1978. Udviklingslinier og tendens.* Copenhagen: Munksgaard, 1980.

Headey, Bruce W. "Trade Unions and National Wage Policies." *The Journal of Politics* (May 1970), 32(2):407–31.

Heckscher, Gunnar. "Interest Groups in Sweden: Their Political Role." Henry Ehrman, ed., *Interest Groups on Four Continents*. Pittsburgh: University of Pittsburgh Press, 1958.

Helander, Voitto. "A Liberal Corporatist Sub-system in Action: The Incomes Policy System in Finland." Lehmbruch and Schmitter, eds., *Patterns*, pp. 163–87.

Henig, Stanley, ed. *Political Parties in the European Community*. London: Allen and Unwin, 1979.

Herman, Valentine and John Pope. "Minority Governments in Western Democracies." *British Journal of Political Science* (1973) 3(2):192–212.

Hermeren, H. "Government Formation in Multiparty Systems." *Scandinavian Political Studies*, (1976) o.s. 11:131–46.

Hodgson, John. *Communism in Finland: A History and Interpretation*. Princeton: Princeton University Press, 1967.

Horowitz, Dan and Moshe Lissak. *Origins of the Israeli Polity: Palestine Under the Mandate*. Chicago: University of Chicago Press, 1978.

Hvidt, Kristian. *Venstre og forsvarssagen, 1870–1901*. Århus: Institut for Statskundskab, 1960.

Husu, Erkki. "The Economic Stabilization Programs and Their Political Consequences in Finland, 1967–1970." *Scandinavian Political Studies*, (1970) o.s.7:254–65.

Ikle, Fred C. *How Nations Negotiate*. New York: Harper and Row, 1964.

Inglehart, Ronald. *The Silent Revolution: Changing Values and Political Styles Among Western Publics*. Princeton: Princeton University Press, 1977.

—— "The Changing Structure of Political Cleavages in Western Society." Dalton, Beck, Flanagan, eds., *Electoral Change in Advanced Industrial Democracies*, pp. 25–70.

—— "New Perspectives on Value Change: Response to Lafferty and Knutsen, Savage and Boltken and Jagodzinski." *Comparative Political Studies* (1984) 17(4):485–533.

Irving, R. E. M. *The Christian Democratic Parties of Western Europe*. London: Allen and Unwin, 1979.

Isaac, Rael Jean. *Party and Politics in Israel: Three Visions of a Jewish State*. London: Longman, 1981.

Jackson, Gabriel. *The Spanish Republic and the Civil War, 1931–1939*. Princeton: Princeton University Press, 1965.

Jarlov, D., L. N. Johansen, and O. P. Kristensen. "The Danish Committee System: A Preliminary Report from a Study of Danish Committees, 1946–1975." Paper delivered to the 1976 Congress of the International Political Science Association, Edinburgh.

Jensen, E. *Danish Agriculture, Its Economic Development*. Copenhagen, 1937.

Jensen, Erik Vagn, ed. *De politiske partier.* Copenhagen: Det danske Forlaget, 1964.
Johansen, Lars N. and Ole P. Kristensen. "Corporatist Traits in Denmark, 1946–1976." Lehmbruch and Schmitter, eds., *Patterns of Corporatist Policy Making,* pp. 189–219.
Jones, W. Glyn. *Denmark.* New York: Praeger, 1970.
Jorberg, L. "The Industrial Revolution in Scandinavia." Carlo Cippola, ed., *Fontana Economic History of Europe,* vol. 4. London: Fontana Books, 1970.
Kaarsted, Tage. *Dansk politik, 1960'erne: Taktik og strategi.* Copenhagen: Gyldendal, 1969.
—— *Regeringskrisen, 1957, en studie: Regeringsdannelsen proces.* 2d ed. Århus: Institute for Press Research and Contemporary History, 1969.
—— *Kilder til valget og regeringsdannelsen, 1968.* Copenhagen: Gyldendal, 1971.
Kalela, J. *Right-Wing Radicalism in Finland During the Interwar Period.*" *Scandinavian Journal of History* (1976) 1(2):121–37.
Kalischer, Rabbi Zvi Hirsch. "Seeking Zion." Arthur Hertberg, ed., *The Zionist Idea: A Historical Analysis and Reader.* New York: Atheneum, 1975.
Kirby, D. G. *Finland in the Twentieth Century.* London: Hurst, 1979.
Knoellinger, Carl Erik. *Labor in Finland.* Cambridge: Harvard University Press, 1960.
Kolding, K. *Danmarks Retsforbund.* Aabenraa: Danskerens Forlaget, 1958.
Krag, Jens Otto and K. B. Andersen. *Kamp og fornyelse, Socialdemokratiets i dansk politik, 1955–1971.* Copenhagen: Fremed, 1971.
Kraines, Oscar. "Israel: The Emergence of a Polity, Part One." *Western Political Quarterly* (1953) 6(3):518–42.
Krosby, H. Peter. *Finland, Germany, and the Soviet Union, 1940–1941: The Petsamo Dispute.* Madison: University of Wisconsin Press, 1968.
Kuhnle, Stein. *Patterns of Social and Political Mobilization: A Historical Analysis of the Nordic Countries.* Beverly Hills: Sage Publications, 1975.
Kvavik, Robert. *Interest Groups in Norwegian Politics.* Oslo: Universitetsforlaget, 1976.
Lange, Halvard M. "Scandinavia." H. A. Marquand, ed., *Organized Labor on Four Continents.* London: Longman, Green, 1939.
Lange, Peter. "Sindicati, partiti, stato e liberal corporativismo." *Il Mulino* (1979), 28:943–72.
Laqueur, Walter. *A History of Zionism.* New York: Holt, Rinehart and Winston, 1972.
Larsen, Axel. *Den levende vej.* Copenhagen: Eget Forlaget, 1958.
Lauring, Paul A. *A History of the Kingdom of Denmark.* Copenhagen: Gyldendal, 1968.
Lehmbruch, Gerhard. "Introduction: Neo-Corporatism in Comparative Perspective." Lehmbruch and Schmitter, eds., *Patterns of Corporatist Policy Making,* pp. 1–29.

Lehmbruch, Gerhard and Philippe Schmitter, eds. *Patterns of Corporatist Policy Making.* Beverly Hills: Sage Publications, 1982.

———, eds., *Trends Toward Corporatist Intermediation.* London: Sage Publications, 1979.

Leieserson, Michael. "Game Theory and the Study of Coalition Behavior." Sven Groenings, E. W. Kelly, and Michael Leieserson, eds., *The Study of Coalition Behavior: Theoretical Perspectives and Cases from Four Continents,* pp. 255–72. New York: Holt, Rinehart and Winston, 1970.

Leonardi, Roberto. "Polarizzazione o convergenza nel sistema politico italiano?" Alerbert Martinelli and Gianfranco Pasquino, eds., *La politica nell' Italia che cambia,* pp. 299–399. Milan: Feltrinelli, 1978.

Lijphart, Arend. *The Politics of Accommodation, Pluralism, and Democracy in The Netherlands.* 2d ed. Berkeley and Los Angeles: University of California Press, 1975.

——— "Political Parties: Ideologies and Programs." David Butler, Austin Ranney, and Howard Penniman, eds., *Democracy at the Polls: A Comparative Study of Competitive National Elections,* pp. 27–42. Washington, D.C.: American Enterprise Institute, 1981.

Lindal, Sigurour. "Political Parties." Johannes Nordal and Valdimar Kristinsson, eds., *Iceland, 874–1974,* pp. 150–59. Reykjavik: Central Bank of Iceland, 1976.

Lindman, L. *Den svenska partibildningen i Finland.* Uppsala: Festkrifts till A. Brusewitz, 1941.

Linz, Juan and Alfred Stepan, eds. *The Breakdown of Democratic Regimes: Europe.* Baltimore: Johns Hopkins University Press, 1978.

Lipset, Seymour Martin. "Radicalism or Reformism: The Sources of Working-Class Politics." Mimeo. Stein Rokkan Memorial Lecture, Copenhagen, June 29, 1982.

Lipset, Seymour Martin and Stein Rokkan. "Cleavages, Structures, Party Systems, and Voter Alignments: An Introduction." Lipset and Rokkan, eds., *Party Systems and Voter Alignments,* pp. 1–64. New York: Free Press, 1967.

Luebbert, Gregory M. "Coalition Theory and Government Formation in Multiparty Democracies." *Comparative Politics* (1983) 15(2):235–49.

——— "A Theory of Government Formation." *Comparative Political Studies* (1984) 17(2):229–64.

Mabille, Xavier and Val Lorwin. "The Belgian Socialist Party." Paterson and Thomas, eds., *Social Democratic Parties in Western Europe,* pp. 389–408.

——— "Belgium." Henig, ed., *Political Parties in the European Community,* pp. 6–28.

Macridis, Roy, ed. *Modern Political Systems: Europe.* 4th ed. Englewood Cliffs, N.J.: Prentice-Hall, 1978.

Macridis, Roy C., Christopher S. Allen, and Winston L. Anselem. "The Mediterranean: The Politics of Instability—An Overview." Macridis, ed., *Modern Political Systems,* pp. 481–514.

Bibliography

Maddeley, J. T. S. "Scandinavian Christian Democracy: Throwback or Protest?" *European Journal of Political Research* (1977) 5(3):267–86.

Mahler, Gregory S. and Richard J. Trilling. "Coalition Behavior and Cabinet Formation: The Case of Israel." *Comparative Political Studies* (1975) 8(2):200–33.

McDaniels, Gerald R. "The Danish Unicameral Parliament." Ph.D. diss., University of California, Berkeley, 1963.

Meijer, H. "Bureaucracy and Policy Formulation in Sweden." *Scandinavian Political Studies*, (1969) o.s. 4:103–16.

Miller, Kenneth. *Government and Politics in Denmark*. Boston: Houghton Mifflin, 1968.

Milward, Alan and S. B. Saul. *The Economic Development of Continental Europe, 1780–1870*. London: Allen and Unwin, 1979.

Moller, P., ed. *De politiske partier*. Copenhagen: Det Danske Forlaget, 1974.

Myers, Charles. *Industrial Relations in Sweden*. Cambridge: MIT Press, 1951.

Nielsen, Vagn Oluf. *Danmarks forste arbejderflertal: Kilder til belysning af det parliamentariske samarbejde mellem Socialdemokratiet og Socialistiskfolkepartiet: 1966–1967*. Copenhagen: Fremed, 1974.

Nilson, Sten Sparre. "Norway and Denmark." Peter Merkl, ed., *Western European Party Systems*, pp. 205–35. New York: Free Press, 1980.

Ninn-Hansen, Erik. *Syv år for VKR*. Copenhagen: De Schønbergske Forlag, 1974.

Norlund, Ib. "Fornyelsen, derblev vaek—om SFs kongres og dets udvikling." *Tiden*. (1967) 22:205–9.

Norman, Edward. "Israel After Two Years." *Foreign Policy Reports*. (1952) 26(5):42–51.

Nousiainen, Jaako. *The Finnish Political System*. John J. Hodgson, tr. Cambridge: Harvard University Press, 1971.

Nyholm, Pekka. "Finland: A Probabilistic View of Coalition Formation." Browne and Dreijmanis, eds., *Government Coalitions in Western Democracies*, pp. 71–109.

O'Connor, James. *The Fiscal Crisis of the State*. New York: St. Martin's Press, 1973.

O'Hegarty, P. S. *A History of Ireland Under the Union, 1801–1922*. London: Oxford University Press, 1952.

Olsen, Johan, ed. *Politisk organisering*. Oslo. NKS-Forlaget, 1978.

Olsen, Johan, Paul Roness, and Harald Saetren. "Norway: Still Peaceful Coexistence and Revolution in Slow Motion?" Jeremy Richardson, ed., *Policy Styles in Western Europe*, pp. 47–80. London: Allen and Unwin, 1982.

Østerud, Øyvind. "Agrarian Structure and Peasant Politics in Scandinavia." Ph.D. diss., London School of Economics, 1974.

Paltiel, Hayyim Zeev. "The Progressive Party in Israel: A Study of a Small Party in Israel." Ph.D. diss., Hebrew University, 1963.

Paterson, William E. and Alastair H. Thomas, eds. *Social Democratic Parties in Western Europe.* London: Croom Helm, 1977.

Pedersen, K. S. "The First Socialist Majority: Denmark's 1966 General Election." *Parliamentary Affairs* (1967) 20(2):144–57.

Pedersen, Oluf. *Erindringer, Fra nimandsudvalg til trekantregering.* Copenhagen, 1967.

Penniman, Howard R., ed. *Israel at the Polls: The Knesset Elections of 1977.* Washington, D.C.: American Enterprise Institute, 1979.

———, ed. *Italy at the Polls: The Parliamentary Elections of 1976.* Washington, D.C.: American Enterprise Institute, 1981.

———, ed. *Italy at the Polls, 1979: A Study of the Parliamentary Elections.* Washington, D. C.: American Enterprise Institute, 1981.

Pesonen, Pertti and Onni Rantala. "Change and Stability in the Finnish Party System." Paper delivered to the Colloquium on Recent Changes in European Party Systems, European University Institute, Florence, December 1978.

Petersen, Gert. "Socialistik folkeparti." Jensen, ed., *De politiske partier.*

Peterson, E. A. "Interest Group Incorporation in Sweden." Paper delivered to the 1977 meeting of the American Political Science Association, Washington, D.C.

Pirenne, Henri. *Medieval Cities: Their Origins and the Revival of Trade.* Princeton: Princeton University Press, 1925.

Pogorelskin, A. "The Politics of Frustration: The Governor-Generalship of N. I. Bobrikov in Finland, 1898–1904." *Journal of Baltic Studies* (1972) 7(3):231–46.

Pridham, Geoffrey. *The Nature of the Italian Party System.* London: Croom Helm, 1981.

Rantala, Onni. "The Political Regions in Finland." *Scandinavian Political Studies,* (1967) o.s. 2:116–40.

Rasila, V. "The Finnish Civil War and Landlease Problems." *Scandinavian Economic History Review* (1962) 1(2):110–42.

Rasmussen, E. and R. Skovmand. *Det radikale Venstre, 1905–1955.* Copenhagen: Det danske Forlaget, 1955.

Regini, Marino. "Changing Relationships Between Labor and the State in Italy: Towards a Neo-Corporatist System?" Lehmbruch and Schmitter, eds., *Patterns of Corporatist Policy Making.*

Reich, Bernard. "Israel's Foreign Policy and the 1977 Parliamentary Elections." Penniman, ed., *Israel at the Polls,* pp. 255–83.

Renier, G. J. *The Dutch Nation: An Historical Study.* London: Allen and Unwin, 1944.

Rhode, P. P. "The Communist Party of Denmark." Anthony F. Upton, ed., *Communism in Scandinavia and Finland.* New York: Anchor Press, 1973.

Riker, William. *The Theory of Political Coalitions.* New Haven: Yale University Press, 1962.
Rimstad, I. A. "De Uafhaengige." Jensen, ed., *De politiske partier.*
Rokkan, Stein, ed. *Approaches to the Study of Political Participation.* Bergen: Christian Michelsen Institute, 1962.
—— "Numerical Democracy and Corporate Pluralism." Dahl, ed., *Political Oppositions in Western Democracies.*
—— "Votes Count, Resources Decide: Relfeksjoner over territorialietet vs. funcjonalitet i Norsk of Europeisk politik." Stein Rokkan, ed., *Et festkrift till Jens Arup Seip,* pp. 214–24. Oslo: Gyldendal Norskforlaget, 1975.
Rose, Richard and Derik Urwin. "Persistence and Change in Western Party Systems Since 1945." *Political Studies* (1970) 18(3):287–319.
Rosenburg, Arthur. *Geschichte der Weimarer Republik.* Frankfurt: Europäische Verlagsanstalt, 1961.
Rubinstein, Elyakin. "The Lesser Parties in the Israeli Elections of 1977." Penniman, ed., *Israel at the Polls,* pp. 173–99.
Ruin, Olof. "Participatory Democracy and Corporatism: The Case of Sweden." *Scandinavian Political Studies,* (1976) o.s 9:171–86.
Rustow, Dankwart. *The Politics of Compromise: A Study of Parties and Cabinet Government in Sweden.* Princeton: Princeton University Press, 1955.
Sachar, Howard. *A History of Israel, from the Rise of Zionism to Our Time.* New York: Knopf, 1981.
Safran, Nadav. *Israel, Embattled Ally.* Cambridge: Harvard University Press, 1979.
Salvati, Michele. "May 1968 and the Hot Autumn of 1969: The Response of Two Ruling Classes." Berger, ed., *Organizing Interests in Western Europe,* pp. 331–66.
Sani, Giacomo and Giovanni Sartori. "Frammentazione, polarizzazione e cleavages: democrazie facili e difficili." *Rivista Italiana di Scienza Politica* (1978) 8(3):339–61.
Sänkiaho, Risto. "A Model of the Rise of Populism and Support for the Finnish Rural Party." *Scandinavian Political Studies,* (1971) o.s. 6:27–47
Sartori, Giovanni. *Parties and Party Systems: A Framework for Analysis.* London: Cambridge University Press, 1976.
—— "Il pluralismo polarizzato: Critische e repliche." *Rivista Italiana di Scienza Politica* (1982) 12(1):3–44.
Savage, James. "Postmaterialism of the Left and Right: Political Conflict in Postindustrial Society." *Comparative Political Studies* (1984) 17(4):431–53.
Scalapino, Robert A. and Masumi Junnosuke. *Parties and Politics in Contemporary Japan.* Berkeley and Los Angeles: University of California Press, 1969.
Schechtman, Joseph B. and Yehuda Benair. *A History of the Revisionist Movement, 1925–1930.* Tel Aviv: Hadar, 1970.

Schmitter, Philippe. "Interest Intermediation and Regime Governability in Contemporary Western Europe and North America." Berger, ed., *Organizing Interests in Western Europe*, pp. 285–327.

Sedgwick, Frank. *The Tragedy of Manuel Azaña and the Fate of the Spanish Republic*. Columbus: Ohio State University Press, 1963.

Shapiro, Yonathan. *The Formative Years of the Israeli Labor Party: The Organization of Power, 1919–1930*. Beverly Hills: Sage Publications, 1976.

Simon, Walter B. "Democracy in the Shadow of Imposed Sovereignty: The First Republic of Austria." Linz and Stepan, eds., *The Breakdown of Democratic Regimes: Europe*.

Sirkin, Ronald M. "Coalition, Conflict and Compromise: The Party Politics of Israel." Ph.D. diss., Pennsylvania State University, 1971.

Skrubbeltrang, F. *Agricultural Development and Rural Reform in Denmark*. Agricultural Studies, no. 22. Rome: Food and Agriculture Organization, 1953.

Snyder, Glenn H. and Paul Diesing. *Conflict Among Nations: Bargaining, Decision Making, and System Structure in International Crises*. Princeton: Princeton University Press, 1977.

Sorensen, Kurt. "Denmark: Politics Since 1964." *Scandinavian Political Studies*, (1967) o.s. 2:263–65.

Stjernquist, Nils. "Sweden: Stability or Deadlock?" Dahl, ed., *Political Oppositions in Western Democracies*.

Strøm, Kaare. "Minority Government and Majority Rule." Mimeo. Political science department, Stanford University, November 1979.

Suhonen, Pertti. "The Finnish Recession Election of 1975." *Scandinavian Political Studies*, (1976) o.s. 11:148–56.

Svensson, Palle. "Support for the Danish Social Democratic Party, 1924–1939—Growth and Response." *Scandinavian Political Studies*, (1974) o.s. 9:127–46.

Tamburrano, Giuseppe. *Storia e cronaco del Centro-Sinistra*. Milan: Feltrinelli, 1971.

Tarrow, Sidney. "Three Years of Italian Democracy." Penniman, ed., *Italy at the Polls, 1979*, pp. 1–34.

Thomas, Alastair. "Social Democracy in Denmark." Paterson and Thomas, eds., *Social Democratic Parties in Western Europe*, pp. 234–72.

Tomasson, Richard F. *Iceland, the First New Society*. Minneapolis: University of Minnesota Press, 1980.

Torgersen, Ulf. "The Trend Toward Political Consensus: The Case of Norway." Erik Allardt and Stein Rokkan, eds., *Mass Politics*, pp. 93–104. New York: Free Press, 1970.

—— "Chapter Six: Political Institutions." Natalie R. Ramsoy, ed., *Norwegian Society*. Oslo: Universitetsforlaget, 1974.

Torgovnik, Efraim. "A Movement for Change in a Stable System." Penniman, ed., *Israel at the Polls*, pp. 143–77.
Tsurutani, Taketsugu. *Political Change in Japan*. New York: McKay, 1977.
Upton, Anthony F. *The Finnish Revolution, 1917–1918*. Minneapolis: University of Minnesota Press, 1980.
Wahlbäck, Krister. *Från Mannerheim til Kekkonen: Huvudlinjer i finlandsk politik, 1917–1967*. Stockholm: Bonniers, 1967.
Walton, Richard F. and Robert B. McKersie. *A Behavioral Theory of Labor Negotiations*. New York: McGraw-Hill, 1965.
Wheeler, Christopher. *White-Collar Power: Changing Patterns of Interest Group Behavior in Sweden*. Chicago: University of Illinois Press, 1975.
Zartman, I. William, ed. *The Fifty Percent Solution*. Garden City: Anchor Books, 1976.
———, ed. *The Negotiating Process: Theories and Applications*. Beverly Hills: Sage Publications, 1978.
Zohar, David M. *Political Parties in Israel: Evolution of Israeli Democracy*. New York: Praeger, 1974.

Index

Abortion as issue, 50, 270–71, 273
Achdut Haavodah (party, Israel), 97, 99, 100, 102–3, 104, 110, 122–28, 129–36, 137, 139, 148
Agrarian-Conservative-Liberal-Christian People's party government (Norway): *1965*, 269–70; *1969*, 270–71
Agrarian-Conservative-Liberal-Swedish party government (Findland, 1964), 214–17 Agrarian government (Finland, 1961), 209–11 Agrarian-Liberal-Conservative-Swedish party government (Finland, 1962), 211–13
Agrarian-Liberal government (Finland, 1957), 202–3
Agrarian Liberals (party, Denmark), 154, 155–56, 158
Agrarian-Liberal-Social Democratic Opposition government (Finland, 1957), 203–5
Agrarian-Liberal-Swedish party government (Finland, 1957), 199–202
Agrarian party (Finland), 190, 193–94, 195, 196, 197–213, 214–17, 223–24, 226, 227, 228, 229, 230, 244
Agrarian party (Norway), 235, 266, 267, 268, 269–71, 272, 273
Agrarian party (Sweden), 235–36, 258, 259, 261, 262, 263, 264, 265

Agricultural and forest land issue: Swedish politics, 259, 263, 265
Agricultural Incomes Law (Finland), 215–16
Agricultural issue: Italian politics, 284; Finland, 199, 200–1, 202, 203, 205, 206, 209–10, 212, 213, 216
Agriculture, commercialization of, 54, 56; Denmark, 152–53; Finland, 188, 192–93, 194, 195
Agriculture, Danish, 155–57
Agudah Yisrael (party, Israel), 95, 97, 103, 104, 109–12, 117, 119, 123, 127, 129, 133, 140, 142, 143, 144, 298*n*1
Alignment-Mapam-NRP-Pagi-Liberal government (Israel, 1965), 136–41
Alignment party (Israel), 136–41, 142, 143
Aloni, Shulamit, 144
Andreotti, Giulio, 219
Andreotti government (Italy), 243
"Andreotti Solution" (Italy), 243
Antidemocratic parties, 11, 55, 70, 233, 236; blackmail potential of, 12–15, 29–30; policy preference of, 53
Antimarket Liberal party (Norway), 272
Anti-Semitism, 95, 124
Antisystem parties, 12–13

Anti-Revolutionary party (Netherlands), 274–79
Anton, Thomas, "Political Culture of Bureaucrats and Politicians," 22, 27
Arabs, 126; in Israel, 101, 103, 108, 116, 130, 133, 134, 137, 141
Asefat Hanivhasim (Assembly of Delegates of the Yishuv), 97–98, 99
Aura I (government, Finland), 229
Aura II (government, Finland), 229
Austria, 15, 16, 249, 251; consensual politics, 34; corporatism, 32, 39; interwar, 43; party competition, 15; transition to democratic rule, 39, 40, 42, 44
Authoritarian interludes, 39–40, 250

Balance of payments, 156–57; deficit issue, Denmark, 159, 161–62, 165, 166, 169, 176, 178
Bank loan issue; Norweigian politics, 269
Bargaining, 51, 52; and limits of tolerance, 62–65
Bargaining relationships, 5, 219, 235–36, 237–38, 239–40, 252, 255; in case summaries, 257, 258; consolidated results, 247T; Danish politics, 184–85; Finnish politics, 217–18; Israeli politics, 128, 147–48; Norwegian politics, 270; policy preferences in, 62–65
Begin, Menachim, 134
Begin government (Israel), 79
Belgium, 16, 56, 249, 251; as dominated-competitive system, 72–73, 82–83; government formation in, 3; issues in, 19; party competition in, 15; policy profiles in, 58, 59; transition to democratic rule, 40, 41, 42, 43; as undominated-competitive system, 85, 86T
Ben-Gurion, David, 100, 105, 110, 117, 119, 120, 121, 123, 126, 127, 130, 131, 132, 134–35, 136; followers of, 136–37, 138
Blackmail, 79, 81, 239; potential for, 12, 13, 14, 29–30
Bourgeois parties, 57; Denmark, 155, Finland, 190, 191, 195; Israel, 101; Norway, 269, 271

Braun, Otto, 48–49
Budget deficit issue: Swedish politics, 262–63

Cabinet(s), 37, 67, 70; Israel, 130, 140; working-class representation in, 245
Caretaker government, 254–55; Belgium, 83; Finland, 227, 229
Case summaries, 257–93
Catholic church, 40, 56
Catholic People's party (Austria), 44
Catholic People's party (KVP) (Netherlands), 59–60, 72, 79, 239, 274–79
Center Democratic party (Denmark), 182–83, 184, 235
Center party (Sweden), 262
Center-periphery issue: Finnish politics, 195–96, 197, 204
Center-periphery profile, 54–55, 57, 58, 59
Central Federation of Trade Unions (Finland), 224–25
Centralization, 31–32, 245
Centrifugal competion, 12, 14, 15, 16, 235, 240; in conflictual democracies, 70–71: in Finnish society and party system, 224, 225, 226
Centripetal competition, 12, 14, 15, 16
CGIL (Union, Italy), 243
"Change of System" (Denmark), 152
Christian Democratic Appeal (party, Netherlands), 59–60, 78, 79
Christian Democratic party (DC) (Italy), 243, 244, 257, 279–93
Christian Democratic Union/Christian Social Union (CDU/CSU) (Germany), 72, 73–76
Christian party (Norway), 235, 266, 267
Christian Historical Union (party, Netherlands), 274–78
Christian People's-Agrarian-Antimarket Liberal party government (Norway, 1972), 272
Christian People's party (Denmark), 182, 183, 184
Christian People's party (Norway), 268, 269–71, 272, 273
Christian Socials (party, Belgium), 82, 83

Citizen's Rights Movement (Israel), 141–46
Civil servant governments (Finland), 205, 214, 217–18, 229, 240
Civil service employment issue: Dutch politics, 275
Civil service reform: Israeli politics, 115, 117
Civil war(s), 39, 188
Civil War (Finland), 191–92, 193, 196
Class conflict, 55
Classes: in Danish politics, 150, 152–54
Cleavages, 233, 249, 255; in case summaries, 258; in Finnish politics, 196–97, 226, 231; social, 53–58, 59
Clergy: Finland, 187
Coalition outcomes, 256; case summaries—Italy, 281, 282, 283, 284, 285, 286, 287, 288, 289, 290, 292, 293,—Netherlands, 277, 278, 279,—Norway, 267, 268, 269, 270, 271, 272, 273,—Sweden, 261, 262, 263, 264, 266; politicians in and, 247; in unconsolidated democracries, 219, 220
Coalitions, governing: and democratic politics, 1–6; literature on, 1–2; party leaders and, 67–89
Coalition situation, classical, 238
Coalition theory, 2–6, 45–46, 84, 89; consolidated results of, 247T; empirically validated, 3; limits of 249–52; predictive successes/failures, 234–35, 236, 237–38, 239–41, 292; *See also* Hypotheses (coalition theory)
Cold War, 56
Commercial television issue: Dutch politics, 278, 279
Communist parties, 10, 13, 142; importance of inclusion of, 243–45
Communist party (Denmark), 157–58, 159, 165, 167, 180, 182
Communist party (Finland), 13, 14, 189, 191, 192, 195 197–98, 200–01, 202, 204, 207–08, 211, 212, 214, 223–24, 225, 226, 227, 228, 229, 230, 231, 244, 246
Communist party (France), 15, 49

Communist party (Italy), 13, 14, 243, 244
Communist party (Norway), 273
Communist party (Sweden), 15, 258, 266
Communist party (Weimar Republic), 15
Competition: bilateral, 240; interparty, 13–16, 93, 94, 242; intraparty, 54, 59–60; *see also* Centrifugal competition; Centripetal competition
Competitive systems (democracies), 10, 19, 43, 87, 233; bargaining relationships in, 64–65; conflict resolution in, 238–39; dominated-to-undominated change, 76–79, 81–82; minority/majority governments in, 87–89; policy formulation in, 67–68; *see also* Dominated-competitive democracies; Undominated competitive democracies
Compromise(s), 21, 22, 63, 81, 256; in confilictual democracies, 70–71, 237; in consensual democracies, 234; corporatism and, 37, 39; negative inducement to, 68–69; transition to democratic rule and, 40; *see also* Explicit compromise; Implicit compromise
Concessions, 4, 68, 86, 234, 239, 241
Confederation of Industry (Norway), 36
Conflict(s), 1, 24–27, 29, 53, 54
Conflict resolution, 40; avoidance of, 247; in competitive democracies, 238–39; in conflictual democracies, 236–38; in consensual democracies, 234–36
Conflictual systems (democracies), 6, 10, 14, 44, 70–72, 84, 233, 241, 246; bargaining relationships in, 64–65; concern of democratic parties in, 207–8; corporatism needed in, 242–46; limit of tolerance in, 198–99, 201, minority/majority governments in, 87–89; nonpolicy relations in, 240; policy formulation in, 67–68; resolution of party conflict in, 236–38; test of hypotheses for, 251; transition from oligarchy to democratic rule, 43
Consensual politics, 238; institutional and historical bases of, 29–44; normative commitment to, 67, 68, 69, 238

330   Index

Consensual systems (democracies), 10, 11–12, 19, 20, 24, 29, 39, 44, 68–70, 84, 178, 184–85, 233, 241; bargaining-relationships; 64–65; conflict resolution in, 234–36; cooperation in, 18: corporation in 42, 234, 238; minority/majority governments in, 87–89; party structure in, 72; policy formation in, 67; test of hypothesis for, 251; transition from oligarchy to democratic rule, 43

Consensus building, 9, 10, 11, 17–21, 22; commitment to, 29–30; mechanisms for, 67–68, 87, 88, 234

Conservative-Liberal-Agrarian-Christian People's party government (Norway, 1963), 268

Conservative party (Denmark), 154, 156, 157, 158, 159, 160, 162, 164, 165, 166, 168, 169, 170, 171, 172, 173, 174–78, 180, 181, 182, 183, 184, 235

Conservative party (Finland), 190, 194–95, 196, 197–98, 200, 201, 202, 203, 204, 209, 210, 211–13, 214–17, 222, 227

Conservative party (Norway), 50, 235, 268, 269–71, 272–73

Conservative party (Sweden), 258, 259, 262–63, 264

Conservatism, 54, 247

Consociational political systems, 19–20

Constitutional profile(s), 54–55, 58

Consumers-producer issue; Finnish politics, 194, 195, 196–97, 201, 204, 206, 212, 216; Norwegian politics, 266

Continuation War (Finland), 191, 192

Convergent policy preferences, 62–63, 64, 69, 70, 71, 81, 84; Danish politics, 235

Convergent relationships, 64, 238, 241, 255; in conflictual democracies, 237; in consensual democracies, 236; in Danish politics, 163, 168, 169, 170, 171, 172, 174, 175; 178, 180, 181–82, 183; in Finnish politics, 198, 199, 201, 203, 207, 215, 216; in Israeli politics, 108, 116, 126, 140; limit of tolerance, 234; in Norwegian politics, 270

Cooperation, 9, 37, 245; interparty, 18–20, 21, 38, 64, 87; normative commitment to, 29; transition to democractic rule and, 40

Copenhagen, Denmark, 57, 151

Corporatism, 11, 18–19, 29, 30–39, 233, 241–46; in consensual democracies, 42, 234, 238; defined, 31; in Finland, 225–29, 230; political consequences of, 37–39; in unconsolidated democracies, 220; see also Hyper-corporatism

Corporatization: Finnish economy, 20–21, 220, 221, 224, 226, 230, 243, 244

Counter-Reformation, 56

Crisis governments, 251; Israel, 140–41

Cultural profile(s), 54–55, 57–58, 266

Dano-Prussian War, 150

Dayan, Moshe, 146

DC Government (Italy): *1957*, 281; *1959*, 283; *1960*, 283–84; *1969*, 289

DC-PRI government (Italy, 1974), 293

DC-PRI-PSDI government (Italy, 1962), 284–85

DC-PRI-PSDI-PSI government (Italy, 1964), 286–87

DC-PSDI government (Italy, 1958), 282

DC-PSDI-PLI government (Italy 1972), 291–92

DC-PSDI-PRI-PSI government (Italy, 1963), 285–86)

DC-PSI-PSDI government (Italy, 1974), 292–93

DC-PSI-PSDI-PRI government (Italy): *1970*, 289–90; *1973*, 292

DC-PSU (PSI + PSDI)- PRI government (Italy, 1966), 287–88

Decay (economic), 59

Decision sites, 37, 67; alternative, 68, 234, 236, 238

Democracies, typology of, 4, 9–44; *see also* Transition from oligarchic to democratic rule

Democratic parties, 71; in conflictual democracies, 207–08; in Israel, 142; majority-relevant, 72–73, 81–82; policy preference of, 47, 53

Index

Democratic reversals, 39, 40
Democrats-66 (party, Netherlands), 12–13, 78
Denmark, 16, 57, 149–85, 249, 251; bilateral competition in, 140; consensual politics in, 11, 17, 18, 20, 34; constitution, 149, 150, 168; corporatism, 32, 39; crises in politics of, 150; government formation in, 3, 5, 89, 234–35; governments in, 158–84, 236, 241; interest groups in, 36; party competition in, 14, 15; transition to democratic rule, 39, 40, 41, 42, 43
Dependent variables (this study), 252
Development, 57, 59–60
Divergent-implicit relationships, 63, 64, 81, 84, 255; in consensual democracies, 236; in Danish politics, 163, 164, 174, 180; in dominated-competitive systems, 109, 239; in Finnish politics, 199, 201–2, 203, 205, 207, 213; in Israeli politics, 108, 109, 113, 116–17, 120, 126, 131, 140, 142, 143, 145, 146, 148; in Italian politics, 284; limit of tolerance, 198–99, 201, 237
Divergent policy preferences, 62, 63
Divergent relationships, 236, 255, 256; in Danish politics, 160, 164, 168, 169, 170–71, 172, 174, 177, 180, 183, 184–85; in Finish politics, 201, 207, 211; in Norwegian politics, 267, 270
Divorce liberalization issue, in Italian politics, 288, 289–90, 291, 292
Dominant party(ies), 72, 78–83, 238–39, 241; in Israel, 134, 135, 136, 141–42
Dominated-competitive democracies, 71–83, 84, 241; conflict resolution in, 238–39; Israel as, 72, 73, 74–76T, 78, 79, 148, 239, 240; limit of tolerance in, 109; test of hypothesis for, 251
Dominated system(s): defined, 72

Economic crises, 10, 241–42, 243
Economic issue, 31, 50, 57; Finnish politics, 197–98, 199–200, 202–4, 205, 206–7, 210, 211–12, 215, 227; in Israeli politics, 103, 106, 108, 110–11, 112, 115, 116, 121, 124, 133, 137–39, 142, 143, 144; in Italian politics, 280–81, 284, 285, 287, 290, 291, 292–93; Swedish politics, 259, 265
Economy (Finland), 224–25, 226, 228
Education issue: Israeli politics, 97, 106–7, 109, 111, 112, 113, 114, 115–16, 118–20, 122, 129, 130, 133, 140; in Italian politics, 282, 284–85, 286–87, 288, 289, 290; Norwegian politics, 270, 273
Education spending issue, Dutch politics, 275
Eduskunta (Finnish legislature), 189, 197, 198, 202, 203, 205, 207, 209, 210, 211, 212, 214, 215, 222, 225, 227, 228, 229
Electoral performance, change, 16, 220
Electoral reform issue: Israeli politics, 115–17
Electoral support, 242
Electoral systems, 53, 249
Empirical procedures (this study), 255–56
Employers' Association (Finland), 198, 213
Employers' associations, 32, 36
Enti Nazionale Indrocarburi (E.N.I.), 280
Eshkol, Levi, 135–36, 140
Estates, 56; Finland, 187, 189
Estrup, J. B., 151
Ethical/religious profile, 54–55, 56
Ethnolinguistic issue: Finnish politics, 187–88, 189–90, 196, 197, 210–11, 212
Ethnolinguistic profile(s), 54–55, 57–58, 59
European Economic Community (EEC) membership issue: in Danish politics, 165, 167, 169–71, 178, 180, 182; in Italian politics, 283; in Norwegian politics, 266, 271, 272–73
European Free Trade Association, 165
Explicit compromise, 63, 64, 69, 71, 84, 255, 256; in Danish politics, 234; in

Index

Explicit compromise *(Continued)*
undominated-competitive democracies, 238
Expropriation issue: Italian politics, 287

Factionalized parties, 61, 62; and policy preferences, 50–52
Faeroe Islands, 158
Fagerholm coalition (Finland), 222
Family allowance issue: in Dutch politics, 276, 277; in Swedish politics, 258–59
Farmers, 34, 55–56
Federal Republic of Germany, *See* Germany; West Germany
Finland, 13, 16, 17, 39, 187–218, 249, 251; agriculture in, 157; as conflictual democracy, 237–38; consensual politics in, 34; corporatism in, 32, 39, 241–46; Diet of the Four Estates, 187, 189; governability of, 5–6; government formation in, 3, 5, 89; governments, 197–217, 240; issues in, 19; party competition in, 13, 14; policy profiles, 57, 58, 59; transition to democratic rule, 39–40, 42, 43; as unconsolidated democracy, 20–21, 29, 212–13, 219–31
Finnish movement (party), 187, 188, 190
Finnish Rural party, 226, 227
Flank parties, 80–81, 239, 240
Flemish Christian party, 82–83
Flemish Christian Social party (FCP) (Belgium), 72
Flemish People's party, 82, 83
Foreign policy issue: in Danish politics, 151, 152, 158, 160, 165, 167, 168; in Finnish politics, 196, 197, 222; in Israeli politics, 105, 110, 112, 116, 121, 123–27, 129, 130, 131, 139, 143; in Italian politics, 283
Foreign policy profiles, 54–55, 56–57, 104
Formateur(s), 51, 52, 69; in competitive systems, 83–85, 86; dominant party, 80–81; policy preferences of, 62, 63–65, 70, 71

Forty-hour week issue: Finnish politics, 212–13
France, 56, 171; Third Republic, 43; Fourth Republic, 15, 17, 43; transition to democratic rule, 40
Francophone Democratic Front (Belgium), 82, 83
Frederik VII, king of Denmark, 149
Free Center party (Israel), 141
Free Democrats (party, Germany), 73–76
Fund for the South (Italy), 282

Gadna (youth organization, Israel), 122
Gahal, 141, 142–43
Gahal list (Israel), 138–39, 140
Gam, Mikael, 169, 171
Gaza Strip, 126, 142
GCIL (union, Italy), 243
General Zionists, 96, 100, 101, 103, 104, 105, 106, 108, 110, 111, 112–22, 127, 130–31, 132, 134, 138, 139, 147, 148
George, Henry, 158
German National People's party, 15
German party, 76
German People's party, 48–49
Germany, 15, 56, 152, 251; as dominated-competitive system, 72, 73–75; political elites in, 27; rearmament issue, 160; transition to democratic rule, 40, 43; as undominated-competitive system, 85, 86T; Weimar Republic, 3, 15, 17, 43, 48–49, 249, 250–51; West Germany, 110, 249; relations with Israel, 125–26, 127, 129, 130, 131; reparations issue: Israeli politics, 110, 116, 119, 123
Glistrup, Mogens, 180, 182
Governability, 6, 242
"Governing formula"(s), 218, 242, 243
Government formation, 3, 9, 13, 30, 87; in conflictual democracies, 70–71; in consensual democracies, 68–70; in dominated-competitive democracies, 71–83; in Finland, 21, 225–29; in Israel, 105–48; policy preferences in, 45, 52, 62; predictions tested against, 5; theory of, 65 (*see also* Coalition

theory); unconsolidated democracy and, 220
Governments, 252; consolidated results, 247T
"Grabski Laws" (Poland), 98
Great Britain, 15, 57, 170, 171, 178; and Israel, 99, 101, 102; political elites in, 27
Greece, 250
"Green Plan" issue: Italian politics, 284
Greenland, 158, 169

Halstein Doctrine, 126
Hansen, H. C., 159, 160–61, 162, 164
Hapoel Hazair (Young Worker party, Israel), 97, 99, 100
Hapoel Mizrachi (party, Israel), 103, 109–22
Hartling, Poul, 182, 183–84
Hashomer Hazair (Party, Israel), 100, 102–3, 104, 110, 124
"Havlaga" (policy), 101
Health insurance issue (Dutch politics), 275, 278
Heckscher, Gunnar, 37
Hedtoft, Hans, 159
Helander, Voitto, 231
Helsinki, Finland, 57, 189, 191, 210, 211, 212, 213, 216
Herut (party, Israel), 78, 102, 103, 104, 108, 110, 112, 113, 114, 116, 117, 119, 121, 125–26, 127, 131, 134, 135, 138, 139, 142–43
Histadrut (General Federation of Jewish Workers), 98, 100, 109, 110, 115, 122–23, 137, 139, 142
Holocaust (the), 97
Home rule issue, Finland, 189
Honka, Olavi, 222
Hot Autumn (Italy), 242
Housing issue: Danish politics, 165–66, 168, 169, 170, 173, 174, 175, 177, 181; Dutch politics, 274, 277–78; Finnish politics, 210; Norwegian politics, 269
Hyper-corporatism, 30, 39, 41–42, 43, 67, 68, 69

Hypotheses (coalition theory), 11–12; consensual democracies, 184–85; dominated-competitive systems, 148; government-formation outcomes, 52, 86, 89; limit of tolerance, 65, 109, 112; tests of, 251–52

Iceland, 3, 85, 86T, 249, 251
Ideology, 42, 61, 62
Implementation (policy), 234
Implicit compromise, 63, 64, 69, 71, 82, 83, 85, 238, 255, 256; in Danish politics, 160, 161, 165, 171, 174, 184–85; in Finnish politics, 216–17; in Israeli politics, 112, 120, 127, 128, 129, 134, 139, 145, 146; in Swedish politics, 235
Incomes policy, 31; Finland, 225, 227; Italy, 243; Norway, 273; Sweden, 264
Independence party (Uafhaengige) (Independents, Denmark), 168, 169, 170, 171, 172, 175
Independent Liberal party (Israel), 138, 140, 141–46
Industrialist, 55–56
Industrialization: Denmark, 156; Finland, 188, 194–95, 196, 210; Scandinavia, 42
Industrial revolution, 54, 56
Interest groups, 4, 9, 34, 67, 68; Finland, 221, 227, 228, 230; integration of, 31–39; with policy vetoes, 29; see also Corporatism
International Monetary Fund (IMF), 162, 292, 293
Ireland, 15, 16–17, 57, 249, 251; transition to democratic rule, 40, 41, 42, 43; as undominated-competitive system, 85, 86T
Irene, princess, Netherlands, 20
Irgun, 102, 103
Israel, 16, 19, 93–148, 249, 251; as dominated-competitive system, 72, 73, 74–76T, 78, 79, 148, 239, 240; factionalism in parties, 51; Fourth Aliyah, 98, 100, 101; government formation in, 3, 5, 89; governments, 105–47, 241; origins of party system in,

Israel (*Continued*)
93–104; party competition in, 15; Second Aliyah, 96, 97, 98; Third Aliyah, 98, 100; socioeconomic development, 60; as undominated-competitive system, 85, 86T
Israel Defense Service Law, 112–13
Issues, 18, 19, 20; determining, in parties' participation, 48, 49–50, 51, 52, 257; government-formation-relevant, 68, 256; party identification with, 54; in party politics, 234
Italy, 13, 16, 17, 218, 249, 251; case summaries, 257; corporatism, 241–46; governance, 6; government formation, 3, 5, 89, 250; governments, 237–38, 240, 279–93; party competition, 13, 14; political elite, 22, 27; transition to democratic rule, 40, 43

Jabotinsky, Vladimir, 101
Jerusalem, 108, 110, 116
Jewish Agency, 99, 100
Jewish Defense Force, 101
Jewish identity issue (Israeli politics), 1217–28, 129, 144
Jewish Legion, 101
Johansen, Lars, 36
Jordan (kingdom), 125, 143
Jorgensen, Anker, 181
Joseph, Dov, 105
Judaism, 97
Justice party (*Retsforbund*) (Denmark), 158–59, 160–69, 180, 182, 183, 184, 185, 234–35
Jutland, 155

Kallio government (Finland), 192
Kampmann, Viggo, 161–62, 164, 166, 167, 168–69
Karelia, 194
Kastner case (Israel), 121–22
Kekkonen, Uhro, 199, 208–9, 213, 214, 215, 217, 219, 221–25, 226–27, 228, 229, 230, 245–46
"King's Bay Affair" (Norway), 268
Knesset, 73, 96, 103, 109, 113, 118, 128, 137, 142, 146; elections, 108, 122, 129, 131, 136, 141
Korean War, 105, 110, 116, 123
Krag, J. O., 169, 171, 172, 177
Kristensen, Knud, 168
Kristensen, Ole, 36
Kulturkampf, 40
KVP (Catholic People's party, Netherlands), 72, 274–79
KVP-ARP-CHU-VVD government (Netherlands): *1959*, 275–77; *1963*, 277–78
KVP-ARP-PvdA government (Netherlands, 1965), 278–79

Labor, 244–45; Israel, 98–99, 100, 101; percent of, in unions, 34–35; *see also* Trade unions
Labor Alignment party (Israel), 60, 141, 142
Labor-employers cleavage (Finnish politics), 212–13
Labor-Independent Liberal-Citizen's Rights Movement government (Israel, 1974), 141–46
Labor issue: Italian politics, 282, 284
Labor-NRP-Independent Liberal government (Israel, 1974), 141–46
Labor parties, 98, 99–100
Labor party (Israel), 72, 78, 141–46
Labor party (Norway), 17–18, 235, 266–67, 268–69, 270, 271–73
Labor Party government (Norway): *1961*, 266–67; *1963*, 268–69; *1971*, 271–72; *1973*, 272–73
La-Merhav (party organ), 127
Land Act (Finland), 194
Land price control issue: Dutch politics, 276, 277, 278
Land reform, 56, 152; Finland, 193, 194
Landed elite, Denmark, 150, 151, 152, 153, 156
Landowner/tenant farmer issue: Italian politics, 280, 281, 286, 287
Language issue: Finnish politics, 187, 210–11, 212, 213, 216
Language Law (Finland, 1922), 210

Index

Lapua Movement (Finland), 39–40
Larsen, Aksel, 167
Lavon, Pinchas, 131
"Lavon affair" (Israel), 131, 132, 134, 135, 136, 137, 148
League of Nations, 99
Lechi ("Stern Gang"), 102, 103
Left (the), 14, 57, 72
Left Socialist party (Denmark), 178
Legislature(s), 37, 47, 72–76
Legitimacy, 9–10, 11, 12–17, 29–30, 88, 233; criteria for, 16–17; party, 70
Lehto ministry (Finland), 214–15, 216, 217
Leksinen, Vainno, 208
Leo XIII, pope: *Rerum Novarum*, 40
Liberal Center (party, Denmark), 175
Liberal government (Denmark, 1973), 180–84, 234–35
Liberal party (Belgium), 82, 83
Liberal party (Finland), 190, 197–209, 210, 211–13, 214–17, 223–24, 227, 230
Liberal party (Israel), 132, 134, 135, 136–41
Liberal party (Netherlands), 78, 278
Liberal party (Norway), 235, 268, 269–71, 272
Liberal party (Sweden), 258, 259, 262, 264
Liberalism, 42–43
Liberals (party, Denmark), 154, 157, 158, 159, 162, 164, 165, 166, 168, 169, 170, 171, 172, 173, 174, 175–78, 180, 181, 182, 183, 234–35
Lijphart, Arend, 19, 20
Likud party (Israel), 60, 78, 114, 141, 142, 143, 148
Limit(s) of tolerance, 230, 252; bargaining and, 62–65; in competitive systems, 73; in conflictual democracies, 71, 198–99, 201–2, 237; in consensual systems, 70, 234; convergent relationship, 234; in dominated-competitive governments, 89, 109, 239; implicit comprise, 112, 126; in undominated-competitive systems, 84–85

Lininamaa I (government, Finland), 229
Lipset, Seymour Martin, 53
LO (trade union organization), 32, 36, 181
Lutheran church, 56

Macridis, Roy, 250
Majority electoral systems, 249
Majority governments, 2, 4, 5, 65, 68, 69, 72, 80, 81, 84, 87–89, 241; consensual democracies, 236; Israel, 142; Norway, 266; undominated-competitive democracies, 238
Maki (Miflaga Communistit Yisraelit party, Israel), 108, 110
Mapai (party, Israel), 99–100, 102–3, 104, 105–28, 129–36, 137, 139, 144, 147, 148
Mapai-Achdut Haavodah-Mapan-National Religious party-Progressive government (Israel); *1955*, 122–26; *1958*, 126–27; *1959*, 129–31
Mapai-Achdut Haavodah-Mapam-Progressive government (Israel, 1958), 127–28
Mapai-Hapoel Mizrachi-General Zionist-Progressive government (Israel, 1952), 112–18
Mapai-Hapoel Mizrachi-Poalei Agudah Yisrael-Agudah Yisrael government (Israel, 1951), 109–12
Mapai-Mizrachi-Hapoel Mizrachi-General Zionizt-Progressive government (Israel, 1953), 118–22
Mapai-NRP-Achdut Haavodah-Poalei Agudah government (Israel, 1961), 131–36
Mapai-Religious Front-Progressive-Sephardim government (Israel, 1950), 105–9
Mapam (party, Israel), 103, 104, 105, 110, 113, 116, 117, 119, 122–28, 129–31, 133–34, 135, 136–41
Market economy, 55
Martens government (Belgium), 83
Meat import issue (Israeli politics), 106, 107, 111

Media, 1
Meir, Golda, 140, 141, 142, 144–45
Merchants, 55–56
Methodology (this study), 249–56
Middle Ages, 56
Middle class, 43, 100–1, 145
Military posture issue, Danish politics, 150, 151, 152, 154, 155, 165
Military strategy, 56
Minimum-winning governments, 65, 76, 79, 84, 85–86, 87; Belgium, 80, 81, 83; Israel, 134, 146
Minorities, excluded, 39, 40
Minority governments, 1, 2, 5, 65, 69, 87–89, 241; in competitive democracies, 238; in conflictual democracies, 236; in consensual democracies, 236; Denmark, 160, 175, 183–84, 185; Finland, 201–2, 204, 209, 211, 229; Italy, 281, 283, 284, 289; Norway, 267, 268, 269, 272, 273
Mitterand, François, 49
Mizrachi (party, Israel), 95, 97, 103–4, 113, 114, 118–22
Monarchists (party, Italy), 279
Monopoly Control Authority (Denmark), 170
Monopoly regulation issue: Italian politics, 284
Moral issue: Norwegian politics, 271
Moral profile: Norwegian politics, 266
Moro, Aldo, 293
Moviménto Unita Italiano Socialists, 283
MSI (party, Italy), 279
Multipartism, 67, 93
Multiparty democracies, 249; varieties of, 9–44; policy preferences in, 46, 50

Nation-state(s), 54
National Bank (Denmark), 167, 175
National Bank (Finland), 199, 200, 202
National Farmers Association (Finland), 198
National health care issue: Israeli politics, 122–23, 125, 126, 127, 129–30, 131, 138, 142, 145
National insurance Fund (Norway), 271–72

National Investment strategies, 56
Nationality issue, Finnish politics, 187
Nationalization issue: Italian politics, 281, 282, 283, 284; Norwegian politics, 266
National Labor Confederation (Finland), 213
National Liberals (Denmark), 149, 150, 151
National Pension Insurance Fund (Sweden), 265
National polity, form of, 55
National Religious party (NRP) (Israel), 104, 120, 122–27, 128, 129–36, 148
National service for women issue, Israeli politics, 111, 112–13, 114, 116, 119, 123, 127, 129, 133, 140, 143
NATO membership issue: Danish politics, 160, 161, 163, 164, 165, 167, 168, 169, 170–71, 174, 180, 182, 185; Italian politics, 283; Norwegian politics, 266, 268, 269, 273
Nazi party, 15
Negotiations: case studies, 60; case summaries, 257–58; policy conflicts in, 45, 52
Netherlands, 15, 16, 249, 251; consociationalism, 11, 19–20; as dominated-competitive system, 72–73, 76–79; government formation, 3, 5, 89; governments, 239–40, 241, 274–79; party competition in, 15; policy profiles in, 56, 59–60; political elites in, 27; transition to democratic rule, 40, 41, 42, 43; as undominated-competitive system, 85, 86T
Neutrality, 56
New Zionist Organization, 101
Nobility, 56, 187
Nonparticipation, 48, 49
Nonpolicy issues, 237, 238, 239, 240; in Danish politics, 185; in Finnish politics, 208–9, 217; in Israeli politics, 111, 117, 118, 126, 137, 147, 148
Nonpolicy relationships, 240
Norway, 16, 249, 251; agriculture in, 157; as consensual democracy, 11;

Index   337

consensus building, 17–18; corporatism in, 32, 39; government formation in, 3, 5, 89, 235, 236, 241, 266–73; interest groups in, 34–37; labor negotiations in, 32–33, 34; opposition parties in, 38; party competition in, 15; policy profiles in, 57, 58, 59; transition to democratic rule, 39, 40–41, 42, 43
Norwegian language, 58
"Note Crisis" (Finland), 222

Old Fins, 188, 190
"Old Mapai" (Israel), 137
Opposition parties, 69; role of, 9–10, 17–21, 38
Oversized governments, 19, 65, 76, 79, 80, 83, 84, 87; in dominated-competitive governments, 239; Finland, 199, 207, 227, 228, 229; Israel, 128, 146

Pacte Communautaire (Belgium), 19
Palestine, 94–95, 96, 97, 101; original mandate territory, 101, 102–3, 125, 127, 131, 142–43
Palestine Communist party, 100
Parliamentarism, 42–43
Parliamentary government: Denmark, 150, 151, 152, 154, 155, 167; Israel, 93
Parliamentary order, Finland, 223
Parliamentary party(ies), 46, 50
Participation, 63, 68; defensive, 70, 236, 238, 239; in dominated systems, 73; Finland, 187–188; policy preferences and, 46, 47–48, 49, 50, 51, 52–53, 60–62
Parties, 1, 2, 37, 67, 233; anti-system, 12–15; expendable, 73–76, 79–80; Finland, 221, 222, 223, 225, 227–29, 230–31; Greece, 250; identification of (this study), 252–55; Italy, 250; left-right scale, 15–16; new, 58, 59; origin of, 250; Weimar Republic, 250–51; *see also* Antidemocratic parties; Democratic parties; Policy profiles
Partito Socialista Italiano de Unita Proletaria, 285

Party leaders, 2, 9, 229, 236, 238; behavior model of, 1, 3; career incentives of, 46, 49–50, 58; contradictory pressures on, 230; Finland, 246; goals of, 46, 65, 69, 72, 73, 84, 219, 233–34; and governing coalitions, 67–89; imperatives of, 45–65; and policy politics, 45–53; and policy preference relationships, 64; and policy profiles, 54, 58, 61; policy principles and, 60–62
Party system(s), 2, 249, 255; Denmark, 149–58, 180, 184; Finland, 187–97, 217, 220–29, 244; Israel, 93–104, 141; Italy, 243; nonpolicy motivations in, 240; number of majority-relevant parties in, 72–73, 81–82; polarized, 16, 242 (*see also* Polarization); and policy profiles, 55–60; structure of, 4, 17–18, 53–54, 68–69, 72; *see also* Unpolarized party systems
Party unity/disunity, 4, 46, 47, 48, 53, 61
PCI (party, Israel), 243, 279, 280, 289
Peasantry, 42; Finland, 187, 192–93
Peel Commission Report, 102
Pension issue: Italian politics, 289, 290; Swedish politics, 261–63, 265
Personal preferences, 21
Petrograd, 190
Pig-breeding issue: Israeli politics, 122, 132, 133
PLI (party, Italy), 279–81, 282, 283, 284, 286, 287, 288, 290, 291–92, 293
Poalei Agudah (party, Israel), 95, 103–4, 113–14, 123, 127, 129
Poalei Agudah Yisrael (Pagi) (party, Israel), 103, 109–12, 113–14, 117, 119, 131–41, 142, 143, 144, 148
Poalei Zion (Workers of Zion party, Israel), 97, 103
Polarization, 16, 40, 43, 233, 242; in conflictual democracies, 70–71, 72, 236, 237; and cooperation, 87; in Finnish politics, 21, 217–18, 223, 225, 229, 230, 231; in Italian party system, 243; and oversized governments, 83; and policy preferences, 51–52; in unconsolidated democracies, 220

Policy choice, 37, 42
Policy dissonance, 4–5
Policymaking, 4, 9–10; corporatist: Finland, 212–13; and imperatives of party leadership, 45–65
Policy politics, 45–65
Policy preferences, 45–53, 58, 60–62, 249, 255; in conflictual democracies, 70–71; in consensual systems, 68–70; decisive, 45–46, 47, 48, 50–51, 61; divergent, 62, 63; in dominated-competitive democracies, 71–83; in Israeli government formations, 148; and party preferences, 60–62; types of, 46–47
Policy profiles, 53–60, 233, 249, 250, 252, 253, 254, 255; in case summaries, 258; in Israeli parties, 104; in Norwegian parties, 267T
Political culture, elite, 1, 4, 234, 238; attitudes of, 21–29; in Denmark, 150–51, 154; in Finland, 21, 231
"Political Culture of Bureaucrats and Politicians" (Anton), 22
Political leaders, 2, 4; policy choices of, 37
Politicians, 2, 4; and coalition making, 4–5; personal attributes of, 247; powerful, autonomous, 219–20, 221, 229–31; satisfaction levels of, 22–29; *see also* Party Leaders
Politics, democratic, 1–6
Polity(ies), 2, 55
Portugal, 15, 17, 249, 250
Postmaterialist cleavage, 60, 220
Po Valley oil and gas issue (Italian politics), 280, 281
Prediction(s) of government-formation outcomes, 5, 21, 64–65, 230; Denmark, 184–85; Finland, 217–18; Israel, 147–48; success/failure (this theory), 234–35, 236, 237–38, 239–41, 292
Presidency, Finland, 21, 220, 221–25, 229–31, 245–46
PRI (party, Italy), 280, 281, 282, 283, 284–88, 289–90, 291, 292, 293

Price supports, 56
Principles of policy direction, 46, 47, 61, 62, 70, 114–15
Producer-consumer profile(s), 54–56
Producer cooperatives, 34
Progressive party (Israel), 103, 104, 105–9, 110–11, 112–28, 129–31, 138, 147
Progress party (Denmark), 14, 180
Proportional representation, 50, 249; in Denmark, 149, 155, 156; in Israel, 93, 96; policy profiles and, 53–54
Protestantism, 56
Prussia, 150
PSDI (party, Italy), 279–81, 282, 283, 284–87, 288, 289–90, 291–93
PSI, *see* Socialist party (PSI) (Italy)
PSU (PSI + PSDI) (party, Italy), 287–88, 289
Public employment issue: Swedish politics, 259, 263
PvdA (party, Netherlands), 274–77, 278–79
PvdA-ARP-CHU-KVP government (Netherlands, 1956), 274–75

Rabin, Yitzhak, 146
Radical-Liberal-Conservative Government (Denmark, 1968), 175–78
Radical Liberals (party, Denmark), 154–55, 156, 157, 158, 159, 160–61, 172, 173, 174, 175–78, 180, 181, 182, 183, 184, 185
Radical party (Denmark), 234–35
Rafi party (Israel), 136, 137, 141, 147
Rational-choice model, 5
Rationing issue: Israeli politics, 105
Reformation, 56
Reform Liberals (Denmark), 154
Refugee's party (Germany), 76
Regime stabilization, 241–46
Regional development issue: Norwegian politics, 267, 269–70, 271; Swedish politics, 264
Regional government issue, Italian politics, 286, 287–88
Regional profile(s), 54–56
Reichstag, 251

Religious Front (Israel), 51, 105–9, 111
Religious issue: Israel politics, 95, 96–97, 103–4, 105, 107–8, 111, 114, 128, 132–33, 139–40, 143–45, 146
Religious parties: Israel, 95, 103–4, 106, 111, 112, 113, 144
Religious policy profiles, 50, 59, 104
Remiss system, 36
Rent control issue, Dutch politics, 274
Rerum Novarum (Pope Leo XIII), 40
Revisionist party (Israel), 101–2, 103
Right (the), 14, 72; in Danish politics, 152, 154
Rigsdag (Denmark), 149, 150, 154, 155, 157, 260; Folketing, 149, 150–51, 152, 154, 158–59, 164, 166, 167, 168, 169, 171, 172–3, 174, 175, 177, 178, 180, 182, 183; Landsting, 149, 150–51
Rogers Peace Plan, 140
Rokkan, Stein, 38, 53
Rosen, Pinchas, 134
Rural/urban conflict, 55–56
Russia, 187; revolution, *1905*, 189; see also Soviet Union
Russian Empire, 188
Russian Revolution, 56, 57, 100
Russification of Finland, 188–89, 190, 191

SAJ (union, Finland), 224
SAK (union, Finland), 224
Sartori, Giovanni, 12
Scandinavia, 56, 156; consensual politics, 17–18, 30, 41, 42; corporatism, 32, 38
Schmitter, Philippe, 31–32, 34
School Agreement (Belgium), 19
Sephardim party (Israel), 105–9
Severing, Karl, 48–49
Sharett, Moshe, 121, 122
Six-Day War, 140, 142
Slesvig-Holstein, 150
Slesvig party (Denmark), 158
Smallholders (Denmark), 153–54, 156
Smallholdings Act of 1899 (Denmark), 153
Smallholdings Act of 1909 (Denmark), 153–54
Sneh, Moshe, 124, 133

Social Democratic-Agrarian government (Sweden, 1956), 235, 258–61
Social Democratic-Agrarian-Liberal-Swedish party government (Finland, 1956, 197–99
Social Democratic-Conservative-Agrarian-Liberal-Swedish party government (Finland, 1958), 205–9
Social Democratic government (Denmark) *1955*, 159–60; *1964*, 171–72; *1966*, 172–75; *1971*, 178–80
Social Democratic government (Sweden, 1957), 261
Social Democratic Opposition party (Finland), 203–5, 206–7, 208, 209–210, 211, 212, 216, 217, 222
Social Democratic party (Denmark), 152, 154, 155, 156, 157, 158, 160–75, 178–84, 185, 234–35
Social Democratic party (Finland), 190–92, 193, 194, 195, 196–99, 200–1, 202, 204, 205–9, 211, 212, 214, 216, 217, 223–24, 226, 227, 228, 229, 230, 243–44
Social Democratic party (Sweden), 18, 235–36, 258–66
Social Democratic-Radical government (Denmark, 1962), 169–71
Social Democratic-Radical-Justice party and Social Democratic-Radical government (Denmark, 1960), 164–69
Social Democratic-Radical-Justice party government (Denmark, 1957), 160–64, 234–35
Social Democrats (Weimar Germany), 48–49
Social Economic Council (Netherlands), 279
Socialism, 174, 193; Israel, 96, 97, 100, 102–3, 104
Socialist Alliance (Norway), 273
Socialist parties, 57, 118–20
Socialist party (Austria), 44
Socialist party (Belgium), 82
Socialist party (France), 12–13, 49
Socialist party (Netherlands), 78, 274, 275, 276, 278–79

Socialist party (PSI) (Italy), 243, 279, 280, 283, 284, 285–87, 288, 289–90, 291, 292–93
Socialist People's party (Norway), 266, 268, 273
Socialist People's party (SPP) (Denmark), 167, 169–73, 175, 177, 178, 179, 180, 181–82, 183
Social security reform issue (Italian politics), 288
Socioeconomic issue: Danish politics, 158, 159, 162–63, 167, 168, 169, 170, 171, 173, 176–83; Finnish politics, 189, 190, 195–97, 204
Socioeconomic profiles, 54–55, 59, 104
South Slesvig, 168
Soviet Union, 123–24; relationships with/interventions in Finland, 191, 192, 208–9, 214, 217, 222, 223, 224, 237, 244
Spain, 17, 58, 249, 250; Republican, 15, 17, 250
Speculation issue (Italian politics), 286
Stagnation (economic), 59
Starcke, Viggo, 160, 164
State Education Law (Israel), 118–19
State List (Israel), 141
Storting, 267, 270, 273
Subsidization of foodstuffs issue: (Norwegian politics), 268
Suffrage, 55; Denmark, 149; Finland, 188, 189; Israel, 93; Scandinavia, 42
Sukselainen (Finnish party leader), 199, 200, 203
Supranational institutions, 56
Sweden, 14, 16, 57, 187, 249, 251; agriculture in, 157; case summary, 258–66; as consensual democracy, 11, 17, 18, 20, 34; corporatism, 32, 39; government formation, 3, 5, 89, 235–36, 241; interest-group participation, 36–37; party competition, 15; policy profiles, 59; political elites, 21, 22–24, 27–29; royal commissions, 36–37; transition to democratic rule, 39, 43
Swedish party (Finland), 187, 188, 189, 197–202, 203, 204, 205–9, 210, 211–13, 214–17, 227

Switzerland, 15, 56
System attributes, 220, 230, 234, 237

Tampere, Finland, 210
Tangential policy preferences, 62, 64, 69, 70, 71, 81, 84, 238, 255; Israeli politics, 126, 127, 140
Tanner, Vainno, 208
Tariffs, 56
Taxation issue: Danish politics, 150, 152, 153, 158, 159, 162, 163, 165–66, 168, 169, 170, 171–72, 173–75, 176, 182, 183; Dutch politics, 274, 277–78; Finnish politics, 225; Israeli politics, 115, 121, 131, 133; Norwegian politics, 267, 268, 271–72; Swedish politics, 259, 262, 263–64, 265
Tel-Aviv, 98–99
Third International, 157
Tindemanns, Leo, 289n9
Tingsten, Herbert, 160
Torah Front (Israel), 104
Torgersen, Ulf, 18–19, 41
Trade unions, 31–34, 36, 198, 224–25, 243; corporatism and, 244–45
Transition from oligarchic to democratic rule, 9, 30, 39–44, 233, 250; rough, 39–40, 41–42, 232; smooth, 39, 40–44, 232
Turku, Finland, 210–11, 212, 213, 216

Unconsolidated democracy(ies), 10, 14, 20–21, 233; Finland as, 20–21, 29, 212–13, 219–31; systemic attributes, 220; transition to democratic rule, 43
Undominated-competitive democracies, 83–96; conflict resolution in, 238; hypothesis, 251–52
Unemployment, Israel, 99
Unions, see Trade unions
United Nations, 102
United Religious Front (Israel), 103–04
United Right (party, Denmark), 151, 153
United States, 15, 27; Jewish emigration to, 94, 95, 98; Korean War, 105, 110, 116, 123

Unpolarized party systems, 18–19, 29–30, 69, 233; in consensual systems, 67, 234, 238

Vaasa, Finland, 211, 212, 213, 216
Vanoni Plan (Italy), 280–81, 282
Venstre (Left, Liberals) (Denmark), 151, 152, 155
VVD (party, Netherlands), 275–79

Wage indexation, 62–63
Wage/price issue: Dutch politics, 274, 276; Norwegian politics, 269
Walloon/Brussels Rally, 82, 83
Walloon Christian Social party (WCP) (Belgium), 72, 82
War of Attrition, 140
War of Independence (Israel), 104
Weizman, Chaim, 105
West Bank (Israel), 116, 143–44, 145, 146

West Germany, *see* Germany
Winter War (Finland), 191, 192
Workers, 55–56
Working class, 42, 57
Working-class parties, 43, 224–25, 244–45
World War II, 56, 102
World Zionist Organization (WZO), 94, 95, 96, 99–100, 101; Fifth Congress, 97; Second World Conference, 100

Yemenites, 109
Yishuv, 93, 94, 96, 97, 98, 100, 101
Yom Kippur War, 140, 141
Young Finns, 188, 190
"Young Mapai" (Israel), 137

Zionism, 95, 96–97, 100, 101, 103, 104, 128; Zionist movement, 93, 94, 95, 96; Zionists, socialist, 96, 97

THE UNIVERSITY OF MICHIGAN

DATE DUE

OCT 1997
SEP 19 1997

MAY 13 2001
APR 23 2001
APR 2 5 2002
AUG 2002
JAN 03 2005
8-18-06

AUG 08